Why Do You Need This New Edition?

If you're wondering why you should buy this new edition of *A Brief Guide to Writing from Readings*, here are a few great reasons!

1. **A new chapter on reading and writing with and about visual texts** helps you read graphs and tables correctly, analyze visual texts, and use visuals appropriately in your own writing (Ch. 8).

2. **Five new student-authored essays** model for you the kinds of papers often assigned in college. The new student texts include an analysis and evaluation of a visual text, a critique of an argument concerning cell phone use in classrooms, an informative synthesis of three film reviews, and two argumentative syntheses addressing the same film.

3. **Instruction in and examples of citing research sources according to both MLA and APA style have been completely updated** in accordance with the 2008 MLA guidelines and the 2007 APA update for electronic sources (Chs. 12 and 13).

4. **Six new professional readings—** three essays examining the issue of banning cell phones from schools and three movie reviews of *V for Vendetta*—allow you to practice analysis, synthesis, and argument using engaging topics (Chs. 6 and 9).

5. **New end-of-chapter flowcharts summarize key writing tasks** to help you see at a glance how to break down a complicated project into clear, effective tasks. (Chs. 4–10).

6. **New examples of integrating quoted material into essays** augments the writing instruction so that you have samples of how to use quotes effectively. (Ch. 2).

7. **New instruction on how to blend original and paraphrased texts as well as combine paraphrasing strategies** gives you more guidance on developing strategies that are critical for successful academic writing that emphasize working with sources. (Ch. 3).

Fifth Edition

A BRIEF GUIDE TO WRITING FROM READINGS

Stephen Wilhoit

The University of Dayton

Longman

New York   San Francisco   Boston
London   Toronto   Sydney   Tokyo   Singapore   Madrid
Mexico City   Munich   Paris   Cape Town   Hong Kong   Montreal

Acquisitions Editor: Lauren Finn
Senior Marketing Manager: Sandra McGuire
Production Manager: Denise Phillip
Project Coordination, Text Design, and Electronic Composition: Electronic Publishing Services
   Inc., NYC
Senior Cover Design Manager/Designer: Nancy Danahy
Cover Image: © Brand X Images/Jupiter Images, Inc.
Senior Manufacturing Buyer: Dennis J. Para
Printer and Binder: R. R. Donnelley & Sons-Harrisonburg
Cover Printer: R. R. Donnelley & Sons-Harrisonburg

For permission to use copyrighted material, grateful acknowledgment is made to the copyright
holders on pp. 318, which are hereby made part of this copyright page.

Library of Congress Cataloging-in-Publication Data
Wilhoit, Stephen
   A brief guide to writing from readings / Stephen Wilhoit. — [5th ed.].
      p.   cm.
   Includes bibliographical references and index.
   ISBN 978-0-205-67459-6 (alk. paper)
1. English language—Rhetoric—Handbooks, manuals, etc.   2. Academic writing—
Handbooks, manuals, etc.   3. Interdisciplinary approach in education.   4. College readers.
I. Title.
   PE1408.W586 2009
   808'.0427—dc22   2008052233

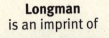

Longman
is an imprint of

www.pearsonhighered.com

4 5 6 7 8 9 10—DOH—12 11 10
ISBN 13: 978-0-205-67459-6
ISBN 10:   0-205-67459-3

CONTENTS

Chapter 3   PARAPHRASE   *47*

Chapter 4   SUMMARY   *59*

Chapter 7   RHETORICAL ANALYSIS   117

Chapter 8   READING AND WRITING ABOUT VISUAL TEXTS   137

Chapter 9   INFORMATIVE SYNTHESIS   157

Chapter 10   ARGUMENTATIVE SYNTHESIS   179

PREFACE

In the fifth edition of *A Brief Guide to Writing from Readings*, my goal remains the same: to help students master one of the most common academic genres—writing from readings. Toward this end, and based on responses from students and faculty using the book, I have made several significant changes to the fifth edition. The changes include the following:

- Six new readings: three essays examining the issue of banning cell phones from high schools and three movie reviews of *V for Vendetta*
- Five new student essays: a critique of an argument concerning cell phones in high schools, an informative synthesis of *V for Vendetta* reviews, two argumentative syntheses addressing the same film, and an essay analyzing and evaluating a visual text
- A new chapter on reading and writing about visual texts
- Additional examples of integrating quoted material into essays
- Instruction on how to combine paraphrasing strategies when writing source-based essays and how to blend original and paraphrased text
- Updated samples of works cited and reference list entries
- Documentation samples that incorporate guidelines established by the 2008 *MLA Style Manual* and the 2007 APA guidelines on citing electronic courses of information

To accommodate these changes, I have removed the chapter on journal writing, which reviewers and students indicated was the least utilized section of the textbook.

Though much has changed in this edition of *A Brief Guide*, much also remains the same. Faculty and students have long noted the collegial tone of the book and the utility of the summary charts located at the end of each chapter in addition to the revision checklists found at the end of the text. These features have all been retained. From the first edition, I have tried to maintain a clear, process-oriented approach to writing instruction, laying out for writers a series of steps they can follow or modify as needed when composing source-based essays. To help students better understand this instruction, in the fifth edition I have reformatted the sections of each chapter that specifically address the writing process.

As in previous editions of the textbook, the sample readings are drawn from a range of disciplines and reflect both academic and popular sources of information. They vary in length and in difficulty, but all are intended to pique student interest and serve as prompts for class discussion. I should also say a few words about the sample source-based essays I include in the text. Although each of these essays can serve as models for students to follow in terms of its thesis, organization, and use of sources, none of them is perfect. Students should be encouraged to read the sample essays in this textbook as critically as they read any other material in school. They may identify several ways each essay might be improved. In fact, instructors might consider asking their students to do just that: to use the instruction offered in *A Brief Guide* to critique and revise these sample essays.

In the end, my hope, as always, is that the instruction offered in this text-book will help students develop the skills they need to successfully complete source-based college writing assignments, to read texts honestly and critically, and to explore connections they find between the material they read and their own knowledge, experience, and beliefs.

SUPPLEMENTS

Instructor's Manual. An Instructor's Manual is available for *A Brief Guide to Writing from Readings*. The Instructor's Manual includes a brief introduction to each chapter, an examination of problems students commonly face when writing each type of source-based essay, and a series of exercises and assignments designed to help students improve their writing.

The New MyCompLab Web Site   mycomplab

The new MyCompLab integrates the market-leading instruction, multi-media tutorials, and exercises for writing, grammar, and research that users have come to identify with the program with a new online composing space and new assessment tools. The result is a revolutionary application that offers a seamless and flexible teaching and learning environment built specifically for writers. Created after years of extensive research and in partnership with composition faculty and students across the country, the new MyCompLab provides help for writers in the context of their writing, with instructor and peer commenting functionality; proven tutorials and exercises for writing, grammar, and research; an e-portfolio; an assignment builder; a bibliography tool; tutoring services; and a gradebook and course management organization created specifically for writing classes. Visit www.mycomplab.com or ask your sales representative for more information.

ACKNOWLEDGMENTS

I would like to thank the following reviewers for their helpful suggestions as I prepared each new edition of *A Brief Guide to Writing from Readings:* Curtis R. Burdette, Central Michigan University; Jennifer Campbell, University of Denver; Jacqueline E. Cason, University of Alaska, Anchorage; Tim Catalano, Marietta College; Jane Creighton, University of Houston–Downtown; Sally Ebest, University of Missouri, St. Louis; Daniel P. Galvin, Clemson University; Karen Gardiner, University of Alabama; Monica E. Hogan, Johnson County Community College; Wesley Jones, University of Mary; Greg Luthi, Johnson County Community College; David D. Knapp, Front Range Community College; Raj Mohan, Cleveland State University; Anne Pici, University of Dayton; Kathy Overhulse Smith, Indiana University–Bloomington; and Mary Trachsel, University of Iowa.

Stephen Wilhoit

Chapter 1

CRITICAL READING

DEFINITION AND PURPOSE

Most successful college writers are also sophisticated, critical readers. They assume a skeptical attitude toward texts: instead of believing whatever they read, they critically examine the author's ideas and their own responses to the reading. They are active, reflective readers who ask questions about the words on the page, mark passages, take notes, and draw connections between the author's ideas and their own experiences and knowledge. They are open to new ideas, but do not accept them without serious, reflective consideration. Unreflective readers, however, tend to accept unquestioningly what they see in print. In their view, if something has been published, it must be accurate. Instead of asking questions about what they read, they tend to accept the author's words at face value.

A major difference, then, between reflective and unreflective readers is the way they try to learn from what they read. Unreflective readers usually believe that the meaning of a text can be found in the words on the page: to understand a text, all a reader has to do is understand the meaning of the author's words. For them, reading is a rather simple, straightforward process: they read through a text, look up any words they do not know, isolate the author's main ideas, perhaps take some notes, then move on to the next reading. They also tend to believe that because the meaning of a text resides in the author's words, students reading the same material ought to come away with the same information; the text should mean roughly the same thing to any competent reader who studies it.

Reflective, critical readers, however, tend to adopt a different view of reading. They believe that the meaning of a text resides in the *interaction* between the reader and the words on the page: to understand a text, readers must be aware of how their own knowledge, feelings, and experience influence their *interpretation* of the words on the page. For them, reading is a rather dynamic, fluid process: they read through a text skeptically, assess the author's words and ideas in light of their own knowledge and experience, jot down some notes that capture their questions and responses, reread the text after they have had some time to consider what the author had to say, then move on.

Viewing reading as an interactive process can help you better understand the complex nature of writing from sources and the need to be an active, critical reader. For example, it helps you understand why a story you read your first year in high school means something different to you when you read it again your first year in college. The words on the page have not changed, you have, and because you have changed, the "meaning" of the story has changed for you as well. This interactive view of reading also helps explain how twenty students in an introductory philosophy class can read the same meditation by Descartes and come away with twenty slightly different interpretations of the piece. Active, critical readers understand that for any given person the meaning of a text results from the interaction between the words on the page and that reader's knowledge, feelings, and expertise; reading involves more than a simple transfer of information from the words on the page to the mind of the reader.

Does this mean that all interpretations of a reading are equally valid? No. While every person forms his or her own understanding of a reading, people can and often do misread texts: they may not read carefully, they may not understand certain terms or ideas, or they may lack the knowledge and experience they need to form an adequate interpretation of the text. As a safeguard against misinterpretation, critical readers discuss the material with others who have read it. Comparing their own reading of a text with a teacher's or a peer's reading can help clarify the material and prevent misunderstanding.

In addition, the author of the piece plays an important role in reading. Good writers try to influence their readers' understanding of and response to a text. When writing, authors manipulate the language, structure, and content of their prose to achieve a certain effect on their audience. Success is never guaranteed, but good writers know that they can at least influence how readers might respond to their work through the choices they make while composing. Critical readers take this into account when approaching a text—they try to be aware not only of what they bring to the reading, but also of the choices the writer has made to achieve a certain goal.

Learning to read material actively and critically can be difficult. However, critical readers tend to understand course material more fully, prepare for class more efficiently, and write from readings more effectively. Below you will find a number of suggestions aimed at helping you become a more active, critical reader. Central to this process is the ability and willingness to ask good questions about your reading of a text and to keep a written record of your responses. Critical readers refuse to sit back passively while they read; they actively question and respond to texts in light of their own knowledge, feelings, and experience.

ASKING QUESTIONS ABOUT WHAT YOU READ

Instead of passively accepting the ideas an author presents, a critical reader attempts to engage in a dialogue with the text, posing and working out answers to tough questions concerning the material's purpose, audience, language, and content.

The most productive critical questions center on the connections that exist between a text's author and his or her audience, subject, and language. Everything you read has been written by someone for someone about something using certain words on a page. Learning how to identify and question the relationship between these various aspects of a reading can help you understand the material more fully and determine its meaning and importance.

Typical questions you should ask of a reading include:

- Who is the author of the piece?
- What is her stand on the issue she's addressing?
- What are her interests, qualifications, or possible biases?
- What was her intent when writing this piece?
- Who is the intended audience?
- How does the author support her contentions?
- What language has she used to convey her ideas on this topic to this audience for this purpose?
- Based on my own knowledge and experience, what do I think about her ideas, intent, language, and support?
- How well does the author achieve her goal?

When you are confronted with conflicting sources of information on a topic (as is frequently the case in college), asking questions such as these is a particularly important way to sort out the authors' different positions, evaluate the worth of each source, and decide who presents the clearer, more convincing case.

Forming a full, critical understanding of a reading requires asking the right kinds of questions about the author, subject, audience, and language of the piece. Below you will find a series of questions to ask before, during, and after your reading. However, these questions are merely suggestive, not exhaustive; they indicate only starting points for your critical assessment of a text. Your teacher and peers may suggest other questions to ask as well. Finally, it is a good idea to write out your answers to these questions. Do not rely on your memory alone to keep track of your responses.

QUESTIONS TO ASK BEFORE YOU BEGIN A CLOSE READING OF A TEXT

Whether you are assigned to read material in history or art, biology or sociology, before you begin you need to ask yourself a series of questions concerning the author and publication in which the piece appeared as well as your own knowledge of and attitude toward the topic. Answering these questions may help you determine any biases present in the reading and help ensure that you remain open to any new perspectives or information the author has to offer.

Questions Concerning the Author

- Who is the author?
- What are her credentials?
- What else has she written on the topic?
- What possible biases might have influenced her work?

Before you begin to read a text, try to assess the credibility and expertise of the person who wrote the piece. Who is the author, and what are his or her qualifications for writing on this topic? If, for instance, you are writing a paper about global warming for your English class and find an article you want to use in your essay, note whether you are reading a research report produced by a scientist who conducted her own studies on the topic, an informative article composed by a reporter who interviewed that scientist, or an opinion piece written by a television star who has no particular expertise in climatology. The first author is probably well qualified to offer expert opinion; the second author, while less qualified than the first, may still be a legitimate source of information. However, approach the third author skeptically: good actors are rarely good scientists. If you plan to use any of these readings to support a position of your own in an essay, understand that academic readers will tend to believe authors with solid, professional credentials and demonstrated expertise in the topic.

Also determine, as best you can, any biases operating in the authors' work. Note who the writers work for, who supported their research, who publishes their results. No writers are completely objective; all writers bring to their work certain biases or preferences—political, religious, methodological. These biases may influence the type of study authors conduct, the type of evidence they use to support their contentions, the language they employ, the conclusions they draw. When researching a paper on abortion, for instance, it would be important to note whether the author of a piece is a member of the National Abortion Rights Action League or Operation Life, even if the writer claims to be presenting the results of an objective study. In college you will often read expert testimony that presents conflicting views and interpretations of the same topic, data, or event. Often your job as a *writer* is to examine these different perspectives, compare their quality or worth, and use them to form and defend a position of your own. However, recognizing potential authorial bias in a reading does not disqualify it as a legitimate source of information: it simply puts you in a better position to read the work skeptically and to ask better, more critical questions.

Most academic journals include brief biographical entries on the authors at the beginning or end of each article or in a separate section of the journal typically labeled "Contributor Notes" or "Contributors." Many popular magazines also include some information on the author of each article they publish. (If you cannot find this information, see a reference librarian for help locating biographical dictionaries. Later, including in your essay the credentials of the authors whose work you are quoting or paraphrasing can help increase the credibility of your assertions.)

Questions about the Publication

- In what regard is the publication held by professionals in the field?
- Toward what type of readership is the publication aimed?
- How long ago was the piece published?
- What, generally, is the editorial stance of the publication?

When assessing the quality of a publication, your first questions ought to address its credibility and audience. Do members of the profession or the academy consider this a reputable journal? Does it publish scholarly work or general interest features? What type of reader is this publication trying to reach: scholars or the general public? Answering these questions can help you determine whether work published in this journal or magazine is appropriate for inclusion in an essay of your own.

To answer these questions about the publication, first consult your teacher. He or she can probably tell you in what regard a particular journal is held by professionals in the field. Also, if you want to consult only scholarly sources of information, you may want to limit your research to scholarly indexes and databases—drawing information from *The Applied Science and Technology Index* or ABI/Inform rather than from *The Readers' Guide to Periodical Literature* and InfoTrac. Again, your teacher or a reference librarian can help you identify scholarly reference works.

Just as individual authors have certain biases or preferences that may influence their writing, publications have certain editorial slants that may influence what they print. Some publications will have definite political or ideological agendas. For example, *The New Republic* and *The National Review* are not likely to publish the same article on gun control. Other publications may exhibit certain methodological biases: they prefer to publish only historical studies or empirical studies or marxist studies of a topic. Determining the editorial or methodological slant of a publication can be difficult: if you have not read widely in a field, you may not know a great deal about its principal publications. Often, your best recourse in gathering this type of information is to scan the titles and abstracts of other articles in the journal to determine its political or methodological preferences or, if you are reading newspaper or magazine articles, to read the editorials.

However, a particular periodical's political or methodological slant does not necessarily make it any more or less valid a source of information. Recognizing these preferences, though, should help you read material more skeptically. A publication's biases may affect the content of the articles it publishes, its authors' interpretations of statistics, even the nature of the graphics and illustrations accompanying the text. When you are thoroughly researching a topic, gathering information from several different sources is one way to guard against one-sided, unbalanced treatments of a topic.

Questions Concerning Your Own Views of the Topic

- What are my beliefs about the issue addressed in the reading?
- How open am I to new ideas on this topic?

Just as every author and publication presents material from a particular perspective, readers, too, bring their own prejudices and preferences to a text. Though absolute objectivity may be impossible for readers and writers to attain, knowing your own predispositions toward the topic an author addresses can help you guard against unfairly judging someone else's arguments or shutting yourself off from potentially helpful ideas.

Author Peter Elbow suggests two frames of mind students ought to assume when reading material. First, he advises students to play the "believing game"—that is, to assume that what the writer has to say is correct. If the author of the piece is right in what he says, how do his ideas influence your current views on the topic? What are the implications of the author's ideas? Can you draw any connections between what the author has to say and what you already know? Next, Elbow suggests that students play the "doubting game"—that is, assume a more critical stance toward the author's ideas. What are the weaknesses in the writer's arguments? What are the limitations of his ideas? In what ways are the author's ideas incompatible with what you already know about the topic?

Being aware of your own stance on an issue *before* you begin to read something for the first time can help you play the believing and doubting games more effectively. First, reading with your own beliefs firmly in mind can help you recognize which ideas are hard for you to accept or even to consider fairly. We all resist ideas that run counter to our beliefs: giving them legitimacy forces us to question our own positions. However, being a critical reader means you are willing to do just that, to consider ideas that you might otherwise ignore or reject. When you dismiss an idea in a source text, consider why: if it is only because that idea runs counter to your views, try playing the believing game before moving on.

Second, reading with your beliefs firmly in mind can help you recognize which ideas are hard for you to question and criticize. We all like to read material that confirms our present positions, because such reinforcement is comforting and reassuring. However, as a critical reader you must be willing to question authors who voice opinions you endorse, to criticize fairly and thoroughly ideas you are predisposed to accept unquestioningly. If you accept information without question, consider why: if it is only because you agree with the author, try playing the doubting game before moving on.

QUESTIONS TO ASK WHILE YOU READ AND REREAD MATERIAL

After you have read material with these questions in mind, reread it. If necessary, read it a third or fourth time—very few of us truly understand a text the first time we read it. When rereading material, though, you should consider another set of questions that focus your attention on the audience, purpose, con tent, and organization of the piece, along with your response to the author's ideas.

Questions Concerning the Audience of the Piece

- What audience does the author seem to be trying to reach?
- What type of reader would be attracted to the author's writing, and what type would be alienated by it?
- How does your sense of the text's audience influence your reading of the piece?

Audience is one of the most important concepts in writing: an author's sense of audience will greatly affect, among other things, the language she uses, the material she includes, and the organizational strategy she employs. However, *audience* can be a difficult term to define. In one sense, it refers to actual people a writer may know. When composing a letter to a friend, for instance, a writer can make fairly accurate predictions about the way her reader will react to what she says or the language she uses.

In another sense, though, *audience* can have very little to do with specific people the author has in mind as he writes a text. Much of what you read in college, for example, was written by people who possessed a much more nebulous sense of audience as they wrote. They knew the *type* of reader they were trying to address (for example, a first-year student taking an introductory geology course) or perhaps the *type* of reader they wanted to interest (for example, people curious about feminist interpretations of literature). When writing, they did not have in mind as their audience a specific, individual reader. Instead, they were trying to produce prose that would attract or interest a particular type of reader.

Therefore, as you read and reread material, try to determine the audience the author is trying to address: how is she attempting to interest or appeal to that type of reader? How successful is she in achieving that goal? Pay attention to the language, content, and organization of the piece, as you try to answer questions such as these:

- Was the author trying to reach a general reader, an educated reader, or a specialist?
- What language does the author use to try to reach this audience? What examples? What graphics?
- What type of reader would actually find the work helpful, informative, valuable, or difficult?
- Would any readers be alienated by the material in the piece? Why?

Answering these questions will help you better understand how the text you are reading came to assume its present form. When writing, authors choose language, examples, and a structure they believe will help them achieve their desired effect on an audience. Part of reading a text critically is determining in your mind how successful each writer has been in making these choices.

Realize, too, that when you read something, you become a member of that writer's audience. *Your* response to what you read is extremely important to note as you try to understand what the author has to say. Is the writer communicating his ideas effectively to you? Do you find the material in the piece interesting or boring, helpful or irrelevant, engaging or alienating? What choices has the writer made that led to these responses? What knowledge or experience do you bring to the text that contributes to your reaction? Understanding the complex relationship between the audience and the writer of a piece can help you become a more sensitive, critical reader.

Questions about Purpose

- What was the author's purpose in writing the piece?
- What is the author's thesis?
- Does the author successfully achieve his or her goals?

Generally, when writing a text, an author will have one of three aims: to entertain, to inform, or to persuade his readers. Many times a work will serve multiple purposes—it will both entertain and inform, inform and persuade. However, as a critical reader, you ought to identify the primary purpose of the piece you are reading. To criticize an article for failing to present an effective argument on a topic would be unproductive and unfair if all the author intended was to write an informative essay.

However, determining an author's purpose or goal can be difficult. In social science and natural science journals, look for the author's stated purpose in his abstract or thesis ("The purpose of this article is . . ." and "The authors seek to prove that . . ."). The conventions of most humanities journals, however, require authors to be less straightforward or declaratory in stating their purpose, but again thesis statements and abstracts are good places to start your search. Even if the author states his or her goal somewhere in the paper or abstract, be wary. When you finish rereading the piece, ask yourself, "Given the content, language, and structure of this piece, what do *I* believe to be the writer's primary goal or purpose?"

Questions about Content

- What are the author's major assertions or findings?
- How does the author support these assertions or findings?

When examining the content of any reading, try first to locate the author's thesis and paraphrase it. A thesis statement will be either stated or implied. If it is stated, you will be able to point to a sentence or two in the reading that serves as the thesis. If it is implied, a general idea or argument unites and guides the writing, but the author never explicitly puts it into words. When you paraphrase this general idea or argument, you have identified the thesis. In either case, as a first step in analyzing a reading's content, restate the author's thesis in your own words to form a clear idea of what the author is trying to accomplish in the piece.

Next, note how the author supports her thesis—identify her primary ideas, arguments, or findings and the evidence, reasons, or examples she offers to support them. As you reread the piece, ask yourself what empirical, philosophical, theoretical, or other type of evidence or reasoning the author has provided to support her thesis and achieve her goal.

Finally, be sure to examine what you already know about the topic—what you have learned in the past, what you are learning now by reading *this* piece. Has the author left out any important information or arguments; has she neglected certain interpretations of evidence others have offered? If so, why do you think that is? How can the reading's content be explained by its author, audience, or purpose?

Questions about Organization

- How is the material organized?
- What headings and subheadings does the author provide?
- What does the organization of the essay tell you about the author's view of the material?
- What gets stressed as a result of the organization?

As a writer composes his piece, he has to make a series of decisions about organization: he needs to determine the order in which he will present his findings, ideas, or arguments. Good writers organize their material purposefully—to make their article clear, to make their book more persuasive, to make their findings more accessible. Through the order in which they present their material and through their use of paragraph breaks, headings, and subheadings, they try to help the reader understand or accept their views.

As you read a source text, think critically about its organization. First, form at least a rough idea of how the writer has organized his ideas. What are the major sections of the text? In what order are the ideas, arguments, or findings presented? You might want to produce a scratch outline or list that captures the reading's organization. Also, use the headings and subheadings the author provides to get a better understanding of how he views his material and how he sets priorities among his findings. For example, what ideas, arguments, or findings get emphasized through the author's selection of headings? How do the headings and subheadings guide you through the piece? Are there any instances in which you think a heading or subheading is misleading or poorly stated? Why?

Questions about the Author's Sources

- How does the author use other people's ideas or findings?
- How credible are the sources the author uses to support his ideas or findings?

As you analyze the content of a reading, examine the sources the author relied on when writing. What is documented? Flip back to the works cited list or bibliography at the end of the piece. Where does the author's information come from? Is the paper based on library research, primary research, interviews? If much of the text's material comes from previously published work, how credible are the sources the author used to support her claims? For example, is the author relying on scholarly sources of information? Is there any apparent bias in the author's use of source material: is most of his material taken from journals that share similar editorial stances, or has the writer tried to draw information from sources representing a variety of political, theoretical, or methodological perspectives? Answering questions such as these can help you determine the credibility and utility of the author's ideas, arguments, or findings.

Questions about Graphics

- How clear are the charts, graphs, tables, or illustrations the author provides?
- How well does the author explain the graphics?
- How well do the graphics support or explain what the author has to say?

Graphics include charts, tables, graphs, drawings, and pictures. While authors may add graphics to entertain readers, most include them to support arguments, summarize findings, or illustrate ideas. As you read a text, try to determine how the author is using graphics in her work and how clear, helpful, or informative you find them.

Questions about Your Reactions and Responses

- How do I feel about the topic, issues, or findings addressed in the reading?
- What is convincing? What is unclear?
- What ideas in the piece contradict my understanding of the topic?
- What ideas in the piece are new to me—which ones do I accept and which ones do I reject?

People's beliefs and knowledge influence how they read material—what they take note of, what they understand the author to be saying, what they remember after they read the piece. Understanding your response to the material you read can help you become a more critical reader and a more effective writer in several ways. First, honestly assessing your response can help you be balanced and fair. As a skeptical reader you need to be both critical of ideas you at first enthusiastically support and open to ideas you at first strongly reject.

Second, examining your response to what you read can help you decide on and develop effective paper topics—your responses may help you identify an interest or question you can later pursue more thoroughly in an essay. Especially consider what you learn from a reading: what information is new? How do the author's ideas or findings confirm or contradict what you have come to think? Examining your answers to questions such as these can result in some interesting essays.

MARKING TEXTS

Look at the books of active, critical readers and you will see pages filled with underlined passages, marginal comments, questions, and reactions. Because they have recognized the close link between reading and writing, they rarely read without a pencil in hand. They underline the reading's thesis statement and any important passages they find. As they question the material they are reading, they annotate the text and write down the answers to the questions they ask so that when they return to the material later they can recall the author's purpose and findings, remember how they responded to the author's ideas, and locate the information they want to use in their papers.

The two most common ways of marking texts are highlighting and annotating. Highlighting typically involves underlining, circling, bracketing, or color coding passages, while annotating involves writing comments or questions in the margin or at the end of the text.

HIGHLIGHTING TEXTS

Highlighting involves underlining, color coding, or in some other way marking important passages in a reading. Most students tend to highlight too little or too much. Some never make a mark in their books. Perhaps in high school they were trained not to mark up readings, or maybe they are concerned about the resale value of their books. For some reason, these students rarely, if ever, highlight material they read. Other students highlight too many passages in a reading—practically every sentence is underlined, almost every paragraph is shaded yellow or pink. You have to be selective in what you highlight: you mark up a reading in order to understand it more clearly and to identify important passages you may return to later when you write your paper.

In order to highlight a reading effectively, you need to develop your own marking system, a kind of code that helps you locate certain types of information in a text. Good writers usually develop unique ways of highlighting readings: they underline certain kinds of passages, place brackets around certain types of information, circle other parts of the text. Later, when they return to the reading to write their paper, they can easily find the information they need. Below are some suggestions about what to mark in a text:

1. Mark an author's thesis, primary assertions, and supporting evidence.
2. Mark the names of authors, dates of studies, locations of research projects, and other important facts mentioned in the reading.
3. Mark key passages you might want to reread, quote, or paraphrase later as you write your paper.
4. Mark words or terms you do not know so you can look up their definitions.

Establish your own way of highlighting a text: circle authors' names; bracket dates; use a yellow highlighting pen to mark any passages you may want to quote, blue ink to indicate questionable statements, whatever. Once you establish your own highlighting system, writing from readings will become much easier for you.

ANNOTATING TEXTS

While you are highlighting a reading, you should also annotate it—that is, *write out* your responses, questions, observations, or conclusions. Generally, there are two types of annotations you will use—marginal and end comments. Marginal annotations are notes that you make to yourself in the top, bottom, or side margins of the page; end annotations are notes that you make at the end of the text.

Marginal Annotations

Marginal annotations are typically short and in many cases may make sense only to the person who wrote them. Generally, they can be divided into content notes, organization notes, connection notes, questions, and responses.

Content notes typically identify the meaning or purpose of the marked passage. For example, after bracketing an author's first argument—that eliminating a particular government program may have negative consequences on the poor, for instance—you may write in the margin, "Argument 1—consequences for poor." When you review a reading to find material you want to use in your paper, content notes help you easily locate what you need, which is particularly important if you are completing a research project involving multiple readings.

Organization notes identify the major sections of a source text. After underlining an article's thesis, you may write *thesis* in the margin in order to find it more easily later, then bracket the first few paragraphs and write *introduction* in the margin. You might draw a line down the margin beside the next few paragraphs and write *first argument* in the margin, then highlight the next section and write *refutation of first argument*. Organization notes help you understand how the author has structured the piece and may help you locate particular sections of the text you would like to review.

Connection notes identify the links you see between an author's ideas and those offered by other writers or between ideas an author develops in different sections of a reading: "this idea echoes Weber's argument," "illustrates first point," or "contradicts teacher's position." As you read an article, you should note how the author's ideas confirm or refute ideas developed by other writers. Note the connections in the margin of the essay you are reading in case you want to examine the link more closely later: do not rely on your memory. If you are reading multiple sources on the same topic, distinctions between the texts can quickly blur; you may have a difficult time remembering who wrote what if you do not write good connection notes. Also, use connection notes to trace the development of each writer's thesis. Note in the margin of the reading the link between the various ideas, arguments, or findings the writer offers and his or her thesis.

Questions can serve several purposes. First, they can identify passages you find confusing: in a question try to capture *precisely* what you find confusing in a passage, especially if you will have a chance to discuss the reading in class. Second, questions can help you identify in a reading the material you want to dispute. Try to capture in a critical question or two why you disagree with what the author has written. Finally, questions can identify where the author has failed to consider important information or arguments. These are typically "what about" questions: "What about the theory proposed by Smith?" "What about people who can't afford day care?" Your goal is to indicate with a question possible limitations to an author's ideas or arguments.

Response notes record your reactions to what you read. These notes may indicate which ideas you accept, which ones you reject, which ones you doubt. They can range from a simple "yes!" or "huh?" to more elaborate and detailed reactions that allow you to explore your response in some detail.

Remember to keep your marginal notes brief. Their purpose is to help you read the text more critically and recall your responses and questions when you reread the material.

End Annotations

End annotations typically make some type of comment on the source as a whole and can assume different forms, including summaries, responses, and questions.

Summaries offer brief, objective overviews of a reading. You may want to write a one- or two-sentence summary at the end of a reading, especially if you are reading several source texts for your paper. The purpose of these summaries is to jog your memory about the reading's content or thesis so you don't have to reread the entire text. These summaries are especially helpful if you have to read several texts with similar titles: it is easy to confuse these readings, and the summaries can often help you find the particular text you need.

Responses capture your reaction to the work as a whole. Try to capture in your note your response to the author's ideas, argument, writing style, or any other aspect of the reading that strikes you as important. These responses can help you form comments to offer in class when you discuss the piece, and often they serve as a good starting point for developing a topic for a paper: you may want to investigate and develop your response more thoroughly and formally in an essay.

Questions written at the end of a reading typically address the source's clarity, purpose, or effectiveness. Your questions might address the reading's claims, evidence, or reasoning, its syntax, tone, or structure. Other questions might address the reading's relationship to what you already know about the topic or what you have already read. These questions help you draw connections between the readings and your own knowledge and experience. Still other questions might indicate specific aspects of a topic you still need to investigate ("I wonder how his ideas might have an impact on part two of my paper—need to reconsider?") or links between two or more authors' claims that need further consideration ("Do her arguments refute the textbook's claims?").

You will usually jot down several different types of endnotes when you finish reading a text. You may write out a brief one- or two-sentence summary, a few questions, and a response. These endnotes can prove very helpful when you return to the material later: they indicate your assessment of the source text's content, strengths, weaknesses, and worth.

Together, highlighting and annotating can help you fully understand a reading and determine the best way to use it in your own writing. A word of warning, though: do not be blinded by your own annotations and highlights. When you review a source text you have already marked and annotated and are now planning to use in your paper, be critical of your *own* highlighting and annotations. Be sure to question whether your highlighting and annotations *really* capture the source's key points. As you review your comments and marked passages, ask yourself whether you feel the same way now about the reading. If you have been engaged in researching a topic, are you now in a better position to assess the value and meaning of the reading before you? Have your views changed? Also, try to answer the questions you asked in the margins or at the end of the article. Reassess your original reactions.

SAMPLE ANNOTATED READING

Below is a sample annotated reading. Your system for marking a reading will likely be different from the system used here. Note, though, how the reader used highlighting and annotations to gain a better understanding of the author's content, structure, language, and purpose.

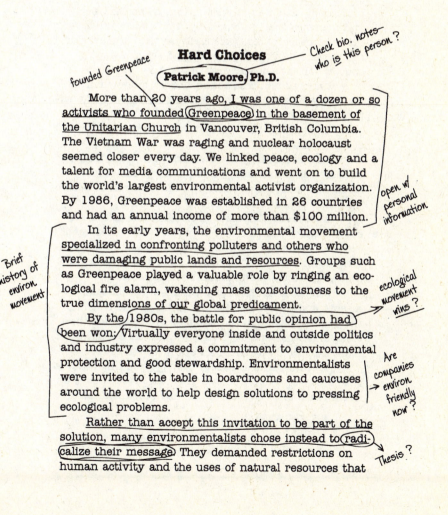

Hard Choices

Patrick Moore, Ph.D.

Check bio. notes — who is this person?

founded Greenpeace

More than 20 years ago, I was one of a dozen or so activists who founded Greenpeace in the basement of the Unitarian Church in Vancouver, British Columbia. The Vietnam War was raging and nuclear holocaust seemed closer every day. We linked peace, ecology and a talent for media communications and went on to build the world's largest environmental activist organization. By 1986, Greenpeace was established in 26 countries and had an annual income of more than $100 million.

open w/ personal information

In its early years, the environmental movement specialized in confronting polluters and others who were damaging public lands and resources. Groups such as Greenpeace played a valuable role by ringing an ecological fire alarm, wakening mass consciousness to the true dimensions of our global predicament.

Brief history of environ movement

ecological movement wins?

By the 1980s, the battle for public opinion had been won. Virtually everyone inside and outside politics and industry expressed a commitment to environmental protection and good stewardship. Environmentalists were invited to the table in boardrooms and caucuses around the world to help design solutions to pressing ecological problems.

Are companies environ friendly now?

Rather than accept this invitation to be part of the solution, many environmentalists chose instead to radicalize their message. They demanded restrictions on human activity and the uses of natural resources that

Thesis?

too "radical"

anti-science ?

not build on earlier successes

far exceed any scientific justification. That tactical decision created an atmosphere in which many environmentalists today must rely on sensational rhetoric and misinformation rather than (good science.) Programs have gone forward without input from more knowledgeable environmentalists and other experts; the public debate has been needlessly polarized as a result of the movement's unwillingness to collaborate with others less radical.

environ. not work w/others ?

In addition to choosing a dubious tactic, the environmental movement also (changed its philosophy) (along the way.) It once prided itself on subscribing to a philosophy that was "transpolitical, transideological, and transnational" in character. Non-violent direct action and peaceful disobedience were the hallmarks of the movement. Truth mattered and science was respected for the knowledge it brought to the debate.

says current movement rejects truth & science

Thesis → That tradition was abandoned by many environmental groups during the 1990s. A new brand of environmental extremism has emerged that rejects science, diversity of opinion, and even democracy. These eco-extremists tend to be:

*Anti-technology and anti-science. Eco-extremists entirely reject machinery and industry; they invoke science as a means of justifying the adoption of beliefs that have no basis in science to begin with.

anti-science

note headings ***Anti-free enterprise.** Although communism and state socialism have failed to protect the environment, eco-extremists are basically anti-business. They have not put forward an alternative system of organization that would meet the material needs of society.

anti-business

*Anti-democratic. Eco-extremists do not tolerate dissent and do not respect the opinions and beliefs of the general public. In the name of "speaking for the trees and other species," we are faced with a movement that would usher in an era of eco-fascism.

point not developed well

anti-democratic

The international debate over clearcutting offers a case study of eco-extremism in action. Groups such as Greenpeace and the Sierra Club have mounted major

example of clearcutting

need clearcutting

campaigns against clearcutting, claiming that it is responsible for "deforestation" on a massive scale in Canada and elsewhere. In fact, no such deforestation is taking place in Canada or the United States, and a ban on clearcutting could do more harm than good.

It is an ecological fact that many types of forest ecosystems thrive most successfully when they are periodically cleared and allowed to regenerate. Fire, volcanic eruptions, windstorms, insect attacks, disease and climate change (ice ages) destroy massive areas of forests, part of a natural cycle of forest destruction and renewal that has existed since long before modern humans arrived on the scene.

ignores diversity— usually replanted w/only one type of tree

The use of hype and myths by Greenpeace and the Sierra Club is symptomatic of the larger problems facing the modern environmental movement. Confrontation too often is preferred over collaboration, and eco-extremism has shoved aside the earlier spirit of tolerance and concern for the fate of humanity. The results have been harmful to the movement as well as to the environment we seek to protect.

hype and myths of Green & Sierra

As an environmentalist in the political center, I now find myself branded a traitor and a sellout by this new breed of saviors. My name appears in Greenpeace's "Guide to Anti-Environmental Organizations." But surely the shoe belongs on the other foot: The eco-extremists who have taken control of the nation's leading environmental organizations must shoulder the blame for the anti-environmental backlash now taking place in the United States and elsewhere. Unless they change their philosophy and tactics, the prospects for a protected environment will remain dim.

he is in political center— how defined?

founder now an enemy?

why a backlash?

Patrick Moore earned a Ph.D. in ecology from the University of British Columbia in 1972. He was a founding member of Greenpeace and for seven years served as director of Greenpeace International.

credentials— but who does he work for?

Summary— "Eco-extremists" reject science, truth, alternative views —> why lose pop. support?

NOTE TAKING

Especially when working on an extended writing project, you may want to take notes on a source text after carefully reading and annotating it. If you are working on a research paper for a class, check with your instructor about any requirements he or she might have concerning your notes. Some teachers, for example, require their students to take notes on index cards following rather specific guidelines. Other teachers set no guidelines concerning notes. It is always a good idea to check with your instructor concerning his or her requirements.

If you take notes on index cards, be sure you indicate somewhere on each card the title and/or author of the work you are reading. If your cards get out of order, you need some way of identifying the source of the information on each card. If you are more comfortable taking notes on paper, try to use only one side of each sheet. Using your notes to write your essay is easier if you are not constantly flipping over sheets of paper to find the information you need.

Some writers like their notes to consist only of quotes; others mix quoted, paraphrased, and summarized material. Some write notes in complete sentences; some use a combination of sentences, sentence fragments, and even single words or diagrams. As with annotations, you will need to work out your own system for taking notes, one that helps you sort out and organize the useful material you find in the sources you read.

Below are some guidelines to keep in mind as you take your notes. Following them can help you avoid problems later as you use your notes to write your paper.

Before Jotting Down Any Notes, Always Write Down the Source Text's Full Bibliographic Information

Whenever you take notes on a reading, be sure to write down the author's full name, the exact title of the piece, the full title of the publication, all the publication information, and the inclusive page numbers. Often students will be completing a paper the night before it is due and realize they used material that needs to be documented. Without having the full bibliographic information with their notes, they have to make a frantic last-minute dash back to the library. If you are careful to write down this information before you take your notes, you can avoid some problems later.

In Your Notes, Carefully Distinguish between Material You Quote and Material You Paraphrase

One of the major sources of unintentional plagiarism is faulty note taking. This problem occurs when, in taking your notes, you copy down a passage word-for-word from a source text but fail to enclose that passage in quotation marks. If you then copy that material directly from your notes into your paper—thinking you originally paraphrased the passage—and fail to quote it in your essay, you will be guilty of plagiarism. You can avoid this problem if you carefully indicate with quotation marks in your notes which passages are exact quotations and which are paraphrases of an author's ideas.

Carefully List Page Numbers

In your notes, be sure to indicate the exact page number of the source text that contains the material you are quoting, paraphrasing, or summarizing. You will need this information later for proper documentation.

Pay Attention to the Punctuation in the Source Text

If you are quoting material in your notes, reproduce the original punctuation exactly as it appears on the page. Many times students misquote material be cause they incorrectly copied in their notes the original punctuation.

In Your Notes, Clearly Differentiate between the Author's Ideas and Your Own

Again, failing to differentiate between what an author says about a topic and what you have to say is a major source of unintentional plagiarism. As you take your notes, you may want to jot down some observations or ideas of your own—reading other people's ideas will often lead you to new insights of your own. However, if you do not make the distinction clear in your notes—if, when reviewing your notes, you cannot tell which ideas were yours and which were the other writer's—you might attribute ideas to authors who never suggested them or take credit for ideas that were originally developed by someone else. To make this distinction clear in your notes, perhaps you could place your ideas and reflections in brackets.

Be Consistent with Your Note-Taking System

Whether you use a notebook, looseleaf paper, index cards, or a personal computer for taking notes, be consistent in how and where you note bibliographic information, page numbers, and your responses to the material. Adhering to a system will make it easier for you to find material in your notes and will help you avoid making mistakes.

Additional Reading

Getting Serious about Eradicating Binge Drinking

Henry Wechsler

Henry Wechsler *directs the College Alcohol Studies program at Harvard's School of Public Health.*

Most of us are aware that binge drinking is a major problem on many college campuses. Since the Harvard School of Public Health's first College Alcohol Study used that term, in 1994, to describe the drinking pattern of significant numbers of American college students, the problem has drawn media attention across the nation. Despite this, the problem has not declined over the past four years. In fact, our latest research findings, released in September, showed little change in the proportion of college students who binge. Among more than 14,500 students surveyed at 116 institutions, 43 per cent reported that they had binged at least once in the preceding two weeks, compared with 44 per cent in the earlier study.

Although the number of students who abstain from alcohol grew to 19 per cent this year from 15.6 per cent in the first study, among students who drink we found an increase in drunkenness, in drinking deliberately to get drunk, and in alcohol-related problems—including injuries, drunk driving, violence, and academic difficulties. For example, among students who drink, 52 per cent said a major motivation was "to get drunk," compared with 39 per cent in the first study. Thus, despite a spate of widely publicized student deaths in alcohol-related incidents, the binge goes on.

Why isn't this behavior decreasing? For one thing, binge drinking has been so deeply entrenched for so long at colleges that it can't be expected to disappear overnight. However, the more important reason that change eludes us is that some colleges have relied too much on one approach to solve the problem— trying to get the binge drinkers themselves to stop, rather than focusing equal attention on factors that make it easy for students to drink too much.

Of course, some campuses use multiple approaches to attack the problem, but many focus most of their energies on educational efforts directed at drinkers, particularly during events such as the recent Alcohol

Awareness Week. Such educational efforts are an important way to teach some students the facts about alcohol abuse. But those efforts overlook the environment around binge drinkers that condones and supports and often even encourages their behavior.

So what are the factors that promote binge drinking at colleges? One is that students who binge tend to think they represent the norm; they argue that they're just doing what most of their peers do. Most binge drinkers don't think they have a problem. They think they are only having fun, and most consider themselves to be moderate drinkers. Doing research into actual behavior and then informing students about how many students actually binge—generally fewer than binge drinkers believe—can help to reduce the behavior.

Another approach to changing student norms is to focus on the disruptive behavior of binge drinkers. Colleges are civic communities, and all too frequently they are disrupted by the behavior of students who drink excessively. Rather than search for contraband alcohol, a college would be wise to engage student leaders in helping administrators work out a clearly worded code of conduct that penalizes drunken behavior—and then to enforce it consistently.

Students who become drunk and disorderly should be made to take responsibility for the messes that they have created: They should have to clean up vomit in the bathrooms made unusable on weekends, help care for drunken students at the college health center, repair damage from vandalism, and pick up litter. The punishment should fit the crime.

But with repeat offenders, colleges need to consider enforcing a "three strikes and you're out" policy for alcohol-related violations of the student conduct code.

At the center of binge drinking on many campuses are fraternities and sororities. While they attract only a small percentage of students nationally, they continue to play a prominent role in campus life at many institutions. Our data shows that in fraternity houses, four of five residents binge, and more than half are frequent binge drinkers. And fraternity parties are attended by many more students than just members. They attract even some high-school seniors—future college students who are introduced to binge drinking as a social norm. Not surprisingly, most of the alcohol-related deaths of college students recently reported in the media involved fraternity parties.

While some colleges have begun to address the drinking culture created by fraternities, many administrators are still hesitant to move strongly against fraternities, for fear of angering alumni donors who fondly remember their own college years of partying. But administrators have a responsibility to protect all of their students against alcohol-related disruptions and injuries, and should not wait for tragedy to strike before they revoke official recognition of fraternities that consistently cause problems. College also can require all first-year students who live on campus to reside in dormitories, and not in fraternity or sorority houses. Of course, then those colleges must work to create interesting alcohol-free activities centered in the residence halls, to show students that out-of-control drinking need not be the focus of social life.

A third impetus for binge drinking on college campuses—one rarely mentioned publicly—involves alumni at tailgate parties during homecoming activities and sporting events. Any alcohol-control measures adopted for students must also apply to visiting alumni. Banning alcohol at home sporting events for everyone except alumni who contribute more than $50, as one college did recently, is not a good way to win students' support for new alcohol-control policies. I would hope that most alumni, if informed that an institution is trying to cope with a serious problem, would cooperate. Colleges that base their decision making on fund-raising concerns must ask themselves: What will cost the college more money—alumni who might decrease their contributions if they're cut off from alcohol at sporting events, or a few large jury awards of damages to families of injured or deceased students?

Another center of college binge drinking is found in athletics programs. Athletes binge more than other students, according to our data. In fact, involvement in athletics—compared with time spent in other activities— increases rather than decreases a student's propensity for binge drinking. Students involved in athletics are one and a half times as likely to be binge drinkers as are other students. This tradition is kept alive through the beer-advertising blitz that surrounds sports. After all, Mark McGwire's 70th home run was hit at Busch Stadium.

As a first step, college athletics officials should stay clear of alcohol-industry promotions and advertising. Further, although coaches at some colleges require team members to abstain from alcohol during the competitive season, relatively few coaches are involved in campus-wide programs to reduce alcohol abuse. Colleges should make it a priority to enlist their coaches and athletics directors in programs designed to reach all students with the message that binge drinking interferes with performance in every area of their lives. The National Collegiate Athletic Association should encourage this. Colleges also should press coaches to stress the institution's commitment to preventing alcohol abuse when they recruit high-school athletes.

Another important point of intervention is at the high-school level. Half of college binge drinkers start in high school. Colleges should begin to address this problem at high schools that send a large number of freshmen to their campuses, by sending college students from those high schools back to talk to the younger students about alcohol and other substance abuse. The volunteers should stress that one in five college students nationally abstains from alcohol, and that another two in five drink, but not to excess.

High-school students are more likely to believe the messages of college students than those of teachers and other adults. Let future freshmen get their first view of college life from these volunteers, rather than from attending fraternity parties or tailgate events. Once freshmen have unpacked and settled in, it may be too late to tell them about college rules on alcohol use. That message should be sent before they even apply.

Colleges also need to focus more attention a block or two away from the campus—on the ring of bars and liquor stores that encircles many institutions. Colleges need to map the density of those establishments; many institutions have more than 50 such alcohol outlets surrounding them. These are formidable competitors for students' attention, and cannot be coped with by the college alone; community leaders must be enlisted to help, particularly in barring the low-price specials that the outlets use to compete with each other: two-for-one offers, cut-rate drinks and free food during happy hours, and free drinks for women on certain nights. Some states and communities already have laws that ban those types of sales. Remember, the problem is not alcohol itself; it is the availability of a large volume of alcohol at a low price, usually to be consumed in a short period of time.

All of the problem areas that I've cited cannot be attacked by every college at once. Some issues may be more pressing than others on particular campuses, and the solutions must be fashioned to fit local circumstances.

Some important actions are being taken by colleges and universities across the country. Many are trying to sever the connection between alcohol and sports by banning advertising in the programs for sporting events and prohibiting alcohol at college stadiums. Some colleges are discontinuing the practice of not holding classes or exams on Fridays, and are no longer allowing local bars to advertise drink specials in campus publications. And some colleges are experimenting with new student-housing arrangements, such as living–learning centers that take faculty members and classes into the dorms, to try to completely change the environments there.

Institutions also are trying to give students more alcohol-free entertainment options. Some are working with neighborhood groups, as well as community and state officials, to find legal and other means of controlling students' behavior off campus. Other colleges are imposing stricter sanctions on students who break the rules—notifying parents after a certain number of infractions, and suspending or expelling repeat offenders.

What institutions need to avoid are one-dimensional programs that focus on particular students but ignore the ways in which colleges help enable some students to continue binging for four years. Not holding classes or exams on Fridays, for example, enables students to binge from Thursday to Sunday without interruption. Making new rules, but not enforcing even the old ones—for example, banning alcohol in the dormitories, but allowing it to be carried in unmarked cups—tells students that the college is not serious about eradicating the problem.

To anyone who thinks that binge drinking is behavior that cannot be changed, I offer the following challenge. At the next meeting you attend, look around and count how many people are smoking. Not many years ago, the room would have been filled with smoke. Today, because of the wide recognition that smoking hurts both the smoker and people nearby, through secondhand effects, the air is clear. Binge drinking can become equally unacceptable on college campuses.

Summary Chart

CRITICAL READING: ASKING QUESTIONS

1. **Questions to Ask Before You Begin a Close Reading of a Text**

   Questions concerning the author

   - *Who is the author?*
   - *What are her credentials?*
   - *What else has she written on the topic?*
   - *What possible biases might have influenced her work?*

   Questions concerning the publication

   - *In what regard is the publication held by professionals in the field?*
   - *Toward what type of readership is the publication aimed?*
   - *How long ago was the piece published?*
   - *What, generally, is the editorial stance of the publication?*

   Questions concerning your own views of the topic

   - *What are my beliefs about the issue addressed in the reading?*
   - *How open am I to new ideas on this topic?*

2. **Questions to Ask While You Read and Reread Material**

   Questions concerning the audience of the piece

   - *What audience does the author seem to be trying to reach?*
   - *What type of reader would be attracted to the author's writing, and what type would be alienated by it?*
   - *How does your sense of the text's audience influence your reading of the piece?*

   Questions concerning the purpose of the piece

   - *What was the author's purpose in writing the piece?*
   - *What is the author's thesis?*
   - *Does the author successfully achieve his or her goals?*

Questions concerning the content of the piece

- *What are the author's major assertions or findings?*
- *How does the author support these assertions or findings?*

Questions concerning the organization of the piece

- *How is the material organized?*
- *What headings and subheadings does the author provide?*
- *What does the organization of the essay tell you about the author's view of the material?*
- *What gets stressed as a result of the organization?*

Questions concerning the author's sources

- *How does the author use other people's ideas or findings?*
- *How credible are the sources the author uses to support his ideas or findings?*

Questions concerning graphics in the piece

- *How clear are the charts, graphs, tables, or illustrations the author provides?*
- *How well does the author explain the graphics?*
- *How well do the graphics support or explain what the author has to say?*

Questions concerning your reactions and responses to the piece

- *How do I feel about the topic, issues, or findings addressed in the reading?*
- *What is convincing? What is unclear?*
- *What ideas in the piece contradict my understanding of the topic?*
- *What ideas in the piece are new to me—which ones do I accept and which ones do I reject?*

Summary Chart

CRITICAL READING: MARKING TEXTS

1. **Highlighting Texts**

   Highlight the text's thesis, primary assertions, and supporting evidence.

   Highlight the names of authors, specific dates mentioned, and principal sources cited.

   Highlight key passages you may want to reread, quote, or paraphrase later.

   Highlight terms you do not understand or want to discuss in class.

2. **Annotating Texts**

   Marginal annotations

   - *Content notes: identify the meaning or purpose of the marked passages.*

   - *Organization notes: identify the major sections of the text.*

   - *Connection notes: identify links between readings and within a reading.*

   - *Questions: identify confusing, controversial, or questionable passages.*

   - *Response notes: identify your reactions to the reading.*

   End annotations

   - *Summaries: convey a brief overview of the reading.*

   - *Responses: convey your overall reaction to the piece.*

   - *Questions: convey your assessment of the reading's clarity, purpose, or effectiveness.*

Summary Chart

CRITICAL READING: NOTE TAKING

1. Before jotting down any notes, always write down the source text's full bibliographic information.

2. In your notes, carefully distinguish between material you quote and material you paraphrase.

3. Carefully list page numbers in your notes.

4. Pay attention to the punctuation in the source text.

5. In your notes, clearly differentiate between the author's ideas and your own.

6. Be consistent with your note-taking system.

Chapter 2

QUOTATION

DEFINITION AND PURPOSE

When you use someone else's words in your paper, you have to place them in quotation marks and supply proper documentation. Quoting and documenting material tells your readers where they can find that *exact* language in the source text. If you make any significant changes in a passage you are quoting, you need to indicate the alterations in your text with ellipses, brackets, or an explanation.

Generally, if you take more than three words in a row from a source text and incorporate them word-for-word in your essay, you need to place quotation marks around the passage. However, there are several exceptions to this general guideline. For example, if you repeat in your paper someone's official title as it appears in the source text (e.g., president of the school board), you do not need to quote the title, even if it is longer than three words. Also, if you use in your paper a *single* word or term from a source text that is significant or unusual, you *may* need to quote it. Learning what to quote and when to quote takes some time, practice, and thought. Making good decisions about quoting can be easier, though, if you keep in mind one of the main reasons for quoting material: you want to acknowledge an author's distinctive language.

When employed properly and judiciously, quotations can add color and credibility to your writing; they can help make your papers clearer, more entertaining, and more persuasive. If used improperly, quotations can give the impression that you cannot think through a topic for yourself or cannot articulate ideas in your own words. Therefore, knowing how to quote material properly is an extremely important part of writing from readings.

GUIDELINES ON WHEN TO QUOTE MATERIAL

You ought to have a good reason for quoting material in your paper. Do not quote material just to fill up space or to avoid thinking about your topic. Instead, you ought to consider how quoting material will help you support your thesis or explain important ideas to your reader. Below are some guidelines to help you decide when to quote a word or passage and some suggestions on how to use that material in your paper. As you plan and draft a source-based paper, consider ways to integrate *a few* carefully selected quotations with your own writing to present your ideas as clearly and effectively as possible.

Quote Passages When the Author Has Written Something in a Distinctive or Especially Insightful or Interesting Way

Often an author will express an idea so well it is difficult or impossible for you to express it better by paraphrasing it. The author may have expressed the idea succinctly, employed especially effective adjectives or metaphors, or supplied an especially interesting example. In such cases, quote the word or passage— it may help make your paper more entertaining or persuasive.

Quote Material That Lends Support to a Position You Are Trying to Make in Your Paper

Letting your readers see for themselves that an expert agrees with a position you are advocating can help persuade them to accept your argument or can help them better understand your position. You must be sure, though, that in your effort to find support for your position, you do not misrepresent an author's thoughts or findings. By leaving words out of a quotation or by adding language to it, you should not misrepresent what the author actually had to say. For example, a few years ago a student of mine quoted an editorial writer as saying, "President Reagan's proposed budget cuts will . . . double the number of people living in poverty." I checked the original editorial; the actual sentence read, "President Reagan's proposed budget cuts will not double the number of people living in poverty." By leaving out the word *not*, this student clearly misrepresented the author's intended meaning. Such changes to a quotation are unethical.

Also, in an effort to find support for your thesis, do not limit your research to those authors who agree with the position you are advancing. For several reasons, this strategy is a mistake. First, in doing research, you should learn about a topic by studying many different views. Quite often writers change their position as they write and rewrite their papers; shifting through the material they have read frequently leads them to rethink and restate their thesis. Second, as you will see below, you may want to quote authors who present ideas that challenge your thesis: doing so can increase your credibility in the eyes of many readers. Finally, by seeking out alternative perspectives and learning more about the topic, you place yourself in a better position to defend your assertions, improving the likelihood that your readers will value what you have to say on the topic because of your expertise. Therefore, do not neglect opposing viewpoints when searching for material to quote in your paper.

When you use expert testimony to support a position in your paper, it is a good idea to mention the person's credentials in your paper:

> According to Helen Carter, former president of the First National Bank, ". . ."

> Milton Friedman, noted economist and winner of the Nobel Prize, contends that ". . ."

Citing the credentials of the experts you quote may help convince your readers to accept or at least seriously consider what they have to say. Again, you do not need to cite the credentials of every author every time you quote from his or her work. You also do not want to cite so many credentials that the sentence is hard to read. Variety is the key to using quotations well—cite the credentials when you think they are significant, and do so in a way that fits the overall tone of your paper.

QUOTE AUTHORITIES WHO DISAGREE WITH A POSITION YOU ARE ADVOCATING OR WHO OFFER ALTERNATIVE EXPLANATIONS OR CONTRADICTORY DATA

Often it is a good idea to quote authors who offer views or data that call into question the position you are advocating in your paper. Many beginning authors balk at this idea. They believe that introducing opposing views will only weaken the impact of their thesis. However, when you include in your paper a variety of perspectives, your readers are more likely to perceive you to be fair and thorough in your treatment of the subject: these quotations demonstrate that you recognize and understand alternative points of view. Second, such quotations allow you the opportunity to examine critically the other person's position, acknowledging its worth or value when needed, criticizing it when appropriate.

If you decide to quote authors who challenge your thesis, you must somehow address their ideas or findings, usually in one of four ways. You need to explain in your own words:

a. how that author's ideas do not seriously damage your thesis;
b. how that author's ideas or findings may actually support your contentions;

c. how your thesis may be altered slightly to accommodate the author's ideas; or

d. how that author's ideas are incorrect or at least questionable.

If you do not somehow address the opposing ideas you quote in your paper, your reader will likely be confused, wondering how that material fits your paper's thesis.

GUIDELINES ON WHEN NOT TO QUOTE MATERIAL

When writing from sources, students often rely too heavily on quoted material: their essays are a string of quotations. These papers more accurately represent the ideas and language of the source texts than they do the ideas and language of the student. To avoid producing a paper like this, consider these guidelines outlining when you should *not* quote material. Use quotations *selectively*; they should never make up the bulk of your paper.

DO NOT QUOTE PASSAGES MERELY TO FILL SPACE

Too often when writing from sources, students try to pad their essays with extensive quotations, and their final papers end up being a patchwork of quoted material. This is especially true when students are writing to meet a length requirement. If a teacher wants a paper eight to ten pages long, some students think the easiest way to reach that length is to keep piling on quotations. However, in college your readers will usually want to know what *you* think about your subject, what conclusions *you* have reached through your research, how *you* understand material. Do not substitute other people's views and voices for your own; use theirs to *support* your own.

DO NOT QUOTE PASSAGES AS A SUBSTITUTE FOR THINKING

In addition to using quotations to fill space, too often students rely on quotations alone to clarify, defend, or substantiate a finding or position. They may introduce an idea in a topic sentence, then string together two or three quotations to substantiate the point they want to make. Instead of presenting their own ideas in their own language, they rely on quoted material to present and defend their case.

The better course to follow is to integrate selected quotations into your essay carefully: their purpose is to advance your argument or support your conclusions or findings. Do not expect a quotation alone to convince your readers to accept some contention you want to make. As you work through a writing assignment, find language that reflects and communicates the conclusions you have drawn and the assertions you want to make. When appropriate, support or illustrate your position with quoted material. Also remember that when you do quote material, in most cases you will need to comment on it, explaining in your own words the quotation's meaning, relevance, or importance.

DO NOT QUOTE PASSAGES BECAUSE YOU DO NOT UNDERSTAND THE AUTHOR'S IDEAS WELL ENOUGH TO PARAPHRASE THEM

As you read material in college, you will often run into words you do not know, ideas that seem strange, arguments that are hard to follow, research methodologies and discussions of findings that seem to be written in a language of their own. If you have to write papers based on these readings, do not rely on quotations as a way to avoid thought. You need to understand the material you quote. As a general guideline, if you cannot paraphrase the material, do not quote it. That is, if you cannot convey that information in your own words, quoting it is probably a bad idea.

INTEGRATING QUOTATIONS INTO YOUR WRITING

There are several ways to place quoted material in your papers. You should study and practice several of these techniques since varying the way you integrate quotations into your writing can make your papers more interesting.

One of the real difficulties in learning to write from readings in college is the fact that different disciplines follow different rules concerning the proper way to document and punctuate quotations. The three primary style manuals used in your college courses are those published by the Modern Language Association (MLA), primarily used in humanities classes such as English and history; by the American Psychological Association (APA), primarily used in social science classes such as psychology and sociology; and by the Council of Science Editors (CSE), primarily used in the natural sciences such as biology and chemistry. Because each of these manuals offers its own set of rules concerning the proper punctuation and documentation of quotations, when you receive an assignment, always ask your instructor which style manual he or she expects you to follow. (See Chapters 12 and 13 for a complete discussion of the documentation guidelines suggested by each.)

TWO BASIC TYPES OF QUOTATIONS

When you quote material, you will either set it off in a block quotation or integrate it into the body of your essay. Your choice depends on length: longer passages must be block quoted, shorter quotations should be integrated.

Properly punctuating quotations can be tricky: again, the rules you follow depend on the academic stylebook your teacher wants you to follow. While the three major style manuals generally agree on how to punctuate integrated quotations, the three offer different guidelines for formatting, punctuating, and documenting block quotations. Pay close attention to how the following sample quotations are punctuated. All of the sample quotations will draw on passages from the following editorial published in *The New Republic*.

Missing Link

"U.S. government wants to sedate Black youth." This headline, in a black-oriented Washington weekly called *New Dimensions*, is part of the publicity that recently led the National Institutes of Health to withdraw funding for a conference on heredity and criminal behavior. As a result, the conference, scheduled for mid-October at the University of Maryland, has been canceled. It's a sad and disgraceful descent into craven racial politics. The episode exhibits several troubling themes: paranoia among many blacks; the surprising cowardice of the NIH; and time-honored confusion about biology and behavior.

Part of the muddle is the conflation of "genetic" and "biological." If the government really does want to identify and "sedate" crime-prone youths—black or white—it can do so without the help of conferences like this one. Such youths are easy to spot (they're the ones in handcuffs), and sedatives are available. But this has no special connection with genetics. The fact that some kids have a disposition toward wrongdoing says nothing about whether genes or early environment did the disposing. Neither does any responsiveness to chemical therapy. All behavioral influences, environmental and genetic, are biologically mediated, and thus all behavior tendencies are in principle subject to chemical intervention. As pharmacology advances, society will increasingly face questions about the chemical treatment of criminals, and of playground troublemakers—but it will face them regardless of whether criminals and troublemakers are born or made.

A second confusion involves genes and race. (Actually, nothing in the conference's literature implied anyone would talk about race. But charges of bigotry are routinely leveled at people who dare use the words "gene" and "behavior" in the same breath.) Young black men in America are more prone to crime than young white men. And individuals probably do differ in their genetic inclination toward aggression, impulsiveness, and other traits correlated with crime. Do these facts together suggest that the high black crime rate lies partly in "black genes"? The answer should be obvious—no, genetic differences among individuals don't imply aggregate differences between groups—but it's worth elaboration.

A five-minute visit to your local underclass neighborhood will leave you with no shortage of non-genetic explanations for the black crime rate. Indeed, given the family structures, the menu of role models, the state of inner-city schools, the bleak economic options and perverse incentives, and so on, it would be weird if black ghettos *weren't* fountains of crime. The American "black gene pool" (if so simple a term can be applied to something that is in fact quite variegated) didn't change appreciably between the 1950's, when black crime wasn't a mammoth problem, and today, when it is. What changed was the environment.

Assume, for a moment, the worst-case scenario—the most depressing and politically uncomfortable news about race that could emerge from the study of genes and crime: suppose scientists found a non-trivial statistical difference in the genetic underpinnings of crime between black and white populations. What would happen?

Certainly nothing *should* happen. Equal treatment before the law is an ideal whose logic transcends both the fact that people are different and the source of those differences. Whatever your color, whatever your genes, you're not a criminal until you've committed a crime. (The idea that we could ever give infants "gene tests" and say that they will or won't become criminals *regardless* of their upbringing betrays an unspeakably crude idea of how genes and environment interact.)

What of the distant, Huxleyan fears of eugenics? In the worst-case scenario, mightn't the government limit the reproductive options of blacks? Obviously, the government should stay out of the business of coercive eugenics. But biotechnology is rendering centralized eugenics obsolete anyway. Parents will one day be able to check embryos (or eggs fertilized in vitro) for behaviorally relevant genes and then decide about abortion (or reimplantation). Eventually, direct manipulation of sex cells—genetic engineering—may give parents much finer tailoring tools. Which manipulations are moral, which legal, and which of the legal ones are covered by government health insurance are massively dicey issues. But in any event, the most likely complaint of blacks will not be that they're subjected to eugenics, but that they're excluded from it—that, being disproportionately poor, black parents often lack the options richer parents exercise.

The truth about genes and human behavior, whatever it may be, is coming. The cancellation of a conference to investigate the subject was a cowardly denial of this reality. We suggest that aspiring defenders of black and any other interests muster the sobriety and moral courage to discern the real issues as they arise.

THE BLOCK QUOTATION

The APA, CSE, and MLA style manuals all agree that longer quotations must be set off from the rest of the text, but they differ in how they define "longer":

- APA states that quotations of 40 words or more must be block quoted.
- CSE advises the use of special typography to set off "longer" quotations but offers no length guidelines.
- MLA says to block quote passages that would be more than four typed lines in your paper.

Regardless of the style manual you follow, you should introduce a block quotation with a colon. You do not add quotation marks at the beginning or end of the passage, and all the punctuation in the source text stays the same in the block quotation.

APA Guidelines

According to the APA style manual, you should start a block quotation on a new line in your paper, setting the left margin of the quotation five spaces or one-half inch in from the original left margin. Subsequent lines of the quotation align on that indent. (If you are quoting additional paragraphs in the source text, indent the first line of each an additional five spaces.) The right margin stays the same, and the whole passage is double-spaced.

Example 1

In "Missing Link" (1992) the editors of *The New Republic* argue that the environment is much more responsible than genes for inner-city crime:

> A five-minute visit to your local underclass neighborhood will leave you with no shortage of non-genetic explanations for the black crime rate. Indeed, given the family structures, the menu of role models, the state of inner-city schools, the bleak economic options and perverse incentives, and so on, it would be weird if black ghettos *weren't* fountains of crime. The American "black gene pool" (if so simple a term can be applied to something that is in fact quite variegated) didn't change appreciably between the 1950's, when black crime wasn't a mammoth problem, and today, when it is. What changed was the environment. (p. 35)

Changes in society, not in biology, are primarily responsible for the sharp rise in the black crime rate over the past few decades.

Analysis

Notice that the period at the end of the quotation precedes the parenthetical citation. (If the quotation runs longer than one page in the source text, use "pp." to introduce the inclusive page numbers.) There are no quotation marks added at the beginning or end of the block quote. The words "black gene pool" are quoted because they have quotation marks around them in the source text. Note also that the word "weren't" is italicized in the block quote because it is italicized in the source text (if you cannot print italics, underline words in your paper that are italicized in the reading). The left-hand margin of the block quotation is indented five spaces.

CSE Guidelines

According to the CSE style manual, block quotations should be printed in a smaller type face and/or with wider margins. The quotation may be single- or double-spaced. CSE suggests writers follow the format used in the journal they hope will publish their work. In Example 2, the "1" enclosed in parentheses after the article title is a part of the CSE's documentation system, explained in Chapter 12.

Example 2

> In "Missing Link" (1) the editors of *The New Republic* argue that the environment is much more responsible than genes for inner-city crime:
>
>> A five-minute visit to your local underclass neighborhood will leave you with no shortage of non-genetic explanations for the black crime rate. Indeed, given the family structures, the menu of role models, the state of inner-city schools, the bleak economic options and perverse incentives, and so on, it would be weird if black ghettos *weren't* fountains of crime. The American "black gene pool" (if so simple a term can be applied to something that is in fact quite variegated) didn't change appreciably between the 1950's, when black crime wasn't a mammoth problem, and today, when it is. What changed was the environment. (p 35)
>
> Changes in society, not in biology, are primarily responsible for the sharp rise in the black crime rate over the past few decades.

Analysis

Note the change in type size and the punctuation at the end of the quotation. As with the APA guidelines, the parenthetical documentation follows the period at the end of the quotation. (Use "p" to introduce the page number of the material, whether that material is located on one or more pages in the source text.) No quotation marks are added to the block quote, but the words quoted in the source retain their original punctuation, as do the words originally in italics. Note the new left margin for the quotation and how the first sentence of the quotation is indented an extra five spaces because it was indented in the reading. If you were to quote material from the middle of a paragraph in the source text, the first line of the block quotation would *not* be indented an additional five spaces (see Example 3).

Example 3

> Genetic engineering raises some troubling questions, especially as parents are increasingly able to predict the biological makeup of their future children:
>
>> Parents will one day be able to check embryos (or eggs fertilized in vitro) for behaviorally relevant genes and then decide about abortion (or reimplantation).

Eventually, direct manipulation of sex cells—genetic engineering—may give parents much finer tailoring tools. Which manipulations are moral, which legal, and which of the legal ones are covered by government health insurance are massively dicey issues. (1, p 35)

Clearly, advances in technology will continue to pose new moral and legal questions: just because a procedure is possible to do, is it right to do?

MLA Guidelines

MLA says to begin a block quotation on a new line, indent the left margin ten spaces on the left (and five more spaces for new paragraphs within the block quote), leave the right margin unchanged, and double-space the block quotation.

Example 4

In "Missing Link" the editors of *The New Republic* argue that the environment is much more responsible than genes for inner-city crime:

A five-minute visit to your local underclass neighborhood will leave you with no shortage of non-genetic explanations for the black crime rate. Indeed, given the family structures, the menu of role models, the state of inner-city schools, the bleak economic options and perverse incentives, and so on, it would be weird if black ghettos *weren't* fountains of crime. The American "black gene pool" (if so simple a term can be applied to something that is in fact quite variegated) didn't change appreciably between the 1950's, when black crime wasn't a mammoth problem, and today, when it is. What changed was the environment. (35)

Changes in society, not in biology, are primarily responsible for the sharp rise in the black crime rate over the past few decades.

Analysis

Note how the parenthetical documentation follows the period at the end of the quotation. No quotation marks are added to the block quote. The words quoted from the original passage retain their punctuation, and words in italics in the original are italicized in the quotation. There is a new left margin, but the right margin remains unchanged.

Example 5

The editors of *The New Republic* raise an interesting scenario concerning race and crime in "Missing Link":

Assume, for a moment, the worst-case scenario—the most depressing and politically uncomfortable news about race that could emerge from the study of genes and crime: suppose scientists found a non-trivial statistical difference in the genetic underpinnings of crime between black and white populations. What would happen?

> Certainly nothing *should* happen. Equal treatment before the law is an ideal whose logic transcends both the fact that people are different and the source of those differences. Whatever your color, whatever your genes, you're not a criminal until you've committed a crime. . . . (35)

The editors believe that even if a genetic link between race and crime is found, people will still be protected by the law.

Analysis

Since this block quotation runs longer than one paragraph, note how the first line of each paragraph is indented an additional five spaces. The word *should* is printed in italics because it appears that way in the source text, and the quoted passage ends with an ellipses and a period because the last sentence of the paragraph found in the source text is left out of the quoted passage.

THE INTEGRATED QUOTATION

Short quotations should be integrated in the body of your essay rather than set off in a block quotation. As you will see, you have several ways to integrate quoted material into your paper. Try to use several of these techniques when writing an essay—such variety can help make your paper more interesting to read.

The APA, CSE, and MLA style manuals generally agree on where to place quotation marks, how to use single and double quotation marks, and how to otherwise punctuate integrated quotations. Remember that all quotations must be documented. Again, see Chapter 12 for a detailed discussion on how to document quotations. In the following samples, I alternate among APA, CSE, and MLA documentation conventions.

Introduce a Quotation with a Verb

Probably the most common way of introducing a quotation is to give the author's name, perhaps his or her credentials, maybe even the title of the work, followed by an appropriate verb—*says, notes, comments, contends, asserts,* and so on. Place a comma after the verb of saying.

Example 6 (MLA Documentation)

> Parenthetically, the authors assert, "The idea that we could ever give infants 'gene tests' and say that they will or won't become criminals *regardless* of their upbringing betrays an unspeakably crude idea of how genes and environment interact" ("Missing" 35).

When you integrate material from a source text that already contains quotation marks (as the words "gene tests" are quoted in the original passage), the regular quotation marks in the original (" ") are changed to single quotation marks (' ') in your paper. Also, the word "regardless" is italicized in the quotation because it is in italics in the original. If your typewriter or computer does not have italic script, underline italicized words in your paper.

Note the punctuation at the end of the sentence; the final period follows the parenthetical citation. If the last sentence of the quotation ends with an exclamation point or a question mark, include it before the closing quotation mark and place a period after the parenthetical citation. This punctuation guideline holds true for the APA, CSE, and MLA style manuals.

Example 7 (APA Documentation)

Early in their editorial "The Missing Link," the editors of the *New Republic* declare, "Part of the muddle is the conflation of 'genetic' and 'biological'" (p. 34).

Again, note how a comma follows the verb (in this case, "declare"), how the material quoted in the source text is placed in single quote marks, and how the final period follows the documentation.

Example 8 (CSE Documentation)

The authors of "Missing Link" maintain, "The truth about genes and human behavior, whatever it may be, is coming" (1, p. 35).

Example 9 (MLA Documentation)

The editors of *The New Republic* argue that "All behavioral influences, environmental and genetic, are biologically mediated . . ." (34).

Introduce a Quotation without a Verb

A more formal way of integrating a quotation into your paper is to introduce it with a colon. Commonly, quotations used as illustrations or elaborations of a point you have just made are introduced this way. Make sure that the colon comes at the end of a complete sentence; leave one space between the colon and the opening quotation mark.

Example 10 (CSE Documentation)

In "Missing Link"[1], the editors of *The New Republic* claim that social, not biological factors are primarily responsible for the rise of crime in some urban African-American communities: "Indeed, given the family structures, the menu of role models, the state of inner-city schools, the bleak economic options and perverse incentives, and so on, it would be weird if black ghettos *weren't* fountains of crime" (p 35).

Example 11 (APA Documentation)

According to the authors of "The Missing Link" (1992), "The truth about genes and human behavior, whatever it may be, is coming" (p. 35).

Example 12 (MLA Documentation)

> If it were discovered, a link between genetics and crime should not impact law enforcement: "Whatever your color, whatever your genes, you're not a criminal until you've committed a crime" ("Missing" 35).

Run Your Sentence and the Quotation Together

This particular technique can be hard to master. Instead of separating your words from the quoted passage with a comma or colon, you run the two together seamlessly, relying on the quotation marks to let your reader know when you begin using someone else's language. Integrating quotations in this way, while sophisticated stylistically, can also lead you to misquote material if you are not careful. As students first learn to run their sentence and the quotation together, they tend to alter the quotation to fit the sentence they are writing rather than to alter their sentence so it fits the quotation. As you practice this method of quoting material, try to craft your sentence so it runs smoothly into the quotation. If you have to change the quoted passage in any substantive way, you must indicate the changes (see the section on "Altering Quoted Material and Avoiding Misquotations," which follows).

When you employ this technique properly and read your essay aloud, a listener would not be able to tell where the quotation started and ended. Note that you do not need to place a comma before the quoted material or insert an ellipsis if you are picking up the quotation in midsentence.

Example 13 (APA Documentation)

> In "Missing Link" (1992) the editors of *The New Republic* claim that "the truth about genes and human behavior, whatever it may be, is coming" (p. 35).

In this example, note that the capital *T* in *The* can be changed to lowercase without the addition of brackets. Also, when using this approach, you do not need to include an ellipsis if you begin a quotation in midsentence.

Example 14 (CSE Documentation)

> In "Missing Link," the editors of *The New Republic* make the point that in the future, African-American citizens may not be able to take advantage of advances in genetics because "being disproportionately poor, black parents often lack the options richer parents exercise" (1, p 35).

Example 15 (MLA Documentation)

> While it is true that some kids seem more likely than others to commit crime, no one is sure whether "genes or early environment did the predisposing" ("Missing" 34).

Pick Out Only Certain Words to Quote in Your Sentence

You do not always have to quote entire passages or sentences in your paper. Often you want to quote only a few key words or phrases. Be sure, though, to include proper documentation even if you quote only one word.

Example 16 (MLA Documentation)

> While certain people may have a "disposition" to break the law, in no way does that indicate whether "genes or early environment" are responsible ("Missing" 34).

This particular example needs only one parenthetical citation because all the quoted material comes from the same page in the source text. If it came from different pages in the source text, parenthetical citations would follow each quoted word or phrase.

Example 17 (APA Documentation)

> The authors of "The Missing Link" (1992) argue that advances in genetics are making "centralized eugenics obsolete" because parents are increasingly able to screen embryos or "behaviorally relevant genes" (p. 35).

ALTERING QUOTED MATERIAL AND AVOIDING MISQUOTATIONS

When you place quotation marks around material in your essay and document that passage, you are telling your readers that if they turn to that page of that source text they will find that passage as it appears in your paper: the words and punctuation have not been changed. If that is not the case—if you have made any substantive changes to material you are quoting—then you need to acknowledge those alterations.

APA, CSE, and MLA all agree that you do not need to acknowledge changing a capital letter at the beginning of a sentence to a lowercase letter if lowercasing makes it easier for you to integrate the quoted passage with your own writing; however, other changes must be acknowledged. Especially important is learning how to indicate that you left words out of a quotation, added words to a quotation, or changed the emphasis given words in a quotation.

Leaving Words Out of a Quotation

Use an ellipsis (. . .) to indicate that you left material out of a quotation. Add a fourth dot to act as a period if you omit the end of a sentence or leave out an entire sentence when block quoting. When you introduce a quotation with a colon, include an ellipsis if you pick up a quotation in the middle of a sentence in the source text.

Example 18 (APA Documentation)

As the editors of *The New Republic* point out, "The American 'black gene pool' . . . didn't change appreciably between the 1950's, when black crime wasn't a mammoth problem, and today, when it is" (1992, p. 35).

Example 19 (APA Documentation)

The conference on heredity and crime unfairly faced charges of bigotry and racism: ". . . nothing in the conference's literature implied anyone would talk about race" ("Missing," 1992, p. 34).

Adding Words to a Quotation

When you add words to a quotation, use square brackets, not parentheses, around the words. Add material to quotations sparingly. Do it only when absolutely necessary to avoid confusing your readers.

Example 20 (CSE Documentation)

According to the editors of *The New Republic*, "The episode exhibits several troubling themes: paranoia among many blacks; the surprising cowardice of the NIH [National Institutes of Health]; and time-honored confusion about biology and behavior" (1, p 34).

Noting Emphasis Added to a Quotation

If you want to emphasize a word or passage in a quotation, put it in italics (if your typewriter or computer does not have italic script, underline the word or passage). The three major stylebooks offer different guidelines on how to indicate the addition of emphasis to a quotation:

- APA style: immediately after the emphasized words, place in square brackets the words "italics added."
- CSE style: immediately after the emphasized words, note in square brackets "italics mine."
- MLA style: after the quotation itself, place in parentheses the words "emphasis added," after the page number (if any). Or place "emphasis added" in square brackets immediately after the emphasized words.

If you do not indicate otherwise, readers will assume any words italicized in a quotation appear in italics in the source text.

Example 21 (APA Documentation)

According to the editors of *The New Republic*, "The fact that some kids have a *disposition* [italics added] toward wrongdoing says nothing about whether genes or early environment did the disposing" ("Missing," 1992, p. 34).

Example 22 (CSE Documentation)

According to the editors of *The New Republic*, "The fact that some kids have a *disposition* [italics mine] toward wrongdoing says nothing about whether genes or early environment did the disposing" (1, p 34).

Example 23 (MLA Documentation)

According to the editors of *The New Republic*, "The fact that some kids have a *disposition* toward wrongdoing says nothing about whether genes or early environment did the disposing" ("Missing" 34, emphasis added).

Summary Chart

GUIDELINES ON QUOTATIONS

1. When to Quote Material

Quote passages when the author has said something in a distinctive or especially insightful or interesting way.

Quote material that supports the assertions you make in your paper.

Quote authorities who disagree with a position you are advocating or who offer alternative explanations or contradictory data.

2. When Not to Quote Material

Do not quote passages merely to fill in space.

Do not quote passages as a substitute for thinking.

Do not quote passages because you do not understand the author's ideas well enough to paraphrase them.

Summary Chart

INTEGRATING QUOTATIONS INTO YOUR WRITING

1. Block Quotations

Employ this method with longer quotations.

Follow guidelines established by the style manual your instructor requires.

2. Integrated Quotations

Introduce the quotation with an appropriate verb.

- *precede with a comma*
- *employ a verb of saying that fits the overall tone of your essay, such as:*

says	holds
states	maintains
asserts	contends
claims	explains

Introduce the quotation without a verb.

- *a more formal way of introducing the quotation*
- *precede with a colon*

Run your sentence and the quotation together.

- *edit your sentence so it fits the tone and syntax of the quoted passage*

Pick out only certain words to quote.

- *quote interesting uses of language such as coined or controversial terms*
- *quote terms to draw attention to them*

Chapter 3

PARAPHRASE

DEFINITION AND PURPOSE

When you paraphrase a passage, you express an author's arguments, findings, or ideas in your own words. Much of the writing you do in college will require you to paraphrase material. Some of these assignments will simply ask you to gather and convey information. To write this type of paper, you study the work of various authors, then paraphrase what they have written, trying to convey to your readers as clearly and accurately as possible what each has to say about the topic.

In other assignments you will rely on paraphrased material to help you develop and defend an argument. Paraphrasing the work of experts who agree with your position in a paper can be quite persuasive. Even paraphrasing the work of authors who *disagree* with a position you have assumed in your essay can be helpful: after you objectively present that opposing view, you can examine its strengths and weaknesses and adjust your position to accommodate ideas you can neither discredit nor dismiss. However, when paraphrasing information as a part of an argument you are advancing, you must fairly represent an author's views. It is always tempting to misrepresent what people say, especially when you disagree with them, either by oversimplifying their position or by employing misleading language. Try to resist these temptations; always try to be fair to an author when you paraphrase his or her work.

Finally, paraphrasing allows you to convey your unique understanding of a reading. Paraphrases of the same material written by different students are not likely to be exactly the same because writing a paraphrase involves a series of choices: each writer decides what information to include, what language to use, what organization to employ. Though you should attempt to be objective in your paraphrase of a reading, the details you choose to include and the language you choose to substitute for the author's will be communicating your unique view of the passage.

QUALITIES OF A GOOD PARAPHRASE

Generally, a good paraphrase of a passage exhibits four characteristics. It is thorough, accurate, fair, and objective:

- *Thorough*—it will include all of the author's primary ideas or findings.
- *Accurate*—it will reflect what the author actually wrote.
- *Fair*—your choice of language will be as even-handed as possible.
- *Objective*—you will avoid voicing your own opinion on the topic or on the quality of the source text.

THOROUGH

A paraphrase of a passage differs from a summary of a passage in its comprehensiveness: in a summary, you try to reduce the source material to its most essential message; in a paraphrase, you try to capture the entire content of the passage. Because you change words and sentence structure when paraphrasing material, your paraphrase of a passage may actually be longer than the original text. Summaries, however, will always be shorter than the original passage. Even though your goal is to be thorough, writing a paraphrase involves making some choices concerning content: you may leave out what you believe to be insignificant details, examples, or explanations found in the source text. Guiding these decisions, though, should be your desire to produce as complete a paraphrase as possible.

ACCURATE

Because you are not quoting authors when you paraphrase their work—because you are substituting your words for theirs—you must take care to be accurate in what you write. Your paraphrase should offer your reader a precise restatement of what the author wrote: though the language is different, your paraphrase should convey the same information or arguments found in the source text. However, accuracy can be hard to achieve. Even slight changes in language can drastically alter the meaning of a passage. Therefore, when writing and revising a paraphrase, check your work against your understanding of the source text. Have you at all misrepresented the *content* of the other writer's piece? Would the author read your paraphrase and agree that you have, indeed, captured what he or she wrote?

FAIR

Being fair in your paraphrase is related to being accurate. Writing a paraphrase involves putting into your own words someone else's ideas, arguments, or findings. When doing so, first you want to be fair to the author whose work you are paraphrasing. In exchanging your words for his or hers, you want to be as even-handed as possible. Avoid language, for example, that implies a judgment on your part or makes an author's work appear more sophisticated or more simplistic than it actually is. Second, you want to be fair to your readers. When people read your paraphrase of an author's work, they expect you to give them a fair and accurate understanding of that material. They do not expect you to censure or praise the source text—that's the function of a critique, not a paraphrase.

For a number of reasons, paraphrases are often inaccurate or unfair. First, students often *misread source texts* and make flatly incorrect assertions about the author's work. This type of problem can be avoided through a careful, critical reading of the source text before you try to paraphrase it and by discussing the reading with others. Second, students often *paraphrase material out of context*. Their paraphrase of a passage is misleading because in the larger context of the work the passage has an entirely different meaning from the one reflected in the student's essay. This type of error frequently occurs if the author of the source text is summarizing opposing views in his work. Students who paraphrase this material out of context will frequently misrepresent the author's views, making it appear the author actually agrees with his critics. When you paraphrase someone else's ideas, be sensitive to the relationship between the passage you are working with and the meaning of source text as a whole. Finally, students often produce unfair paraphrases of a source text by *relying on emotionally charged or heavily connotative language*. If an article talks about "presidential aides" and you substitute "presidential cronies," "presidential lackeys," or "presidential co-conspirators," you probably are not being entirely fair in your paraphrase.

OBJECTIVE

A good paraphrase does not take sides. Students often fail to be objective in one of three ways. First, as discussed above, they may employ language that clearly editorializes. In writing a paraphrase, try to use language that fairly and accurately captures the meaning and intent of the source text, not language that reflects your views of the topic or the quality of the source text itself. Second, in writing a paraphrase, sometimes students want to comment directly on the topic the author is addressing—when paraphrasing an author's views on abortion rights, for instance, they may want to articulate their stand on the issue. That material does not belong in a paraphrase, where your goal is to communicate someone else's views. Finally, students sometimes want to include in their paraphrase comments on the quality of the author's work—that they found the argument convincing or faulty, that the author's style was cumbersome or flowing, that the article was "good" or "bad." These types of comments are appropriate for a critique, not for a paraphrase. Your goal in a paraphrase is to be as objective in your content and language as possible.

Before you try to paraphrase someone else's ideas, though, be sure you understand what he or she has written. Again, one of the most common causes of inadequate paraphrasing is failing to grasp the meaning of the source text. Therefore, whether you are paraphrasing a sentence, paragraph, chapter, or essay, you need to understand fully what the author has written before you attempt to put that person's ideas into your own words. Your paraphrase of that person's ideas or findings must be complete, accurate, fair, and objective. It cannot meet these standards if you are confused or at all uncertain about what the author has written.

However, paraphrasing a passage can also be an effective way of determining its meaning. If you are not sure what a passage means, try paraphrasing it. Putting someone else's ideas into your own words is often the best way for you to understand what the author has written. Always be sure to then reread your paraphrase and the source text to be sure you have been thorough and fair, especially if the paraphrased material is going to be a part of a paper you are turning in.

HOW TO PARAPHRASE MATERIAL

Generally, you paraphrase material by changing words, changing sentence structures, or changing the order of ideas in a passage. More often than not, you will make all three types of changes each time you paraphrase someone's ideas.

CHANGING WORDS

One way to paraphrase a passage is to substitute your words for the author's. However, finding appropriate synonyms for words in the source text can often be challenging. Many students are tempted to turn immediately to a thesaurus for a list of possible replacement words. However, it is usually better to try to come up with appropriate synonyms on your own. Remember, writing a paraphrase involves putting someone else's ideas into *your* own words. If you can come up with replacement words that are fair, accurate, and appropriate for the tone of your paper, use them. If you cannot come up with a new word on your own, then turn to a thesaurus. However, after you look up a possible substitute word in the thesaurus, check its definition in a dictionary to see if the word accurately reflects the meaning you want to convey. The words you find in a thesaurus are not always interchangeable; there are often subtle differences in meaning you can determine by checking the definition of each term in a good dictionary.

Whether you rely on your own resources or on a thesaurus, using synonyms in a paraphrase raises similar concerns:

a. Does the new word convey the author's original idea accurately and objectively?
b. Does the new word fit the overall tone of the rest of your essay? Is it too formal or informal? Too technical or too general?

Often, it may be impossible to find an adequate substitute for a word or phrase in a passage: perhaps the author coined a phrase or used an unusual or shocking term. In such cases, it is appropriate for you to quote the language found in the source text (see Chapter 2 for guidelines on quoting material). When paraphrasing material, though, try to keep the number of quotations to a minimum. Also, remember that *all* paraphrased passages you include in your papers must be documented—even though you change the language of the source text when you paraphrase, you need to acknowledge through your documentation the source of the *ideas* you are discussing.

Below are examples of passages paraphrased primarily through word substitution. You will find the original passage, a rough-draft paraphrase, and a final paraphrase. The original passages in all of the following examples are drawn from the readings included in Chapters 1 and 2.

Example 1

A. *Original*

"Whatever your color, whatever your genes, you're not a criminal until you've committed a crime."

B. *Rough-Draft Paraphrase*

No matter what your race or genetic background, you're not considered a criminal until you've committed a crime.

C. *Final Paraphrase (CSE Documentation)*

Whatever your race or genetic background, you're a criminal only if you break the law (1).

Discussion: In my rough draft, I began trying to change a few words: "whatever" became "no matter what" and "genes" became "genetic background."

I also tried to rephrase the second half of the sentence, adding the word "considered," but my first attempt was still too close to the wording of the original. In my final draft, I changed "no matter what" back to "whatever" because I thought the wording in my rough draft was too clumsy. I was satisfied with the words "race and genetic background" so I worked on the second half of the sentence. I changed the negative statement "you're not a criminal" to the positive claim "you're only a criminal" and altered "until you've committed a crime" to "if you break the law." The basic sentence structure has remained the same; I've only tried to change some of the words.

Example 2

A. Original

"Indeed, given the family structures, the menu of role models, the state of inner-city schools, the bleak economic options and perverse incentives, and so on, it would be weird if black ghettos *weren't* fountains of crime."

B. Rough-Draft Paraphrase

Given the problems with family structure, role models, education, and real economic opportunities, it would be strange if black ghettos didn't generate a lot of criminal activity.

C. Final Paraphrase (APA Documentation)

Given all their problems—fractured family structures, negative role models, poor education, and depressed economic opportunities—black ghettos, not surprisingly, generate crime ("Missing," 1992, p. 35).

Discussion: This was a difficult passage to paraphrase because so many ideas had to be reworded. In the rough draft, I began by trying to find another way to restate the problems the author enumerated, choosing, first, just to list them: "family structure, role models, education, and real economic opportunities." In the second half of the sentence I changed "it would be weird" to "it would be strange" and "fountains of crime" to "generate a lot of criminal activity." However, I was not happy with my wording, especially at the beginning of the sentence. I did not capture the negative tone of the original passage. In my revision, I added language to reflect the author's tone—"fractured family structures, negative role models." In the second half of the passage, I changed "it would be strange" to the shorter "not surprisingly" and changed the wordy "criminal activity" back to "crime."

CHANGING SENTENCE STRUCTURE

Besides changing words, when composing a good paraphrase of material, you may also need to alter the sentence structure employed in the source text.

Often such changes involve rearranging the order of ideas in a sentence or altering the order of dependent and independent clauses.

Example 3

A. Original

"Although communism and state socialism have failed to protect the environment, eco-extremists are basically anti-business."

B. Rough-Draft Paraphrase

"Eco-extremists" oppose business interests even though communism and state socialism have failed to protect the environment.

C. Final Paraphrase (MLA Documentation)

"Eco-extremists" oppose business even though communist and socialist governments have permitted environmental degradation (Moore 16).

Discussion: In my rough draft, I first changed the order of the ideas in the sentence. I could not think of an appropriate substitution for "eco-extremist" so I quoted it and changed "anti-business" to "oppose business." In my final draft, I had to find a better way of addressing the second half of my paraphrase. I started by changing "communism and state socialism" to "communist and socialist governments" and reworded the idea about failing to protect the environment to "have permitted environmental degradation." Looking at it now, I think "degradation" might not be the best word—some additional changes might be needed.

COMBINING SENTENCES

When you paraphrase longer passages, you will often have to "combine" sentences in the source text to paraphrase the material adequately. After you read the entire passage, you may feel that you can condense the information into fewer sentences while still being thorough and fair in your paraphrase. By changing words, altering sentence structures, and combining in your sentences information found in two or more source sentences, you can often achieve a smooth, effective paraphrase of material.

Example 4

A. Original

"In addition to choosing a dubious tactic, the environmental movement also changed its philosophy along the way. It once prided itself on subscribing to a

philosophy that was 'transpolitical, transideological, and transnational' in character. Non-violent direct action and peaceful disobedience were the hallmarks of
the movement. Truth mattered and science was respected for the knowledge it
brought to the debate."

B. *Rough-Draft Paraphrase*

In recent years the environmental movement has adopted a new philosophy. It once believed its philosophy cut across political, ideological, and national lines. While its adherents believed in direct action
and peaceful disobedience, truth also mattered, as did science, which
brought knowledge to the debate.

C. *Final Paraphrase (APA Documentation)*

According to Patrick Moore (1995), the environmental movement
has changed its guiding philosophy. They used to believe their ideas
cut across political, ideological, and national lines. They also believed
in peaceful protests, respected the truth, and valued science for the
information it brought them.

Discussion: In my rough draft, I condensed the four sentences found in the
source text into three sentences in my paraphrase. I was especially interested in
combining the last two sentences. At the same time, I was trying to change some
of the words. For example, I altered "transpolitical, transideological, and transnational" but let stand much of the language in those last two sentences. To begin
my final draft, I added the author's name and dropped "in recent years," which I
had added in the rough draft. In the next two sentences I tried to echo the term
"philosophy" with the word "believed" and achieve parallel structure by using
"They" twice. I continued to change some of the terms, substituting "peaceful"
for "non-violent" and again tried to achieve some sense of parallel structure in my
last sentence (which combines two sentences in the source text).

"UNPACKING" SENTENCES

Sometimes a sentence in a reading may be so densely written, so full of ideas,
that in your paraphrase you may need two or three sentences to convey the
same information. When "unpacking" a sentence like this, your goal remains
to convey the author's ideas fairly and thoroughly in your own language. Be
sure first, though, that you fully understand the source passage—densely
written material is often hard to read.

Example 5

A. *Original*

"All behavioral influences, environmental and genetic, are biologically mediated,
and thus all behavior tendencies are in principle, subject to chemical intervention."

B. Rough-Draft Paraphrase

Everything that influences our behavior, whether arising from the environment or from our genetic makeup, does so biologically: our behavior is biologically determined. Thus, in theory, all behavior can be altered chemically, since chemical intervention can alter the way our bodies respond biologically.

C. Final Paraphrase (CSE Documentation)

Everything that influences our behavior, whether arising from our environment or our genes, does so biologically—it influences our behavior by altering our biology. It holds, therefore, that behavior can be altered chemically, since chemicals can alter our biology, the ultimate source of our behavior (1).

Discussion: I found this a hard passage to paraphrase. First, I had to read the original sentence several times to understand what the author wrote. I decided I could paraphrase the passage in two sentences. As I worked to rewrite the passage, I knew my paraphrase would be longer than the original. It seemed to me the author was making, essentially, a cause-effect argument in the form of a syllogism: since all behavior is biologically based and since chemicals affect biology, chemicals can affect behavior. In my two sentences, I tried to capture this line of thought.

COMBINING STRATEGIES: PARAPHRASING LONGER PASSAGES IN SOURCE TEXTS

There may be times when you have to paraphrase passages from a source text that are several sentences or even several paragraphs long. When this is the case, you will likely need to employ all of the strategies discussed in this chapter. The original passage is taken from Henry Wechsler's "Getting Serious about Eradicating Binge Drinking" (pages 20–24).

Example 6

A. Original

At the center of binge drinking on many campuses are fraternities and sororities. While they attract only a small percentage of students nationally, they continue to play a prominent role in campus life at many institutions. Our data shows that in fraternity houses, four of five residents binge, and more than half are frequent binge drinkers. And, fraternity parties are attended by many more students than just members. They attract even some high-school seniors—future college students who are introduced to binge drinking as a social norm. Not surprisingly, most of the alcohol-related deaths of college students recently reported in the media involved fraternity parties.

While some colleges have begun to address the drinking culture created by fraternities, many administrators are still hesitant to move strongly against fraternities, for fear of angering alumni donors who fondly remember their own college years of partying. But administrators have a responsibility to protect all of their students against alcohol-related disruptions and injuries, and should not wait for tragedy before they revoke official recognition of fraternities that consistently cause problems. College also can require all first-year students who live on campus to reside in dormitories, and not in fraternity or sorority houses. Of course, then those college must work to create interesting alcohol-free activities centered in the residence halls, to show students that out-of-control drinking need not be the focus of social life.

B. Rough-Draft Paraphrase

Even though only a small number of students join fraternities and sororities in college, they are responsible for much of the binge drinking on U.S. campuses. In fact, one study showed that four or five fraternity and sorority members binge drink, more than half, frequently. In addition, high-school students sometimes attend Greek parties, introducing them to binge drinking even before they enroll in college. Recently, several students have even died after becoming drunk at fraternity parties.

Although they know fraternities are often the site of binge drinking, college administrators are often reluctant to crack down on them because they are afraid of angering alumni donors who themselves were Greeks. However, in doing so, administrators fail to uphold their responsibility to protect all students. One way to attack the problem would be to require all freshmen to live in dorms, but schools would then also have to provide alcohol-free recreational opportunities to demonstrate that students do not have to get drunk to have fun.

C. Final Paraphrase (MLA Documentation)

In the United States, while only a small number of students join fraternities and sororities in college, they are responsible for much of the binge drinking. One study showed that four out of five fraternity and sorority members binge drink (over fifty percent, frequently) and often introduce binge drinking to high-school students who attend their parties. Although administrators know that fraternities are often the site of binge drinking (and that some students have died after getting drunk at fraternity parties), they are reluctant to crack down on them—many potential alumni donors were Greeks and may object to such action. To address the problem, administrators could prohibit freshmen from living in Greek housing, but they would also have to provide alcohol-free recreational opportunities to demonstrate that students do not have to get drunk to have fun (Wechsler 21–22).

Discussion: As I moved through the rough draft into the final paraphrase, I tried to condense and simplify the sentences in the source text while remaining comprehensive. I ended up with one paragraph instead of two, although the order of the ideas in my paraphrase still follows the order of ideas presented in the original. I'm still not sure that I like substituting "Greek" for "fraternities and sororities" in the paraphrase of the expression "crack down on them" (it may be too informal). To condense the material, I used parentheses twice to enclose material I thought was of secondary importance. Also note that I need to provide documentation only once, at the end of the paraphrased passage.

BLENDING YOUR WRITING WITH PARAPHRASED MATERIAL

Often in academic writing you will be blending your writing with material you're paraphrasing from source texts. Through documentation and attribution, you will guide your readers through the passage, clarifying which prose is yours and which is paraphrased. I have numbered the sentences in Example 7 below to make it easier to discuss the passage.

Example 7 (Using APA Documentation)

[1]Clearly, binge drinking is a problem on many college campuses, but who is to blame? [2]Author Henry Wechsler lays part of the responsibility at the feet of fraternities and sororities. [3]According to Wechsler, although only a small number of college students actually "go Greek," fraternity and sorority members account for a disproportionate number of binge drinkers. [4]Fraternities, in particular, seem to promote binge drinking, since four out of five students living in a fraternity house report that they binge drink (21). [5]If college administrators know that fraternities and sororities are a major site of binge drinking on their campuses, why don't they act to stop that behavior? [6]Wechsler believes it comes down to money. [7]They are afraid to offend alumni donors who were themselves Greeks by cracking down on fraternities and sororities (21). [8]If these alumni feel that the administration is unfairly targeting Greeks, they will be less likely to donate money to the school.

Discussion: In this example, sentences 3, 4, and 7 are paraphrased from the source text and are therefore documented. Sentences 1, 2, 5, 6, and 8 are ones I wrote and therefore do not need to be documented. Note how citing the source text at the end of sentence 4 provides sufficient documentation for sentences 3 and 4.

DOCUMENTATION

Remember that any material you paraphrase from a source must be properly documented. Failing to document paraphrased material is a form of plagiarism. While the various forms of documentation you will encounter in college are discussed in Chapter 12, remember that every discipline expects writers to document all paraphrased material properly.

Summary Chart

HOW TO A PARAPHRASE MATERIAL

1. **Read, reread, and annotate the material.**
   - *Use a dictionary to find the meaning of any words you do not know.*
   - *Form your own opinion about the meaning of the passage.*

2. **Change words in the passage.**
   - *Substitute synonyms for key terms in the passage.*
   - *Substitute pronouns for nouns when appropriate.*
   - *Change the verbs.*

3. **Change the sentence structure in the passage.**
   - *Rearrange the order of ideas presented in the source text.*

4. **Combine sentences found in the source text.**
   - *Combine into single sentences ideas presented in two or more sentences in the source text.*

5. **Unpack sentences found in the source text.**
   - *Convey in two or more sentences ideas presented in one sentence in the source text.*

Chapter 4

SUMMARY

DEFINITION AND PURPOSE

Summarizing a reading involves two separate processes: (1) identifying the important material in the text and (2) restating the material in your own words. Because part of your job when writing a summary is deciding what to include from the reading and what to leave out, summaries are always shorter than the source text. Like paraphrases, summaries are always written in your own words (you can use quotations in a summary, but only sparingly), and they should be as objective as possible (you do not include in a summary your own opinions, beliefs, or judgments, and you try to use neutral language).

The ability to summarize readings is fundamental to academic, source-based writing. You will likely be summarizing information when you prepare a lab report, review a movie, write a research paper, or take an essay test. Instructors will often ask you to summarize articles or book chapters to be sure you can read carefully and critically, identify key ideas and important supporting evidence or arguments, and express that information clearly in your own words.

Sometimes summaries are part of a longer work. In a history research paper, for example, you may summarize the work of several different theorists while presenting an argument of your own. Other times, though, summaries will be "freestanding," graded as independent formal essays. These freestanding, informative summaries are often called "reports." Your goal in writing them is to convey in your own words only the most important ideas, arguments, or findings in a reading. To write these types of assignments, you need to form a clear understanding of the source text, decide what to include in your summary and what to leave out, and choose language that clearly and objectively conveys the author's ideas.

Other times, though, you will use summaries to support a larger argument you are advancing in an essay. First, you may summarize the arguments or findings of experts who agree with the position you have assumed in your thesis: readers may accept your position if they see that other authorities support it as well. Second, you may summarize the work of experts who call into question your thesis. Doing so will help your work appear informed and balanced, again improving your credibility in the eyes of many academic readers. Be sure, though, that if you do summarize opposing views in your essay you then somehow address them. For example, following your summary, you can critique that information—pointing out its strengths and weaknesses—and explain how the opposing ideas affect the validity of your thesis.

Whether your summary is part of a longer work or stands on its own, it must make sense to someone who has not read the source text. If, for example, you are working as a loan officer in a bank and your boss hands you a financial report to summarize, she wants to be able to understand your summary without having to read the report herself. She wants *you* to read the report carefully and distill from it the information she needs to know.

TYPES OF SUMMARIES

In college you will probably write two different types of summaries: informative and explanatory. An informative summary simply conveys the author's main ideas, data, arguments, and supporting material; an explanatory summary conveys this information as well, but also indicates the overall structure of the source text, explaining how the author developed his or her assertions. Informative summaries are often shorter than explanatory summaries and are usually incorporated into longer works; explanatory summaries frequently mention the author's name, usually follow the organizational scheme of the source text, and are frequently independent, freestanding essays.

Below are two different summaries of the opening lines of the Gettysburg Address, one informative and one explanatory. As you read them, note the differences in content, structure, and word choice.

Example 1

Source Text

Four score and seven years ago our fathers brought forth on this continent, a new nation, conceived in Liberty and dedicated to the proposition that all men are created equal. Now we are engaged in a great civil war, testing whether that nation, or any nation so conceived and so dedicated, can long endure. We are met on a great battlefield of that war. We have come to dedicate a portion of that field, as a final resting place for those who here gave their lives that that nation might live.

Informative Summary

Eighty-seven years ago the United States was founded on the idea that all people are created equal. Currently a civil war is testing whether such a nation can survive. A portion of this battlefield is to be designated as a cemetery for those who fought in the war.

Explanatory Summary

Lincoln opens the Gettysburg Address by remarking that eighty-seven years ago the United States was founded on the idea that all people are created equal. He next points out how the country is engaged in a civil war that will determine whether such a nation can survive, then acknowledges the occasion of the speech: to dedicate part of a great battlefield as a cemetery for the combatants.

Notice that the point of the informative summary is simply to capture in your own words the important ideas found in the source text. In an explanatory summary, though, you repeatedly refer to the author of the work and indicate how the piece was organized through your choice of verbs ("opens," "points out") and transition words ("next," "then").

QUALITIES OF A GOOD SUMMARY

Informative and explanatory summaries need to be comprehensive, brief, accurate, neutral, and independent.

- *Comprehensive*—it conveys all the important information in the reading.
- *Brief*—it conveys this information concisely.
- *Accurate*—it correctly conveys the author's ideas, findings, or arguments.
- *Neutral*—it avoids judgments concerning the reading's topic or style.
- *Independent*—it makes sense to someone who has not read the source text.

COMPREHENSIVE

Your summary needs to include all of the important ideas, assertions, or findings contained in the source text as well as the most significant information or arguments the author provides to support them. When you paraphrase a passage, you try to capture in your own language everything the author has written. However, when you summarize that same passage, you have to be more selective in choosing material to include. You need to identify what you believe to be the most important material in the passage and include only that in your summary. In this way your summary is comprehensive—you have not left any important information out of your summary.

Does that mean that if a number of people were summarizing the same article, all of their essays would be identical, at least in content? No. Determining what to include in a summary requires judgment. Each individual writer must decide what is most important in the source text. Some writers will make good choices; some will make poor choices. Even those making good choices may decide to include different information. Consequently, students assigned to summarize the same reading will likely produce slightly different essays. You will probably produce a comprehensive summary if you carefully and critically read the source text before you begin to write your summary and if you check your work against the source text before you turn it in to be sure you have included all of the important information.

BRIEF

In writing a summary, you have to balance two concerns: you want your summary to be comprehensive, but you also want it to be brief. The point of writing a summary is to *reduce* a text to its most essential information. In a summary, brevity is usually achieved through carefully selecting your content and words. First, when writing your summary you need to include (1) the reading's primary ideas, arguments, or findings, and (2) the primary means of support the author offers for his or her contentions. Second, in writing and rewriting your summary, you must always be concerned about word count: if you can say something gracefully in four words rather than five, say it in four; if you can condense material by cutting unnecessary prepositions or adjectives, cut them. Composing a good summary requires disciplined writing.

ACCURATE

Your readers depend on you to be accurate in your summary. You have to be careful not to misrepresent—purposefully or accidentally—what the author wrote. Instead of reading the source text, your readers are depending on you to provide them a thorough, accurate, and fair overview of the piece. Misrepresenting an author in your summary is unfair to both your reader and the writer. However, accuracy can be hard to maintain. Because in a summary you are substituting your language for the author's, even slight changes in words can drastically alter the meaning of a passage. Therefore, when you review your summary, check it against the source to be sure you have accurately represented what the author wrote. Make sure you have not misrepresented the author's ideas or findings either by omitting some important information or by using inaccurate, slanted, or vague language.

NEUTRAL

Summaries should be objective. No matter how much you would like to praise or criticize an author's argument, interpretation of data, or style of writing, such comments do not belong in a summary. In a summary you do not present your views on the topic the author is addressing, you do not comment on the quality of the author's argument or writing, and you do not voice any of your opinions at all. Instead, you try to present what the author has written accurately and objectively. When reviewing your summary, make sure you have not included your own opinions and that you have used objective language. By avoiding highly charged or judgmental terms, you can help ensure that your summary is neutral, balanced, and fair.

When there are problems with objectivity in a summary, more often than not they appear in one of three places: at the beginnings of paragraphs, in the middle of long paragraphs, and at the very end of the piece. At the beginnings of paragraphs, students sometimes react to the material contained in the previous paragraph: instead of moving on to summarize the author's next point, they respond to the previous one. In the middle of paragraphs, students sometimes begin to debate the author. They may notice that the author has presented a weak argument, for example, and feel compelled to point that out. Such criticisms are appropriate for a critique, not for a summary. Finally, at the end of summaries, students sometimes add the kind of concluding line commonly found in high school book reports, "Overall, I really liked this book because . . ." or "Though I found the author convincing, sometimes I had a hard time . . ." Such statements do not belong in an objective, neutral summary.

INDEPENDENT

Your summary ought to make sense to someone who has not read the source text. Keep in mind the purpose of a summary. If, for instance, your employer asks you to summarize a report, she wants to learn from your summary the main points of the report without having to read the original text. Your summary must be able to stand on its own; read independently, it has to make sense. To achieve this goal, you need to pay special attention to word choice when drafting your summary. For example, are there any terms that, taken from the context of the source text, will need to be defined in your summary? Have you included in your summary any pronouns that refer to an antecedent in the source, not to an antecedent in your summary? Have you referred to people who were identified in the source but are not identified in your summary?

To make sure your summary is independent, before you turn it in for a grade let someone read it who has not read the source text. Ask that person to mark any words or passages he or she finds confusing.

HOW TO SUMMARIZE A TEXT

READ, REREAD, AND ANNOTATE THE SOURCE TEXT

Obviously, the first step in writing a summary is to read the material you are summarizing. As you read through it for the first time, try to get a sense of the passage's main ideas and structure—a sense of what the author covers and the order in which the ideas are presented. Next, read the material again, only more slowly this time. As you reread, carefully mark the passage, highlighting important material and in the margin taking notes that identify the main points and key supporting information as well as the structure of the piece.

If you are summarizing a paragraph, locate and mark the topic sentence. If there is no topic sentence, paraphrase the main point of the paragraph in the margin. If you are summarizing an entire essay or article, locate the thesis. If the author states the thesis, underline it and make a note in the margin. If the thesis is implied rather than stated, paraphrase the main point of the piece at the end of the passage. If the source text has headings and subheadings, note how they help structure the piece.

SUMMARIZE EACH SECTION OF THE SOURCE TEXT

Identify the major sections of the piece—where the author discusses one idea or develops one argument or explores one finding. These sections may consist of a single paragraph or a group of paragraphs. In the margin of the passage or on a separate sheet of paper, briefly summarize each section of the text. Using your own words, note the primary idea, assertion, or finding being developed in each section along with the primary supporting material the author provides—the most effective example, the most telling statistic, the most important authority cited.

WRITE YOUR FIRST DRAFT

As you write the first draft of your summary, keep in mind the following suggestions.

- In the **opening section** of your summary—usually the first paragraph or two—introduce the topic of the source text, give the title of the piece you are summarizing, give the name and credentials of the person who wrote the piece, and give your thesis. In a summary, your *thesis* will likely be a paraphrase of the source text's thesis. (Do not quote the source text's thesis to serve as your thesis—restate the reading's thesis in your own words.)
- In the **body** of your summary, present in your own words the author's primary assertions, conclusions, or findings, as well as the supporting examples

or statistics you believe your readers will need to know to understand and appreciate the author's contentions. Use as a guide the brief summaries of each section of the text you wrote earlier.

- Generally, summaries do not need a **conclusion**: simply end your essay with a summary of the author's last point. If you want or need a formal conclusion, make it a brief restatement of the author's thesis.

CHECK THE DRAFT AGAINST THE SOURCE TEXT

Once you finish your rough draft, reread the source text. Check to see if your summary is comprehensive, brief, accurate, neutral, and independent. This would be a good time to have someone else read your summary, preferably someone familiar with the source text who can offer constructive comments on your essay.

REWRITE THE SUMMARY

When you rewrite your summary, concentrate on correcting any problems with the content or tone you discovered when checking your first draft against the source text. Remember that your summary must stand on its own—it must read smoothly and make sense to someone who has not read the source text. Also, pay particular attention to the transitions you use to help guide your reader through your essay. If you are writing an explanatory summary, be sure to use narrative transitions (i.e., "first," "next," "then,"), especially at the beginning of your paragraphs, to help your reader follow the development of your summary. Next, check your paragraph breaks: while summaries of short readings may well be only one paragraph long, summaries of longer pieces will require multiple paragraphs. Finally, check to be sure your language is as objective and clear as possible. Inappropriate word choice can easily cause your essay to lose the appearance of objectivity. Also, see that you do not fall into the jargon of the source text. If you are summarizing highly technical or jargon-laden material, try to simplify the language without distorting the author's message.

DOCUMENTATION

Summarized material should be documented. Many students do not feel they need to document summaries because they are using their own language to convey the author's ideas. However, when you write a summary, you still need to give the author credit for those ideas, arguments, or findings. Documentation also tells your readers where they can locate the source text if they want to read the whole piece themselves.

SAMPLE SUMMARIES

Below are two summaries—one informative and one explanatory—of the following article, "AIDS and Population 'Control,'" by Gerard Piel, published in *Scientific American*.

AIDS and Population "Control"

Gerard Piel

Gerard Piel *is chairman emeritus of* Scientific American.

The now worldwide AIDS pandemic finds its ugliest manifestation in the proposition that AIDS has arrived in time to stop the population explosion. One hears it voiced by otherwise blameless people. Some see AIDS as the solution, in particular, for the "problem" of Africa. There the rate of population growth is highest and poverty deepest. Epidemiologists of the World Health Organization estimate that Africans constitute about 10 million of the 15 million people infected worldwide with the human immunodeficiency virus (HIV) and so fated to die of AIDS.

The AIDS proposition scants history and grossly underestimates the durability of the human species, Africans included. At its present rate of transmission, HIV will infect some 200 million people by 2010. The African share of the casualties might then approach 100 million. That, as a disciple of Thomas Malthus observed of the million Irish who perished in the 1845–50 potato famine, would scarcely be enough.

The Black Death, to which proponents of this cure for population growth hopefully compare the AIDS pandemic, carried off more than half the people of 14th-century Europe. By the middle of the 17th century, the European population had arrived at the point on the growth curve to which it would have increased by that time without deflection by the Black Death.

The paroxysm of violence that seized the industrial world through the three decades from the start of World War I to the end of World War II killed 200 million people. That was more than 10 percent of all the people who lived in those years. Their absence was not remarked in 1970, when the rate of world population growth reached its all-time peak, at around 2 percent.

It was Malthus who made economics the dismal science, but he also made this branch of moral philosophy a science. He rooted economics in what had been the unrelieved experience of humankind from the time of the agricultural revolution and the opening of the first village markets. "Apart from short exceptional periods," Alfred North Whitehead observed, "the normal structure of society was that of a comparatively affluent minority subsisting on the labors of a teeming population checked by starvation and other discomforts."

At the very time Malthus set out his baleful equation, however, industrial revolution had begun to make the growth of production outrun population. Within 20 years of Malthus's death, moreover, John Stuart Mill discovered from inspection of baptismal records that the birth rate of England had begun to decline. This discovery did not shake the conviction, which Mill shared with Malthus, that population growth was the "dynamics of political economy," for the population of prospering England was exploding.

The population of all the European countries undergoing industrial revolution was exploding during this period. Now, after this gigantic increase, which multiplied the number of Europeans 20 times over that in 1600 and avalanched them onto all continents, the populations of all the industrial countries are at or approaching zero growth. These lucky 1.25 billion people—counting the Japanese, the first non-European, in their number—are completing the so-called demographic transition. From near-zero growth in 1600 at high death rates and high birth rates with life expectancy at 25 years, they are arriving at near-zero growth again but at low death rates and low birth rates with life expectancy at 75 years.

Recent history gives every reason to expect that the other three quarters of the world population will make the demographic transition. The leading edge of industrial revolution—mass education, sanitation and primary medicine, and the green revolution—has brought down death rates and lengthened life expectancy throughout the preindustrial world. The rest of humankind has entered the first phase of the demographic transition. Hence the ongoing swelling of the population.

Entrance into the second phase is marked for some few developing countries by decline in their birth rates. These are countries where industrial revolution has proceeded furthest and where its increasing product is most widely shared—small countries like Costa Rica and Sri Lanka and also the biggest countries, India and China.

Whitehead cited India and China as "instances of civilized societies which for a very long period in their later histories maintained themselves with arrested technology . . . . They provided the exact conditions for the importance of the Malthusian Law." By the turn of the 19th century, when Malthus published his *Essay on Population*, they were the world's most populous countries.

Since the end of World War II, India and China have been engaged in industrial revolution, China leading. With life expectancy lengthening to

60 years in India and to 70 years in China, their huge populations have more than doubled. In both countries, calories per capita now meet the daily requirement, and potable water is available to three quarters of their citizens. India has reduced its child death rate to 142 per 1,000 live births, and China to 42. In India, 27 percent of the population lives in cities, in China, 33 percent. Literacy among the female population is 34 percent in India and 62 percent in China. Contraceptives are in use in 43 and 71 percent of their households, respectively. As these statistics suggest, both nations have entered the second phase of the demographic transition. The fertility rate in India has declined from more than six (infants per female reproductive lifetime) to four; in China it is 2.3, close to the zero growth rate of 2.1.

How to hasten the passage of the preindustrial world through the demographic transition was the principal topic before the United Nations Conference on Environment and Development, the Earth Summit, held in Rio de Janeiro in the summer of 1992. The major product of the conference, Agenda 21, is now the agenda of the United Nations. It sets out a program of "sustainable development" to bring human numbers and appetites into accord with the finite resources of the earth before the end of the next century. The AIDS pandemic can only divert physical resources and human energy from this hopeful and urgent enterprise. Delay portends a larger ultimate world population. Industrial revolution has set the terms of a morality different from that implied by the Malthusian equation. It is people living, not dying, who bring population growth to a stop.

SAMPLE INFORMATIVE SUMMARY

In "AIDS and Population 'Control,'" author Gerard Piel rejects the idea that AIDS will serve to control population growth, especially in Africa and other underdeveloped areas of the world. Piel suggests, instead, that industrialization leads countries through a "demographic transition" that results in zero population growth and greater longevity.

In the past, epidemics, wars, and natural disasters have had no long-term effect on population growth. Thomas Malthus had theorized that because the world's population would grow faster than our capacity to develop resources, such calamities were needed to curb overpopulation. However, the Industrial Revolution fundamentally changed the conditions on which Malthus based his theories. The experiences of Western Europe and Japan show that industrialization leads, at first, to a rapid rise in population as nutrition and health care improve (the "first phase" of the demographic transition) then to near-zero population growth as birth rates fall and life expectancy rises.

Today, India and China are going through such a shift. Both countries are becoming more industrialized, and their population is beginning to stabilize. Since the 1940s life expectancy has increased in both countries, child death rates have fallen, and fertility rates have declined.

The participants at the 1992 Earth Summit in Rio de Janeiro agreed that the United Nations needs to develop a plan to help newly industrial nations balance population growth and the demands on natural resources. AIDS is not a factor in controlling population growth—industrialization is (76–78).

SAMPLE EXPLANATORY SUMMARY

In "AIDS and Population 'Control,'" author Gerard Piel attacks the idea voiced by some that AIDS will serve to control rapid population growth, especially in less industrialized areas of the world such as Africa. Piel suggests, instead, that the preindustrialized world is now entering a period of "demographic transition," which the West experienced years ago, a change that will lead to zero population growth and a better quality of life for all.

Piel opens his essay by pointing out how previous epidemics, wars, and natural disasters have had no long-term effect on population growth. This fact counters the theories of Thomas Malthus, who had suggested that such calamities are needed to check population growth. Piel notes that at the time Malthus was writing, the Industrial Revolution was moving Europe into the "first phase" of a demographic transition—a period of rapid population growth generated by an equally rapid increase in the nation's ability to feed and care for its people. Following this period in Europe and Japan, birth rates fell, life expectancy rose, and near-zero population growth was achieved as these areas entered the final phase of the transition.

Piel next offers evidence that industrializing countries today are experiencing similar changes, focusing primarily on recent changes in India and China—countries Malthus used to support his earlier theories on population growth and epidemics. Since the 1940s both China and India have followed a course of steady industrialization. In both nations, life expectancy has increased (to 60 years in India, 70 years in China), child death rates have fallen, female literacy rates have increased, and fertility rates—due to more widespread use of contraceptives—have declined (from around 6 children per woman in India to about 4, and in China to 2.3). As each country has industrialized, it has also become better able to

provide adequate food and water for its people, improving their
quality of life.

   Piel closes his essay by noting that those attending the 1992
Earth Summit in Rio de Janeiro urged the United Nations to
develop programs to help developing nations reconcile their
population growth and their use of natural resources. AIDS is not
the key to controlling population growth, as some have suggested.
Instead, Piel contends, industrialization, which leads to longer,
better lives, will eventually solve the world's population
problems (76–78).

Summary Chart

HOW TO WRITE A SUMMARY

1. **Read, reread, and annotate the material.**

   Carefully read the material, paying particular attention to the content and structure of the piece.

   Reread and annotate the material, being sure to note:
   * *the thesis;*
   * *the primary assertions, arguments, or findings; and*
   * *the primary means of support for each point.*

2. **Write one-sentence summaries of each section of the text.**

   Identify the major sections of the reading, in which the writer develops one idea before moving on to the next.

   In your own words, restate the main point developed in each section of the text and primary means of support the author provides.

3. **Write the first draft of your summary.**

   Introduce the topic of the reading.

   Include, early in your essay, the author's full name and the full title of the piece.

   In the body of your summary, elaborate on the one-sentence summaries, clearly explaining the important content of the reading.

4. **Check the rough draft of your summary against the source text. As you review your work, make sure your summary is:**

   Comprehensive—you have included in your summary all of the author's important ideas, assertions, or findings.

   Accurate—in choosing words and selecting material for your summary, you have not misrepresented the author's positions or findings.

   Neutral—in choosing words and selecting material for your summary, you have attempted to be objective and fair.

   Independent—your summary will make sense to someone who has not read the source text.

5. Rewrite your summary.

Based on your evaluation of your rough draft, make any needed changes in the content, organization, or language of your summary.

If you are writing an explanatory summary, include any transition words you need to guide your reader through your work.

Chapter 5

RESPONSE ESSAYS

DEFINITION AND PURPOSE

Response essays ask you to examine, explain, and often defend your personal reaction to a reading. In this type of essay you explore why you liked the reading, agreed with the author, found the piece informative or confusing—whatever your response might be. There are no necessarily "right" or "wrong" reactions to material; instead, response essays are usually evaluated on the basis of how well you demonstrate an understanding of the reading and how clearly you explain your reactions.

Sometimes teachers grade response essays the same way they grade any other assignment. Other times they assign ungraded response essays—usually as a way to help students develop material for graded essays. Still other teachers combine response essays with other types of papers; for example, they ask students to summarize then respond to a reading, or to respond to a reading then critique it. Sometimes teachers will specify which aspects of the text they would like you respond to in your essay (for example, the author's thesis or use of figurative language); other times they will leave the choice of content up to you. In short, the response essay is a very flexible assignment employed widely by teachers in college. Writing this type of paper helps you understand your personal reaction to what you read: what you think about the topic, how you judge the author's ideas, how the words on the page affect you as a reader.

Effective response essays demonstrate a strong connection between the source text and your reaction. Your responses are triggered by what you read, by certain words on the page. It is important to keep that connection strongly in mind as you compose your response essay. First, you need to put into words your responses to the source text. Second, you need to identify which words on the page triggered those responses. Third, you need to determine, then explain for your reader, why and how those words triggered those responses.

In writing this type of essay, you cannot simply state your response and move on: "I liked this. I didn't like that." "This interested me; that puzzled me." Instead, you must develop and explain your response: what, *exactly*, is your response; what part of the text triggered it; what, *exactly*, is the relationship between the words on the page and your reactions to them? While the idea of "developing" your response may seem odd, remember that you are writing for a reader, not just for yourself. You want your reader to be able to understand and appreciate both your response and what led you to have it. Clearly, writing a response essay is more difficult than it might first appear.

QUALITIES OF A GOOD RESPONSE ESSAY

Part of what makes a good response essay difficult to write is that it must be honest, informed, clear, and well supported.

- *Honest*—it reflects your true responses.
- *Informed*—it reflects an accurate and thorough understanding of the source text.
- *Clear*—it makes sense to your readers.
- *Well supported*—it demonstrates a close link between your responses and the source text itself.

HONEST

A response essay should focus on your sincere, thoughtful reactions to what you read. You want to identify your responses to the material and explore their relationship to the text itself: What gives rise to your reactions? How do they affect your reading of the author's work? These essays are highly subjective—you focus on *your* reactions to the text. Consequently, you should not pretend your responses are other than what they truly are. If you found a work boring, for example, do not claim that you found it intriguing simply because you think that is the way you are *supposed* to respond.

INFORMED

Can your responses, then, ever be "wrong"? In one sense, they cannot—your responses are your responses. That does not mean, though, that all responses to a reading are equally informed. If, for example, your response is based on a misunderstanding of the source text—if you criticize an author for saying something she never said—then your response is misguided. Responses can also be naive, shortsighted, or biased. These responses are not, in a sense, "wrong," but neither are they very insightful. Informed response essays are based on a clear understanding of the source text: the more you know about a topic, author, or reading, the more likely your response will be informed.

Take, for example, an experience I had a few years ago. I asked a group of students to respond to a satirical political essay before we discussed the piece in class. The students who recognized the satire produced fine response essays. However, the students who did not understand that the author was being satirical terribly misread the piece and produced misguided essays. Their responses were honest—the responses accurately reflected their reading of the text—but they were not informed.

CLEAR

When your readers finish your response essay, they should understand (1) how you reacted to the reading and (2) how your reactions are tied to the source text. Problems with clarity often arise from weak content, weak organization, or poor word choice.

Problems with clarity involving **content** occur when the person writing the response essay fails to state clearly the nature of his or her response, fails to identify which aspect of the source text gave rise to that response, or fails to explain the relationship between his or her response and those aspects of the text. Without all three being clearly stated and explored, readers are often left confused about the nature of your response to the reading.

Other problems with clarity involve **organization**. Be sure that your essay has a fully developed opening and closing section and a clearly stated thesis. A good response essay also explores only one reaction at a time and provides clear transitions between the various sections of the paper. Problems with clarity can occur when you shift too quickly from discussing one response to discussing another—without a good transition, the change of focus might not be clear to your reader.

Finally, problems with clarity often involve the **language** used in response essays. Too often students use vague language to explore their reactions—words that mean something to them but nothing to their readers. Though response essays are highly subjective, when you turn them in for a grade, they must be addressed to a more public audience. Good response essays can be difficult to write for just this reason: you have to find language that clearly and efficiently communicates to others your subjective responses to a reading.

WELL SUPPORTED

In good response essays, students support and explain their reactions to the text with specific, elaborated examples. If, for example, a student claims that she was offended by an author's illogical assertions, she should quote some of those passages and explain why she finds them illogical. If another student reads the same work and finds the same passages convincing because they match his experiences, he should also quote some examples and explain why he finds them convincing. In either case, the student supports her or his responses by citing from the source text examples that gave rise to them and then clearly explaining the relationship between those examples and their responses.

WRITING THE RESPONSE ESSAY

CAREFULLY READ THE MATERIAL

The problem with many response essays is that the students have not *fully* understood the source text before they begin to write. Some students respond to only part of the reading, without indicating they understand how the material fits into the author's overall thesis. As a result, their responses often seem limited or even biased; their work tends to ignore important issues raised in the source text. Other students simply misread the source text—basing their response on something the author neither wrote nor intended.

Therefore, when you are assigned to respond to a reading, read it several times and briefly summarize it before you write your essay (see Chapter 4 for advice on writing summaries). Summarizing the piece first can help ensure that your response will be based on a full and accurate understanding of the text's content, structure, tone, and thesis.

Explore Your Responses to the Reading as You Annotate the Text

To develop material for your response essay, as you read and annotate the text, note your responses briefly in the margin of the piece. Sometimes just jotting down a key word or two will do; other times you may need to write out a question you have. Even punctuation marks, such as exclamation points or question marks, can help you keep track of your reactions. When you are finished, expand on these notes at the end of the reading or on a separate sheet of paper. Your goal is to capture in a few sentences your overall response to what you have just read. These notes will form the basis of your response essay. In deciding what to mark and what kinds of comments to write as you read the source text, try answering the following questions.

How Do You React Emotionally to What the Author Has Written?

Your subjective, emotional reaction to a reading is a good place to start generating material for a response essay. Does the text make you angry? Excited? Bored? To explore these reactions, ask yourself several questions:

1. What, exactly, has the author written that makes you feel this way?
2. At what point in your reading did you have these reactions?
3. Which words on the page or ideas cause this response?
4. In short, what has the author done to make you respond this way? Examine the choices the writer made concerning content, organization, and style. What aspects of the text contribute to your response?

As you try to capture your responses in writing, carefully examine your reactions and, when possible, tie them to specific words, passages, or graphics in the text.

How Do the Ideas Offered in the Reading Compare with Your Experience or Your Sense of Reality?

We have all had the experience of hearing or reading something that has a ring of truth or falsehood. Something in a reading makes sense to us because it squares with our experience; it sits right with what we have come to understand about the world. As you reread and annotate a reading, note which of the author's ideas you tend to agree with or question based on their match to your own experience.

There is a real danger, though, in judging what others say by the standards of our experience alone. All of us bring to a reading important but limited experiences. When an author's statements do not match our sense of reality, we should not act defensively and immediately dismiss her ideas. Likewise, simply because we tend to agree with an author does not mean we ought to accept her ideas uncritically. Writing a response essay will give you the chance to question what you believe in light of what the author writes, to understand how your experiences influence the way you react to new ideas.

How Do the Ideas Offered in the Source Match What Others Have Had to Say on the Topic?

When you read a source, you bring with you not only what you think and feel based on your own experience, but also what you know, what you have already learned from your reading and education. There is no reason to ignore this knowledge when you write your response essay. In fact, whether the source text confirms or contradicts what you already know about the topic may be one of the reasons for your reaction to the piece. Be sure to note any reactions you have based on the match between the author's ideas and those proposed by other authors you have read.

COMPOSE YOUR ROUGH DRAFT

When you write your response essay, you will need to introduce the source text, provide your reader with a brief summary of its content, then develop and clarify your reactions.

Introduce Your Topic, Source Text, and Thesis

When composing the opening of your response essay, you have four goals: introduce the topic of your essay, introduce your source text, state your thesis, and capture reader interest. Once you introduce the source text's topic, provide its title and its author's full name. Your thesis for this type of essay will be a statement of your overall response to the reading and, if you like, an indication of how you will develop or explore that response in the body of your paper. If you employ an "open" thesis statement for your essay, you will indicate your overall response to the piece:

- I found parts of the essay confusing.
- Reading this essay proved to be an emotional challenge.

If you employ a "closed" thesis statement for your essay, you will indicate your overall response to the source text and also indicate how you will develop that response in the body of your paper:

- I found parts of the essay confusing, especially its structure and many of its allusions.
- Because members of my family have been touched by the issues the author discusses, reading this essay proved to be an emotional challenge.

Either type of thesis can work equally well. Finally, to capture reader interest you may want to use one of the following strategies:

- Open your essay with a provocative or interesting question raised by the reading or your response to it.
- Open your essay with an interesting quotation from the reading.
- Open your essay with a personal anecdote or hypothetical story related to the topic of the reading.
- Open your essay with a reference to a current controversy or public issue related to the topic of the reading.

Summarize the Source Text

After introducing the source and stating your thesis, give a brief summary of the reading. Generally, this summary will be only a paragraph or two long, highlighting the reading's most important findings, conclusions, or arguments. In the summary, anticipate what you will address in the body of your response. For example, if you know you will be questioning the validity of some of the author's claims, summarize his claims in this part of your essay. When they come up again in the body of your response, your reader will likely remember them and will be able to follow your assertions more easily.

State and Explain Your Responses Clearly and Concisely

In the body of your essay, you explore your responses, clearly and thoroughly, one at a time. This process might sound simple, but clearly and thoroughly stating and explaining your response to a reading can be difficult primarily because it is *your* response. The language you use when describing your reaction may make perfect sense to you but might well be unclear to your reader. For instance, if you were reading someone else's response essay and the writer complained that the source text made her feel "wheezy," would you really know what the person meant? Perhaps her explanation would make it clear, but the language she uses to characterize her response may hinder her readers' ability to understand her reaction. Therefore, a first step in clarifying your response for a reader is to choose language that others can understand. Likewise, explain the terms you use. For example, if you contend that a source is confusing, explain what you mean by "confusing"—that is, whether you had difficulty understanding the writer's language, findings, structure, or some other aspect of the text.

Next, be sure to provide specific examples from the source text to help your reader understand each response. When you have a particular response to a reading, something on the page triggered it. In your essay, identify those "triggering" passages before you explain the dynamics of your response. For example, if you contend that a source text is confusing, identify and perhaps quote a passage you cannot understand, then explain what it is about the writing you find difficult to follow (the logic of the passage? the wording? the structure?).

WRITE YOUR CONCLUSION

With a response essay, your conclusion should restate your overall response to the source text, echoing your thesis. To give a sense of closure to your essay, you should also try to mirror the strategy you employed to capture reader interest in the opening of your essay. For example, if you opened your essay with a question, return to that question in your conclusion and provide an answer. If you opened with an anecdote or story, refer back to it in your conclusion, perhaps indicating how that anecdote or story turned out. If you opened with a quotation from the source text, consider closing with a quotation as well.

REVISE YOUR ROUGH DRAFT

As you revise the rough draft of your response, pay particular attention to your assertions, organization, language, and support.

Review Your Assertions

When you review the assertions you make in your response essay, your primary concern is accuracy:

- Have you truly captured your reactions to the reading?
- Have you openly, honestly, and thoroughly explored your response to the material?
- Does your essay offer an accurate representation of your reaction?

- When other people read your essay, will they be able to understand and appreciate your reaction?

To check your assertions, first reread the source text and see whether you still feel the same way about it. Even a short time away from a reading may enable you to reconsider your reactions—maybe your views have changed. If they have changed, revise your essay. Also, in reviewing the source text, be sure you reread the annotations you originally made. Have you addressed the concerns, questions, and reactions you noted as you earlier annotated the piece?

Review Your Support and Explanations

As you revise your response, examine the way you illustrate and explain each of your responses. Remember that your responses should be tied to specific aspects of the source text, such as words, images, and graphics. When you compose your response, you need to explain for your reader the link between the source text and your reaction. In the body of your essay, you should state a response, point out what aspect of the reading led to that reaction (perhaps quoting the passage), then explain clearly and thoroughly how that material led you to that response. As you revise your draft, make sure you accomplish all three goals in each section of your essay.

Review Your Organization

Next, when you review the organization of your rough draft, check to be sure you have fully developed opening and closing sections and have a clearly stated thesis. In the body of your essay, be sure that you are developing only one response at a time. Often when you write your rough draft, examining one reaction will lead you to a new response, one you have not previously considered. That is one of the real powers of writing: it not only helps you capture ideas in words but often will help you generate new ideas as well. When this happens, some writers will follow that new idea even if it does not belong in that part of the essay, knowing that in the next draft they can place it elsewhere. Other writers prefer to write a note to themselves to explore that new idea later, not wanting to lose track of the idea they are currently exploring. When you review your rough draft, check to see that you are developing only one response at a time in your essay.

Finally, be sure you indicate to your reader—through paragraph breaks and transition words—when you shift focus from one response to the next. Adding these signals to your paper makes it easier for your reader to follow your line of thought. Since you are writing about *your* responses, you know when you have changed focus; your readers, though, may have a harder time recognizing the structure of your essay. Adding appropriate paragraph breaks and transitions can help.

Review Your Language

As indicated earlier, word choice—finding and choosing appropriate terms to express your reactions—can be truly problematic when you are writing response essays. First, your initial reactions to what you read may be so emotional or so abstract that you cannot put them into words. You may struggle to find appropriate language. Second, your first efforts at finding words may result in highly "private" writing; since they arise from your own knowledge and experience, the terms you use may make sense only to you. In this case, you need to find terms that can communicate your responses to others. Before you turn in the final draft of your response essay, be sure to have someone else read your work, someone you trust to give you an honest appraisal of your language. Ask that person to indicate any part of the response he or she does not understand because of the words you are using.

SAMPLE RESPONSE ESSAY

These two sample essays are responding to the article "AIDS and Population 'Control'" by Gerald Piel found in Chapter 4 of this book. If you are unfamiliar with the article, read it before you read the following response essays. In the first essay, the writer responds primarily to Piel's argument, evidence, and reasoning; in the second essay, the writer offers an emotional response to Piel's piece.

SAMPLE ESSAY 1

A Response to "AIDS and Population 'Control'"

Overall, I found the argument presented in "AIDS and Population 'Control'" interesting and informative. Author Gerard Piel presents a clear thesis and supports it well with logical examples and sound reasoning. However, I also found parts of the essay confusing, especially some of the allusions, which makes me wonder about the intended audience of the piece.

"AIDS and Population 'Control'" examines the claim advanced by some that AIDS will serve as a check on population. Piel rejects this idea, pointing out that past epidemics have had little long-term effect on population growth. Instead, he believes that industrial development curbs overpopulation. Citing the experiences of Europe and Japan as examples, Piel puts forward the idea that as countries industrialize and improve their standard of living, birth rates fall and life expectancy rises. As a result, industrialized nations reach near-zero population growth. Piel claims such a process is now occurring in countries such as China and India—industrialization, he claims, controls population, not diseases such as AIDS.

Generally, I found Piel's argument convincing. First, he offers several examples to support his contention that famine and disease have little effect on population growth. For example, Piel points out that Europe overcame the effects of the Black Death in three centuries and that all the death and destruction associated with the two world wars again had a negligible effect on population growth. By 1970 the world's population was growing at a record pace (66). I thought these specific examples clarified Piel's position and added credibility to his thesis: he is relying on historical facts that can be verified.

His examination of industrialization and population was also interesting, but I found it more difficult to follow. For example, he refers repeatedly to the "second phase" of the "demographic shift" without fully explaining what a "demographic shift" is and without explaining how many "phases" are involved in such a phenomenon.

More informative was the analogy Piel draws between the experiences of Europe and Japan and the current condition of India and China (67–68). I know the history of Europe more thoroughly than I know the history of India and China—the comparisons he draws give me some context for understanding what is happening in the lands and cultures I know less well. Particularly compelling was his use of specific statistics—on child death rates, life expectancy rates, and fertility rates. These figures bring into sharp focus and make more concrete the current state of affairs in these countries (especially the fact that China's current fertility rate is 2.3 children per woman with 2.1 representing zero population growth) (68). What is missing, though, are some comparison figures. How have these figures changed over the past few decades? How do they currently compare to European or Japanese figures? Without more of a context, the figures Piel provides are not as effective and informative as they could be.

I had more trouble with some of Piel's allusions. He refers frequently to the work of Thomas Malthus and twice cites the words of Alfred North Whitehead. I think readers unfamiliar with the theories proposed by Malthus (that population growth will outstrip our means of production) would have a hard time following Piel's argument. I wonder what type of reader Piel had in mind when he wrote this piece. He obviously assumes his audience is well read, that they are familiar with Malthus's ideas and with European history. Readers who understand Piel's allusions will get the most out of his work. However, even if they do not catch all the references, they will still come away with a clear idea of how industrialization might affect population growth far more than will AIDS.

SAMPLE ESSAY 2

AIDS, Population Control, and the Need for Public Action: A Response to Gerald Piel

How seriously should the world take the fact that millions of African citizens are infected with the immunodeficiency virus (HIV) and will likely die from AIDS? Should citizens of the Western World be concerned or should we just see this as just one more epidemic that periodically assaults human kind? If fact, can the AIDS outbreak in Africa actually be a blessing in disguise, acting as a means to control over population on the continent? In "AIDS and Population 'Control,'" Gerald Piel, chairman emeritus of *Scientific American*, argues against the idea that epidemics actually control population growth. In modern times, industrialization has accomplished that goal, not disease. Piel presents a logical argument supporting his position, but his analytical (and often sarcastic) tone and academic indifference left me angry and disappointed. Behind all the statistics Piel cites are real people dying horrible deaths in Africa.

In his article, Piel argues against the idea that "AIDS has arrived in time to stop the population explosion" in Africa (66). To support his position, he states that past epidemics, such as the Black Death, only temporarily halted population growth. Today, the population is growing at insupportable rates only in pre-industrialized areas of the world. In the industrial West and Japan, growth rates are near zero. Piel predicts the same growth rate for China and India once they have fully industrialized their economies. All of these countries have passed through what Piel calls "the demographic transition": a rise in population coinciding with a rise in industrialization which will be followed by longer life spans and near zero population growth. According to Piel, those interested in controlling the world's population growth should expend their efforts on hastening industrialization, not fighting AIDS. In fact, "The AIDS pandemic can only divert physical resources and human energy from this hopeful and urgent enterprise" (68).

If I had read Piel's essay a month earlier than I did, my response would have been different than it is now. I might have been convinced by his carefully reasoned argument and not thought any more deeply about his position. But now Piel's essay makes me angry. Though he is clearly an educated man, Piel apparently lacks compassion—he does not seem to appreciate the human suffering behind the AIDS epidemic, the 10 million tragic stories of the 10 million African citizens infected with HIV.

My views on AIDS and HIV in Africa changed last month when a missionary visited our church to talk about her experiences in Nigeria and the Ivory Coast. This missionary, who is also a doctor, worked in several African villages for over two years and shared her heart-breaking stories about the devastating effects of AIDS. She brought slides and showed us one village where almost all of the adult men and women are infected. Over half of the people living there have died, and she expects that in a few years the entire village will be wiped out. She then showed us slides of the babies who are born infected with the disease. These innocent victims have virtually no chance of surviving because the villages do not have access to modern health care and medicine. The doctor said the missionaries do what they can to help, but they know that most of their villagers will die. She asked all of us to help by becoming more informed about AIDS, by supporting World Health Organization efforts to bring needed medicines to Africa, and by urging our political leaders to devote more resources to the fight against HIV. I think everyone leaving church that day had a new attitude toward the plight of the African people.

After listening to this doctor, I have to agree with Piel that viewing AIDS as a way to control the population in Africa is an ugly position to maintain (66). What upsets me about Piel's essay, though, is the fact that after discussing Africa in the opening paragraphs of his essay, he never again addresses its suffering people. I understand that the focus of his essay is "population control," but using the plight of AIDS-infected Africans to help him make his point just seems cold. Any suggestion that fighting AIDS is a diversion of "physical resources and human energy" is morally reprehensible. It indicates a callous indifference to the kind of suffering I saw and heard about that Sunday. Perhaps Piel is right about the effects of industrialization—that as countries become more industrialized, health care increases and both mortality and birth rates decrease. However, industrialization is not coming any time soon to the villages the doctor serves; it is a long-term solution, at best. In the mean time, physical resources and human energy need to be pouring into Africa to help those suffering and dying.

So how seriously should the world take the fact that millions of African citizens are infected with HIV and will likely die from AIDS? Much more seriously than Gerald Piel seems to take it in "AIDS and Population 'Control.'" At best, Piel offers a long-term solution to the problem of over-population and the spread of AIDS, but he seems to discount actions that need to be taken immediately to help those in need. What we do, how we act, *today* is the real test of our humanity.

Summary Chart

HOW TO WRITE A RESPONSE ESSAY

1. **Carefully read the material.**

   Your goal is to form a clear understanding of what the writer has to say.

   Identify and be able to paraphrase the writer's thesis and main assertions or findings.

2. **Reread and annotate the text.**

   As you reread the material, begin to examine your responses by asking yourself the following questions:
   - *How do I react emotionally to what the author has written?*
   - *How do the ideas offered in the source text match my experience and my sense of reality?*
   - *How do the ideas offered in the text match what others have had to say about the topic?*

   Note in the margin your responses to these questions using some combination of the following:
   - *key words*
   - *questions*
   - *statements*
   - *punctuation marks*

   When you are finished, write out in a few sentences your response to the material.

3. **Compose your rough draft.**

   Introduce the topic, your source text, and the full name of the author or authors.

   Summarize the source text.

   State and explain your responses clearly and concisely one at a time.
   - *State your response.*
       For example, the material made you angry.
   - *Explain the terms you are using.*
       What do you mean by "angry"?

Summary Chart: Critical Reading: Note Taking *(continued)*

- *Tie that response to some aspect of the source text.*
  What material in the reading made you feel that way?
- *Explain how that material gave rise to that response.*
  Why or how did that material make you feel angry?
- *Write your conclusion.*
  What was your overall response to the material?

4. **Revise your rough draft.**

   Review your assertions about your reactions.
   - *Are they honest?*
   - *Are they informed?*
   - *Are they clear?*
   - *Are they well supported?*

   Review your organization.
   - *Are your opening and closing sections constructed well?*
   - *Are you addressing one response at a time?*
   - *Are there clear transitions between the responses you explore?*
   - *Are your responses tied to some guiding thesis?*

   Review your language.
   - *Are you using terms your readers are likely to understand?*
   - *Are you invoking a consistent tone, not becoming too informal, too angry, or too satiric when that does not match the tone of your response as a whole?*

   Review your support.
   - *Have you tied each response to some aspect of the text?*
   - *Have you added enough textual references to make clear the connections between the reading and your response?*
   - *Have you attempted to explain those connections?*

Chapter 6

CRITIQUE

DEFINITION AND PURPOSE

While response essays focus on your personal reactions to a reading, critiques offer a more formal evaluation. Instead of responding to a reading in light of your experience and feelings, in a critique you evaluate a source text's quality or worth according to a set of established criteria. Based on your evaluation, you then assert some judgment concerning the text—whether the reading was effective, ineffective, valuable, or trivial. Critiques, then, are usually argumentative. Your goal is to convince your readers to accept your judgments concerning the quality of the reading.

These judgments will be based on certain criteria and standards. **Criteria** are certain aspects of a reading that serve as the basis of your assessment—for example, the text's style or use of evidence. **Standards** serve as the basis for evaluating a criterion—what makes a certain "style" good or bad, acceptable or unacceptable? What counts as "valid" evidence in a reading? When you critique a reading, you will employ either **general** academic criteria and standards (those used to evaluate source material in many fields) or **discipline-specific** criteria and standards (those used by scholars in a particular field of study and generally not applicable to material studied in other disciplines).

In college composition courses you may learn how to critique a source text using general evaluative criteria—for example, how to assess the quality of a reading based on its structure, style, or evidence. These criteria can help you evaluate source material in a variety of classes. In your other college courses you may learn discipline-specific evaluative criteria typically used to assess source material in that field of study. For example, in an English literature course you may learn the criteria used by scholars to critique a poem or a play; in an accounting class, you may learn to employ the criteria and standards experts in that discipline use to critique a financial report or prospectus.

Students often find the idea of writing a critique intimidating: they are not sure what the assignment is asking them to do, how to generate material for their paper, what to include in their essay, how to support their assertions, or what tone to assume. However, you are probably more familiar with this type of writing than you realize since you are often exposed to one special form of critique: the movie review. If you ever listened to Siskel and Ebert argue over a film, you are familiar with the basic structure of a critique. If you ever discussed the strengths and weaknesses of a movie and tried to get a friend to go see it (or to avoid it), then you have already engaged in critique. Examining how a film critic writes a review of a movie can help you understand how to write a critique of a reading.

THE FILM REVIEW AS CRITIQUE

First, consider the nature of a movie critic's job: he watches a film, analyzes and evaluates what he sees, forms some judgment based on that analysis and evaluation, then writes his review, trying to clarify and defend his judgments with specific references to the film and clear explanations of his assertions. In writing his review, the critic does not address every aspect of the film; he addresses only those aspects of the movie that best support his judgment of it. If, for instance, he thought a film was wonderful, he would address in his review only the aspects of the film that, in his opinion, made it exceptional— for example, the direction, the photography, and the acting. If he thought the film was uneven—some parts good, other parts weak—he would offer in his review examples of what made the film effective (maybe the plot or the lighting) and examples of what made it ineffective (maybe the musical score and the special effects).

Think about the way you discuss a film with someone. Maybe the conversation runs something like this:

"So, did you like the movie?"

"Yeah, pretty much. I wasn't too sure about some of the dialogue— sounded pretty lame sometimes—but the special effects were good and the acting was ok."

"The acting was just 'ok'? What didn't you like? I thought the acting was great."

"Well, there was that scene early in the film, right before he shot the guy; I just didn't buy it when he . . ."

In this conversation, one friend asserts a position about the film, is challenged, then begins to defend or explain her view. To convince her friend to accept her judgment, she will likely discuss specific aspects of the film she believes best illustrate her views.

Most of us are accustomed to talking about movies, television shows, or CDs this way—we form and defend judgments about what we see, hear, and read all the time. However, we are usually more comfortable evaluating movies than we are critiquing arguments, book chapters, or lab reports. First, when it comes to movies, we are probably familiar with many of the source texts—we have seen lots of films—and most of us feel we can knowledgeably discuss what we have seen; we can generate, fairly easily, lots of examples from a movie to support our views. Second, we know *how* to talk about films: we know how to identify and discuss particular aspects of a movie—certain criteria—that influence our judgment. We know that when we analyze a movie we can address the dialogue, the acting, the special effects, and so forth. Finally, we know the standards usually applied to evaluate various aspects of a film; we know what passes for good dialogue, good acting, good special effects, and so on. In short, when we discuss a movie, we know how to *analyze* it (what parts to focus on for review), *evaluate* it (what kinds of questions to ask of each part when assessing its quality), and *defend* our assertions (how to examine specific scenes from the film that support our judgments).

These are the same basic skills you employ to critique readings in college. To critique readings, you need to engage in:

- *Analysis*—break readings down into their essential parts.
- *Evaluation*—assess the quality of those various parts.
- *Explanation*—link your judgments to specific aspects of the readings and make those connections clear and convincing to your reader.

Even though you have probably engaged in this process quite often when discussing movies or television shows, you may have a hard time using these skills to critique readings. First, you are probably less familiar with how critiques look and sound than you are with how movie reviews look and sound. When you are assigned to write a critique, no model may come to mind. Second, the readings you are asked to critique in college can be hard to understand. You cannot critique a reading until you are certain you know what it has to say. Finally, you are probably less familiar with the criteria and standards used in college to analyze and critique readings than you are with the criteria and standards used to review films. When you are asked to critique a philosophical essay on the nature of knowledge, do you know how to break that reading down into its key parts and what kinds of questions to ask of each part to determine its quality? When asked to critique a chapter of your history book, do you know what to look for, what questions to ask? Learning how to critique readings such as these is a central goal of your college education, a skill you will obtain through practice in many different disciplines.

Examining how a movie critic organizes a review can also help you understand how to structure a critique. For example, a critic typically opens her review with a "thesis" that captures her overall assessment of the film. This thesis may take the form of a statement early in the review, a graphic placed beside the review—for example, five stars or two stars—or frequently a comment at the end of the review. Sometimes the critic will love the film; she will give it five stars and a rave review. Sometimes she will hate the movie; she will give it one star and a terrible review. Still other times she will have a split decision; she will give it two and a half stars and in her review acknowledge the strengths and weaknesses of the movie. Next, the critic will typically offer a brief summary of the film so her readers can follow what she has to say in the review. Then, in the body of the review, she will address only the aspects of the film that best illustrate or defend her thesis: she will introduce a particular element of the film (for example, the special effects), comment on its quality (claim they were especially effective), describe a specific example or two from the film (perhaps the climactic battle scene), and explain how that specific example illustrates or supports her judgment (what made the special effects in that battle scene especially good).

Writing a critique involves much the same process. After reading the text, you'll form a judgment of its quality or worth based on some set of criteria and standards. This judgment will form the thesis of your critique, which you will explain or defend in the body of your essay, with specific references to the reading. As you draft your thesis, keep in mind the range of judgments open to the film critic. To critique a reading does not necessarily mean only to criticize it. If you honestly think a reading is weak, based on your evaluation of its various parts, then say so in your thesis. If, however, you think the writing is quite strong, say that. If your judgments fall somewhere in the middle—some parts are strong while others are weak—reflect *that* in your thesis. Your thesis should reflect your carefully considered opinion of the reading's overall quality or worth, whatever that judgment may be.

Next, you will offer a brief summary of the text so your reader can follow what you later have to say about the piece. In the body of your critique, you will choose for examination only the parts of the reading that best illustrate or defend your thesis: you will introduce a particular aspect of the reading (for example, its use of statistical evidence), describe a specific example or two from the reading (perhaps the way statistics are used to support the author's second argument), and explain how that specific example illustrates or supports your judgment (what makes the statistical evidence especially compelling in this section of the text).

Your goal, then, in writing a critique mirrors in many ways the goal you would have in writing a movie review. Your task is to analyze and evaluate a reading according to a set of established criteria and standards, pass judgment on the reading's quality or worth, then assert, explain, and defend that judgment with specific references to the reading.

WRITING A CRITIQUE

Writing a critique typically involves five steps:

1. Read and annotate the text.
2. Analyze and evaluate the piece: break it down into its primary parts and judge the quality of each part.
3. Write your thesis and decide which aspects of the reading you will focus on in your essay.
4. Compose your rough draft.
5. Rewrite your critique.

This is only a general guide. Throughout college you will learn much more specific, specialized ways to critique readings.

STEP 1—CAREFULLY READ AND ANNOTATE THE SOURCE TEXT

Before you start to write a critique, you first need to develop a clear understanding of the reading you are about to analyze and evaluate. The material you read in college is often challenging; you have to work hard to understand exactly what the author is asserting. However, this work is unavoidable: it makes little sense to evaluate a piece of writing when you are not completely sure what point the author is attempting to make. As you annotate a reading for a critique, keep in mind the following suggestions.

Note the Author's Thesis, Primary Assertions, and Primary Means of Support

Be sure that you mark the author's thesis, highlight and summarize each major point the author makes, and highlight and summarize how the author supports each idea, argument, or finding. Are the thesis and primary assertions clearly stated? Does the thesis direct the development of the paper? Are the assertions supported?

Note the Author's Use of Graphics, Headings, and Subheadings

What graphics does the author provide? What are their function? How do the headings and subheadings organize the piece? Are the headings and graphics effective? How so?

Note the Author's Diction and Word Choice

Consider the kind of language the writer is employing. Is it formal or informal? Is it overly technical? Is it appropriate? Do you notice any shifts in diction? Are some sections of the text more complicated or jargon laden than others? Note any strengths or weaknesses you see in the author's language.

Note the Author's Tone

What seems to be the author's attitude toward the topic? Is he being serious, comical, or satiric? Does the tone seem appropriate, given the writer's topic and thesis? Are there any places in the text where the tone shifts? Is the shift effective?

Note the Author's Audience

When you finish the piece, determine what the writer seemed to assume about his or readers. For example, is the writer addressing someone who knows something about the topic or someone likely reading about it for the first time? Is the author assuming readers agree or disagree with the position being forwarded in the piece? Judging from the content, organization, diction, and tone of the piece, which type of reader would tend to accept the author's position and which would tend to reject it?

Note the Author's Purpose

Decide, in your own mind, the primary aim of the piece. Is the author attempting to entertain, inform, or persuade readers? Where in the text has the author attempted to achieve this aim? How successful are those attempts? Note at the beginning or end of the reading your comments concerning the author's purpose.

Summarize the Piece

After you have read and studied the text, write a brief summary of the piece, either at the end of the reading or on a separate sheet of paper (see Chapter 5 for tips on summarizing a reading).

When you have finished reading, rereading, and annotating the source text, you should have a clear understanding of its content, organization, purpose, and audience. Try to clear up any questions you have about the reading before you attempt to critique it. You want your critique to be based on a thorough and clear understanding of the source text.

STEP 2—ANALYZE AND EVALUATE THE READING

Think back to the process of putting together a movie review. When a movie critic watches a film, she forms a judgment of its quality based on certain things she sees or hears. As she watches the movie, she will examine and judge certain aspects of the film, including its

acting	scenery	lighting
direction	costuming	plot
special effects	dialogue	action
theme	pacing	makeup
cinematography	stunts	music

Her evaluation of these various elements of the film—either positive or negative—will form her overall judgment of the movie, her thesis.

What, then, should you look for when analyzing a reading, what parts of a text should you be isolating for evaluation as you read and reread the piece? In part, the answer depends on the course you are taking: each discipline has generally agreed-on ways of analyzing a reading. As you take courses in anthropology or physical education, you will learn how experts in those fields analyze readings. However, analyzing certain general aspects of a reading can help you better understand material in a wide variety of classes. Regardless of the course you are taking, you might start to analyze a reading by identifying its:

- thesis and primary assertions or findings,
- evidence and reasoning,
- organization, and
- style.

Once you have analyzed a reading, isolating for consideration its essential elements, your next task in writing a critique is to evaluate the quality of each element. Here, writing a critique differs from writing a response essay. In a response essay, your goal is to articulate your personal, subjective reaction to what you have read. In a critique, though, you are expected to evaluate the reading according to an established set of standards. Think about the movie critic's job again. Most reviewers employ similar criteria and standards when evaluating a film. If a reviewer decides to critique the musical score of a film, she knows the types of evaluative questions one usually asks about this aspect of a movie: How did the music contribute to the overall mood of the film? Was it too intrusive? Did it add humor or depth to the scenes? Did it heighten drama? Was it noteworthy because of the performers who recorded it? Her answers to these questions will lead to her final assessment of this particular aspect of the film. (Of course, another reviewer employing the same criteria and applying the same standards could come to a different judgment concerning the quality of the music in the film; for example, one reviewer might think it heightened the drama in a particular scene while another might think that it did not.)

In college, you will quickly discover that the criteria and standards used to evaluate readings vary from discipline to discipline. Teachers often employ evaluative criteria unique to their field of study, especially in upper-level courses in which the professor is preparing students to enter a profession. In lower-level courses designed to introduce you to a field of study, you may encounter a different sort of problem. Teachers in different fields may be asking you to employ the same or similar criteria, but their standards are very different. Suppose, for example, you are asked to evaluate the style of a particular reading in both an education and an English course. Your job is the same—determine, stylistically, whether this is a well-written essay. Your answer might be different in each class. According to the stylistic standards advocated by the school of education, you might have before you a well-written essay; according to the standards advocated by the English department, though, the same piece of writing might not fare so well. As always, work closely with your teacher when evaluating a reading to be sure you are applying an appropriate set of criteria and standards.

Below are a series of questions you can ask to begin your analysis and evaluation of a reading's thesis, assertions, evidence, reasoning, organization, and style. They are meant to serve only as general guidelines. Your teacher may have much more specific questions he would like you to ask of a reading or evaluative criteria he would like you to employ. Together, analysis and evaluation enable you to critique a reading. After breaking a reading into its essential parts and judging their effectiveness, you will form the thesis of your critique—a judgment of the reading's quality or worth—which you will develop and defend in your essay.

Analyzing and Evaluating a Reading's Thesis and Primary Assertions or Findings

Sometimes identifying an author's thesis can be relatively easy—you can point to a specific sentence or two in the text. Other times, though, an author will not state his thesis. Instead, the thesis is implied: some controlling idea is directing the development of the piece even though the author never puts it into words. If this is the case, you will need to identify and paraphrase this controlling idea yourself and evaluate it as if it were the thesis.

Many times, identifying the author's primary assertions or findings can be easy, too. For example, if the author has made effective use of paragraph breaks, topic sentences, headings, or graphics, you can usually locate his primary assertions fairly easily. However, do not rely on these means alone to identify the author's main ideas. Not every source text is well written. Often, important assertions get buried in an article; key findings may be glossed over. As you analyze a reading, make up your own mind about its primary assertions or findings independently of what the author may assume to be the case. Also, be sure to distinguish between primary assertions and their evidence or support. Very often a student will identify as a primary argument of a reading some statistic or quotation that the author is using only as a piece of evidence, something to support the actual assertion he is trying to make. In short, to analyze a reading's thesis and primary assertions, consider the following questions:

- What is the author's thesis? Is it stated or unstated? If stated, highlight it; if unstated, paraphrase it.
- What are the primary assertions in the reading? Highlight each one and paraphrase it in the margin of the text.
- What is the primary means of support offered to illustrate or defend each assertion? Again, highlight this material.

In determining the quality of a reading's thesis and primary assertions or findings, you can begin by questioning their clarity, effectiveness, and organization. The thesis, whether stated or implied, should direct the development of the piece. Each major finding or assertion should be clearly stated and linked to that thesis through the effective use of transitions, repetition of key terms, or headings. To evaluate an author's thesis and findings, you might begin by asking the following questions. If your answers are positive, you can likely claim that the author has effectively presented and developed his thesis; if your answers are negative, be sure to articulate exactly where the problems exist.

- Is the thesis clearly stated? Does it control the organization of the piece? Is it consistently held or does the author shift positions in the essay?
- If the thesis is implied rather than stated, does it still serve to direct the organization of the piece? Are you able to paraphrase a comprehensive thesis on your own, or does the material included in the piece preclude that?
- Are the author's assertions or findings clearly stated?
- Are the author's assertions or findings somehow tied to the thesis?

Analyzing and Evaluating a Reading's Evidence and Reasoning

Here you identify two separate, but related, aspects of a reading: (1) the evidence an author provides to support or illustrate her assertions and (2) the author's reasoning process or line of argument.

First, try to identify the types of **evidence** the author uses to support her thesis. (At this point do not try to evaluate the effectiveness of the evidence—that comes later.) The types of evidence used to support a thesis vary greatly in academic writing, so again be cautious when using these guidelines to analyze the readings in any particular course. However, to begin your analysis of the evidence an author employs, you might try asking yourself this series of questions:

- In supporting her assertions or findings, what kinds of evidence has the author employed? Has the author used any of these forms of evidence:

statistics	empirical data	precedent
expert testimony	emotional appeals	case histories
personal experience	historical analysis	analogies

- Where in the article is each type of evidence employed?
- Is there a pattern? Are certain types of evidence used to support certain types of claims?
- Where has the author combined forms of evidence as a means of support?

Analyzing an author's **reasoning process** is more difficult because it is more abstract. First, you identify how the author uses evidence to support her thesis and how she develops and explains her ideas, her line of reasoning. Second, you examine the assumptions an author makes concerning her topic and readers. As she wrote the piece, which aspects of the text did she decide needed more development than others? Which terms needed clarification? Which argument or explanation needed the most support? In analyzing the author's reasoning process, these are the kinds of questions you might ask:

- In what order are the ideas, arguments, or findings presented?
- What are the logical connections between the major assertions being made in the piece? How does one idea lead to the next?
- What passages in the text explain these connections?
- What assumptions about the topic or the reader is the author making?
- Where in the text are these assumptions articulated, explained, or defended?

Standards used to assess the quality of an author's evidence and reasoning will vary greatly across the disciplines. For example, you might want to determine whether an author offers "adequate" support for his or her thesis. However, what passes for adequate support of a claim will be quite different in an English class from what it will be in a physics course or a statistics course: these fields of study each look at "evidence" and the notion of "adequacy" very differently. In other words, a good general strategy to employ when critiquing a reading is to determine the adequacy of its evidence; however, how that strategy is implemented and what conclusions you reach employing it can vary depending on the course you are taking. Part of learning any subject matter is coming to understand how scholars in that field evaluate evidence; therefore, answer the following questions thoughtfully:

- Does the author support her contentions or findings?
- Is this support adequate? Does the author offer enough evidence to support her contentions?
- Is the evidence authoritative? Does it come from legitimate sources? Is it current?
- Does the author explain *how* the evidence supports or illustrates her assertions?
- Has the author ignored evidence or alternative hypotheses or explanations for the evidence she offers?
- In developing her position, are there any problems with unstated assumptions? Does the author assume something to be the case that she needs to clarify or defend?
- Are there problems with logical fallacies such as hasty generalizations, false dilemmas, or appeals to false authorities?
- Has the author addressed the ethical implications of her position?
- Is the author's reasoning a notable strength in the piece? Is it clear and convincing?

Your answers to these questions will help you determine whether there are serious problems with the evidence and reasoning employed in the reading.

Analyzing and Evaluating a Reading's Organization

Here you want to identify how the author orders the material contained in the reading. As the author develops a set of findings or ideas, lays out his reasoning for the reader, offers examples and explanations, what comes first? Second? Third? How has the author attempted to mold these parts into a coherent whole? When analyzing the organization of a reading, you might begin by considering the following questions:

- In what order are the ideas or findings presented?
- How has the author indicated that he is moving from a discussion of one point to the discussion of another point?
- What is the relationship between the thesis of the piece (stated or unstated) and the order in which the assertions or findings are presented?
- How has the author tried to help the reader understand the organization of the reading? Identify where in the text the author has used any of the following to help guide his readers through the text:

headings and subheadings	repetition of key terms
transition words or phrases	repetition of language from the thesis
transition paragraphs	repetition of names or titles

If any aspect of a reading's organization makes it difficult for you to understand the author's message, you may want to examine it in your critique. Clearly explain the nature of the problem and how it damages the reading's effectiveness. Likewise, if the organization is especially strong, if it significantly enhances the reading's clarity or effectiveness, you can point that out in your critique and explain how it helps the text. Here are some questions to consider when evaluating the source text's organization:

- Is there a clear connection between the major assertions of the essay? Does there seem to be some reason why one idea precedes or follows another?
- Are all the assertions clearly related to the overall thesis of the piece?
- Has the author provided headings or subheadings to help readers follow his line of thought? How effective are they?
- Has the author provided adequate transitions to help readers move through the writing and see the logical connection between the assertions he is making? How effective are they?

Analyzing and Evaluating a Reading's Style

Stylistic analysis is a complicated process, an academic specialty in and of itself within the field of English studies. In most of your college courses, though, when analyzing style you will likely focus on issues of clarity and convention. First, when you critique a reading, you might comment on its clarity. You will want to identify which aspects of the writer's word choice and sentence structure help you understand what she has to say or which serve to complicate your reading of the text. Other times, you may ask a different set of questions concerning style, especially in upper-division courses. Your assignment will be to assess how well an author adheres to the stylistic conventions of a discipline. For example, you might explore whether the author's language, tone, and syntax are appropriate for a particular type of writing or field of study. To begin your analysis of style, here are some questions you might ask about a reading:

- What level of diction is the writer employing (how formal is the prose)?

  formal?   conversational?
  informal?   a mixture?

  Identify which words or passages lead you to this conclusion.
- What is the tone of the piece (what is the author's apparent attitude toward the topic)?

  serious?   satiric?   involved?
  humorous?   angry?   detached?

  Identify which words or passages lead you to this conclusion.
- What kind of language is used in the piece? Identify any passages using specialized language, emotional language, or jargon.
- What types of sentences are used in the reading?

  simple, compound, complex, complex-compound?
  long or short?
  active or passive?
  a mixture of types?

When critiquing a reading's style, you evaluate elements of the author's prose such as diction, tone, word choice, and syntax. Again, stylistic standards vary greatly across the disciplines. While teachers in various disciplines may use similar terms when describing "good" style in writing—that it should be clear and concise, for example—how they define their criteria is likely to vary. Clear and concise writing in a chemistry lab report may have little in common, stylistically, with clear and concise writing in a philosophy research report. Below are some questions that might help you begin to evaluate certain aspects of an author's style. Remember, though, that your answers may well depend on the stylistic standards accepted by a particular discipline:

- How would you characterize the diction of the piece: formal, informal, or somewhere in the middle? Is it consistently maintained? Is it appropriate? Does it contribute to the effectiveness of the piece?
- How would you characterize the tone of the piece? Is it inviting, satiric, or humorous? Is it appropriate, given the topic and intent of the piece? Does the tone enhance or damage the effect of the writing?
- Is the author's word choice clear and effective? Or does the writer rely too heavily on jargon, abstractions, or highly technical terms?

- Is the author's word choice needlessly inflammatory or emotional? Or do the words convey appropriate connotations?
- Are the sentences clearly written? Are any of the sentences so poorly structured that the source is difficult to read and understand?
- Are the sentence types varied? Is the syntax appropriate given the audience and intent of the piece?

STEP 3—WRITE YOUR THESIS AND DECIDE WHICH ASPECTS OF THE READING WILL BE THE FOCUS OF YOUR ESSAY

At this point you need to develop your thesis and decide which aspects of the reading you will use to develop your critique. To formulate your thesis, you need to decide which elements of the source text best illustrate or defend your judgment. You want your reader to understand and accept your thesis, but this acceptance can come about only if you clearly explain each claim you make about the reading and offer convincing examples from the text to illustrate and defend your contentions.

In your critique, you do not need to address every aspect of the source text. Remember how the movie critic supports her assertions about a film. No review addresses every aspect of a movie. Instead, the critic chooses to discuss in her review only those elements of the movie she thinks most clearly and effectively illustrate her judgment. Maybe she will address only the acting and direction, perhaps only the dialogue, plot, and special effects. Perhaps she will choose to mention, only briefly, the costuming and musical score, then concentrate more attention on the film's cinematography.

Follow the same line of thinking when you decide which aspects of the reading to address in your critique. To illustrate and defend your thesis, you may choose to look only at the logic of the piece and its structure. However, you may choose to ignore both of these and concentrate, instead, on the writer's style. Maybe you will decide to look briefly at the evidence the author offers, then concentrate most of your attention on the organization of the piece. Your decisions should be based on two fairly simple questions: (1) Which aspects of the reading most influenced your judgment of its quality and worth? and (2) Which aspects will best illustrate and support your thesis? Choose only those aspects of the reading for examination in your critique.

Your thesis in a critique is a brief statement of what you believe to be the overall value or worth of the source text based on your analysis and evaluation of its parts. In stating your thesis, you have several options. You can say only positive things about the reading, only negative things, or some mixture of the two. Your main concern at this point is that your thesis honestly and accurately reflects your judgment.

Also, your thesis statement can be either open or closed. In an open thesis statement, you offer your overall judgment of the piece and nothing else. In a closed thesis statement you offer your judgment and indicate which aspects of the reading you will examine when developing your essay. Below are some sample open and closed thesis statements for a critique—positive, negative, and mixed.

Positive Thesis Statement

Open

Jones presents a clear, convincing argument in favor of increased funding for the school district.

Closed

Through his use of precise examples and his accessible style, Jones presents a clear and convincing argument in favor of increased funding for the school district.

Negative Thesis Statement

Open

Jones's argument in favor of increased funding is not convincing.

Closed

Because there are numerous lapses in reasoning and problems with the organization, Jones's argument in favor of increased funding is not convincing.

Mixed Thesis Statement

Open

Though uneven in its presentation, Jones's argument in favor of increased funding for the school district is, finally, convincing.

Closed

Even though there are some problems with the organization Jones employs in his report, his use of expert testimony makes his argument for increased funding for the schools ultimately convincing.

STEP 4—WRITE YOUR ROUGH DRAFT

While there are many ways to structure a critique, the suggestions that follow can serve as a general guide.

Introductory Section

- Introduce the topic of the reading.
- Give the title of the piece and the name of its author.
- Give your thesis.
- Summarize the source text.

In the opening section of your critique you should introduce the topic of the reading and give your reader its exact title and the full name of its author. You will also include here your thesis and a brief summary of the reading (one or two paragraphs long). The exact order you choose to follow when covering this material is up to you. Some writers like to begin with the summary of the source text before giving their thesis; some prefer to give their thesis first. Overall, though, your introductory section should only be two or three paragraphs long.

Body

- Examine one element of the reading at a time.
- Cite specific examples of this element from the reading.
- Explain your evaluation of each example you offer.

State the Criteria and Your Judgments

In the body of your critique you will explain and defend the judgment you made in your thesis, focusing on one aspect of the reading at a time. Topic sentences in a critique usually indicate the element of the reading you will be examining in that part of the essay and whether you found it to be a strength or liability—for example, "One of the real strengths of the essay is the author's use of emotional language."

Offer Examples

Whatever aspect of the reading you are examining—logic, word choice, structure—give your readers specific examples from the source text to clarify your terms and demonstrate that your judgment is sound. For example, the student who hopes to prove that the author's use of emotional language is one of the reading's strengths will need to quote several examples of language from the text he believes is emotional. Offering only one example might not be convincing; readers might question whether the student isolated for praise or criticism the single occurrence of that element in the text.

Explain Your Judgments

After you have specified the aspect of the reading you are examining in that part of your critique and have offered your readers examples from the text, you will need to explain and defend your judgment. After the student mentioned above cites a few specific examples of the author's emotional language, he will need to explain clearly and convincingly *how* that language strengthens the author's writing. Simply saying it does is not good enough. The student will have to explain how this type of language helps make the author's article clearer or more convincing.

In this section of the critique you will likely develop and explain your unique perspective on the reading. Suppose you and your friend are critiquing the same reading. You could both agree that it is effective and could even choose to focus on the same elements of the reading to defend and illustrate this judgment; for example, you could both choose to focus on the author's use of evidence. The two of you will probably differ, though, in your explanation of how and why the author's use of evidence is strong. You will offer your individual assessments of how the writer effectively employed evidence to support his thesis.

Conclusion

- Wrap up the paper.
- Reassert the thesis.

In your concluding section, try to give your reader a sense of closure. Consider mirroring in your conclusion the strategy you used to open your critique. For example, if you opened your essay with a question, consider closing it by answering that question; if you began with a quotation, end with a quotation; if you opened with a story, finish the story. You might also consider restating your thesis—your overall assessment of the piece—to remind your readers of the judgments you developed in the body of your essay.

STEP 5—REWRITE YOUR CRITIQUE

In rewriting your critique, check to make sure your work is accurate, thorough, organized, and clear.

- *Accurate*—it reflects your true assessment of the source text.
- *Thorough*—you completely explain your assertions.
- *Organized*—readers can easily follow the development of your critique.
- *Clear*—you have explained all the terms you need to explain and supported any assumptions that might reasonably be questioned.

Check for Accuracy

When reviewing your work, first check for accuracy. You want to be sure that your essay reflects your honest assessment of the source text. Starting with your thesis, look through your essay to make sure the assertions you make, the supporting material you employ, and the explanations you offer accurately reflect your point of view.

Check the Development of Your Assertions

Next, make sure you have been thorough in developing your critique. Check to be sure you have offered examples from the source text to support and illustrate your claims and that you have explained your reasoning clearly and completely. Add material—quotations, examples, and explanations—where you think they are needed.

Check the Organization

As you review the organization of your critique, make sure your thesis guides the development of your essay. Are you examining only one aspect of the reading at a time? If not, move material around to improve the organization in your essay. Have you provided adequate transitions to help your reader move through the piece? Do you repeat key terms or provide transition words that remind your reader of your thesis or signal the relationship between the various assertions you make?

Check for Clarity

Check your critique for clarity. Have you used any terms that need to be defined? Have you made any assertions that readers would find unclear? Have you made any assumptions that need to be explained or defended? When necessary, change the content, word choice, or sentence structure of your essay to make your ideas more accessible to your readers.

READINGS

The essays "Should Cell Phones Be Banned from Classrooms? Yes," by Josh Allen, and "Should Cell Phones Be Banned from Classrooms? No," by Liz Kolb, both appeared in *Learning & Leading with Technology*. Following the readings is a sample critique of Allen's essay.

Should Cell Phones Be Banned from Classrooms? Yes

Josh Allen

Josh Allen holds a master's degree in education and educational technology. He is the instructional technology facilitator for Papillion-La Vista Schools in Papillion, Nebraska.

I am all for the proper integration of as much technology as possible into our classrooms. I am, however, absolutely, fully, totally against cell phone use as a teaching tool. Cell phones do not have a place in our classrooms as such. Although it would definitely be part of a school board's discussion on integrating cell phones into their schools, I'm not going to spend time on the fact that students would use them for purposes other than educational. They already do that, even when they are not being used as a tool. There are plenty of other negatives to focus on.

No true best practice has started out with, "Have students bring their cell phones to class." Parents can find plenty of unnecessary ways to spoil their children. The new LeBron shoe. The latest Justin Timberlake album. Any phone that is worthy of being called an educational tool is not on the "buy one, get one free" plan. You cannot expect students to come to school with a Blackberry. If they have a Blackberry . . . OK, I'll just stop there, because the discussion on why a parent bought their child a BlackBerry is so ridiculous my head may explode.

Schools should find that the money they would spend on student cell phones, if they chose that route instead of having students bring their own, would be much better utilized for other technology purchases. Laptops, just to touch on one small slice of a district's technology budget, are much more versatile yet uniform than cell phones. When discussing the money that districts would spend on cell phones, don't think about just purchasing the phone. You will also be paying for some type of plan that would probably include text messaging and Web access if you were to get the most out of what you have. Any monies spent on phones and plans would be much better served with any number of other technologies. In this day and age of shoestring budgets and federal funding only for specific curriculum, every penny is scrutinized.

The goal of an educational setting should be to give students the proper tools to succeed once they step into society. The time students spend in a classroom setting is increasingly being divided between curriculum, pedagogy, assessing, and so on. Every year a new "best practice" author is making a buck from "trendsetting" administrators who feed the book to staff members before the ink dries. There comes a time when the school day will begin to explode if it is not relieved of some of the content. So how can instruction including a cell phone even be considered for that valuable block of time? Nothing that you can do on a cell phone will inspire students as they make their way into the world. I cannot think of a job where "cell phone operation" was a skill. Employers are much more concerned about a student's computing and critical thinking skills than their phone skills. Hopefully you are as well.

Should Cell Phones Be Banned from Classrooms? No

Liz Kolb

Liz Kolb is an adjunct assistant professor at Madonna University in Michigan as well as a doctoral student in learning technologies at the University of Michigan.

While schools are struggling to finance the newest hardware and software, they are overlooking that many secondary students already own a technology tool that can be integral not only in school learning, but in the students' future professional lives. Additionally, schools are often criticized for not connecting learning to the real world. What better way to connect students' classroom learning with their everyday lives than a tool they already enjoy using? Instead of using the cell phone as social toy, students can learn how to use their phone as a tool for knowledge construction. As an alternative to spending time and money creating policies to fight cell phone use in schools, teachers and administrators could spend their time finding useful ways to integrate these devices as knowledge construction, data collection, and collaborative communication tools in order to help students become more competitive in the 21st century.

Currently a basic cell phone has the ability to be the students'"Swiss Army knife" of technology. Cell phones can be audio recorders, digital video camcorders, still cameras, note-taking devices, calculation devices, scheduling and management tools, phone conferencing devices, Internet researching tools, faxing and scanning devices, blog and Web page editors, or even audio assessment recorders. Cell phones can also be assistive technologies for special needs students. For example, using a free Web-based software called Jott, a hearing impaired student can record audio on a cell phone to create text-written e-mails. Furthermore, cell phones can couple with many free Web 2.0 tools such as Flickr for innovative classroom projects. For example, students can use their cell phones to take pictures during a field trip, send them to the class Flickr account, and then create a digital slideshow in Flickr.

Considering that it is more common for students and parents to have access to a cell phone than Internet at home, including cell phones in learning would provide more opportunities for better communication with parents and students. For example, teachers can create text message alerts to send information about school assignments or activities to parents.

Teachers who are concerned that cell phones will be distracting inside the classroom can set up a social contract with their students defining the structure and rules around cell phone use in the classroom. For example, the teacher can collect the cell phones at the beginning of class and return them to the students when it is time in class to use them. Furthermore, students do not even need to bring the cell phone into the classroom to use it as a learning tool. They can use them for homework or on class field trips.

Part of an educator's job is to help students safely navigate the media world. There are businesses that are completely mobile, and job interviews that are done via phone. Students need to learn how to use their social devices as a professional tool if they want to be competitive in the future. Currently, students are unaware of cell phone etiquette. Allowing cell phones to become learning tools will give teachers the opportunity to introduce appropriate cell phone etiquette to students as well as show them how their toy can become an essential professional tool.

SAMPLE CRITIQUE

An Unconvincing Argument against Cell Phones

In ever-increasing numbers, high-school students today own cell phones. While they use them to talk to and text-message their friends, high-school students also use cell phones for other reasons as well, for example, to keep in contact with their parents, to take pictures, and to download information from the Internet. Several schools and school systems around the country have banned cell phones, believing they only serve to distract students from their studies. While many teachers oppose these bans, others support them, including Josh Allen who works as an instructional technology facilitator for the Papillion-La Vista Schools in Papillion, Nebraska. In his article "Should Cell Phones Be Banned from Classrooms? Yes," Allen argues that cell phones should be banned from high schools because they serve no educational purpose. However, Allen's argument is seriously hampered by his unsupported assertions, his unwillingness to acknowledge opposing views, and his sarcastic tone.

Allen opens his argument with a very clear statement of his position: "I am all for the proper integration of as much technology as possible into our classrooms. I am, however, absolutely, fully, totally against cell phone use as a teaching tool. Cell phones do not have a place in our classrooms as such" (103–104). In fact, he believes that children who own cell phones are merely being spoiled by their parents. Allen then asserts that schools could find better uses for their funds than purchasing cell phones for students, pointing out that districts would also have to pay for a cell phone plan that would support text messaging and Internet access. He believes that, because schools are already required to address "curriculum, pedagogy, [and] assessing"(104), there would be little time left for instruction on cell phone use. Finally, Allen maintains that the purpose of school is to help prepare students for the real world and he "cannot think of a job where 'cell phone operation' was a skill" (104).

For a number of reasons, Allen's argument against cell phones in high schools is not convincing, including his failure to support many of the assertions he makes. For example, early in his essay Allen claims that if school systems were interested in purchasing cell phones for their students, they would have to buy expensive models since "Any phone that is worthy of being called an educational tool is not of the 'buy one, get one free' plan" (104). However, he fails to explain which features on a cell phone might be essential for educational purposes or to demonstrate that lower-priced phones lack those features. Later, Allen claims that "Any monies spent on phones and plans would be much better served with any number of other technologies" (104), but he again fails to indicate what those other technologies might be. Unsupported, unexplained assertions like these are not convincing.

A related problem involves Allen's unwillingness to acknowledge opposing views in his argument, which often makes it appear that Allen knows less about the topic than one would expect. For example, Allen asserts that "No true best practice has started out with, 'Have students bring their cell phones to class'" (104). This sweeping assertion ignores a great deal of published research, "best practice" articles that have explained how cell phones can be used successfully for educational purposes in schools. Toward the end of his argument, Allen claims, "I cannot think of a job where 'cell phone operation' was a skill. Employers are much more concerned about a student's computing and critical thinking skills than their phone skills" (104). Again, little critical thought is necessary to identify several occupations where strong cell phone skills are essential—sales, customer service, and technical support just to name a few. Additionally, Allen asserts "Nothing that you can do on a cell phone will inspire students as they make their way into the world" (104). This sweeping generalization fails to acknowledge all of the creative ways cell phones are already being used in the classroom: to communicate with teachers and peers regarding class projects, to download material from the Internet, to take and send pictures on field trips, or to record class lectures. While Allen is correct in stating that students may use cell phones for nonacademic purposes in a classroom, he fails to acknowledge all of the ways they can be used to support a student's education.

Allen's unwillingness or inability to acknowledge opposing points of view in his argument is a fatal flaw. Several explanations for this shortcoming are possible. First, Allen may truly believe that one-sided arguments will sway critical readers, a misguided assumption at best. Second, he may purposefully be writing an unfair argument. That is, he knows about the opposing points of view but is simply leaving them out, hoping that his readers do not know about them and will find his assertions convincing. A third explanation, which is perhaps the most damaging, is that Allen simply does not know enough about the topic to understand all of the positive ways that cell phones can be used in classrooms. If this is the case, then Allen loses his credibility as a reliable authority on the topic. Whatever the explanation, Allen's argument is not convincing because it is one-sided and appears to be uninformed.

A final problem with Allen's argument is his willingness to resort to sarcasm to make his point. For example, when characterizing parents who purchase cell phones for their children, he writes, "If they have a BlackBerry . . . [sic] OK, I'll just stop there, because the discussion on why a parent bought their [sic] child a BlackBerry is so ridiculous my head may explode" (104). Allen's attempt at humor here falls flat. He may not see any reason for a student to have a BlackBerry, but parents may want to provide one to their children if those children have certain learning disabilities or medical needs that require the types of communication that BlackBerries can provide. Allen then mocks school administrators who support the use of cell phones in the classroom: "Every year a new 'best practice' author is making a buck from 'trendsetting' administrators who feed the book to staff members before the ink dries" (104). Whatever truth lies behind Allen's assertion is lost in the sarcasm. Some administrators may be too quick to promote the latest "hot trend" in education, but ridiculing them makes it hard for readers to accept Allen's criticism. The sarcasm makes Allen appear egotistical, as if he knows better than those "best practice authors" or "trendsetting administrators." Again, Allen's tone is more likely to alienate readers rather than to convince them that his argument is sound.

So, should cell phones be banned from classrooms? Strong arguments likely exist on both sides of the question, but Allen's is not one of them. Critical, thoughtful readers are likely to reject his argument because Allen employs many unsupported claims, fails to demonstrate his knowledge of the topic by examining alternative points of view, and frequently lapses into sarcasm to dismiss opposing views.

Additional Reading

Crafting a Workable Cell Phone Policy

Ellen R. DeLisio

Ellen R. DeLisio *is news editor for* Education World.

With so many families depending on cell phones, banning them from schools became pointless. Now the debate is how to regulate phone use in schools, as more students own camera phones and ones that can send text messages and connect to the Internet. Included: Sample cell phone policies.

Just a few years ago, it looked like regulating cellular phone use in schools was getting a lot easier. Cell phones had become ubiquitous and innocuous, and making it a school offense or even a crime to possess them on school grounds didn't make much sense anymore.

But just as states and school districts were relaxing their policies, along came a new generation of cell phone — with cameras, Internet access, and text messaging — that it seems every teen must have. Now administrators are wrestling with how to permit the legitimate use of phones, while preventing possible privacy violations and cheating.

"Cell phones still are an issue, but not the same issue," said Dr. William Scharffe, president of the American Association of Policy Services, a work-a-like group with the National School Boards Association (NSBA), and director of bylaw and policy services for the Michigan Association of School Boards. "The main concern is prohibiting use during instructional time and not disrupting the school atmosphere. . . . As the cell phone industry improved the product, it became more problematic for schools."

Technology Evolution

When cell phones, pagers, and beepers began to spread into the mainstream in the late 1980s and early 1990s, most districts and even states moved to ban them from school grounds. Beepers and pagers were associated with the drug trade, and it was feared if a student had one or the other, he or she was or wanted to be a drug dealer.

Some of the regulations originally were not written to apply to phones, but many were expanded to cover phones by including electronic devices among the banned items.

Technological and social changes and national events within the past six years, though, have prompted a review of policies. Advances in cell phone technology and the explosion of the industry made phones less of a luxury item and more a convenience, particularly for working parents trying to keep track of children. The other influences were more sudden and jarring: the shootings at Columbine High School in April 1999 and the terrorist attacks of September 11, 2001.

People watched and heard as cell phones linked victims and potential victims to their loved ones and the outside world. Parents now wanted to be in closer contact with their children and argued to school districts that cell phones were necessary for safety.

Still, some school administrators are wary of opening the gate. The New York City Public Schools, the largest district in the U.S., and one most affected by the terrorist attacks, still forbids students to have any electronic devices in their possession. But school officials are reviewing the policy and may revise it to allow students to carry cell phones, as long as the devices are turned off during the school day, said Marge Feinberg, a spokeswoman for the district.

"One reason we are looking at the policy is because of 9/11," Feinberg said. "Some cell phones still were able to operate that day."

But in most places, change has come.

"We have gotten a lot of information about major changes and school districts looking at policies," according to Naomi Gittins, staff attorney for the NSBA. "Many states are repealing the laws [regulating cell phones in schools] and are throwing the issue back at the local districts."

Local Discretion

That is the case in Connecticut, whose state legislature revised its law regulating cell phone possession in schools to give local districts more latitude in dealing with the issue, said Vincent Mustaro, a senior staff associate for policy for the Connecticut Association of Boards of Education (CABE).

"School officials around the U.S. began to say that an outright ban was not realistic," Mustaro told *Education World*. "Parents are encouraging kids to carry phones." One high-school principal estimated that 70 percent of the kids in his school had phones. "I think the change is connected to school violence and a desire by parents to be more in touch with their kids, and the popularity and availability of phones continue to grow."

"There are more important things we want administrators involved in," than policing cell phone possession, Mustaro added.

At the same time, CABE is making it clear to school districts that cell phones should not be visible or used during instructional time.

"The position we take is that cell phones don't belong in classroom settings unless there is a specific reason, such as a medical disability that requires students to be in touch with a parent," he said. "They are a disruption and shouldn't be on during instructional time. They are not allowed in classrooms, and if they are there, they are confiscated."

CABE also recommends that camera phones be banned from schools because they can be secretly used to take pictures of people and violate privacy and be used for cheating, he said.

Dr. Scharffe said he recommends similar policies to schools in Michigan. "I advise them that they can allow phones if they wish, but to limit their use; there should be no use during instructional time, they are a disruption to instruction and the school atmosphere. Most schools are not going to make a big deal about it. You can bring the phone to school, but you can't use it."

He also suggests banning camera phones or ones that can send text messages, even if students or parents argue that those are the only type of phone a student has. "If safety is the issue [for owning a phone], just give them [youngsters] phones that make and receive calls," Dr. Scharffe said. "Most schools ban camera phones and those with Internet connections."

As for whether screening for different types of student phones could create more headaches for administrators, Dr. Scharffe said once the policy is clear, students have to live with the consequences. "If they use them [camera phones], they lose them," he said. "If they bring camera phones to school, someone will talk, and it will be discovered."

The National Association of Secondary School Principals (NASSP) agrees that districts and schools should decide the policies, said spokesman Michael Carr.

"From our perspective, it is better left up to the local level to set policies," Carr told *Education World*. "It's not as much an issue of calling now as it is cameras and text messaging. We hear some talk among members about trying to make it work — balancing the priorities."

Revamping Policies

Middleburg High School in Middleburg, Florida, has seen its cell phone policy change twice in three years as the state laws eased. Up until recently, state law required disciplinary action if a student had a wireless communication device on school grounds.

Middleburg students had a hand in changing the law last year, researching the state law and then urging legislators to change the regulations. Now the state allows students to possess a wireless communications device while on school property or in attendance at a school function, and it is up to each school board to adopt rules governing the use of wireless communications devices.

As of this school year, Middleburg students are allowed to carry cell phones, but they must be off at all times. If a student is found using a phone during the school day, the punishment is an automatic three-day, out-of-school suspension, principal Dr. David McDonald said. The school does not prohibit camera phones or those that can send text messages.

Just three years ago, a student could receive a ten-day suspension for having a phone in school, although the length of the suspension could be reduced at the discretion of the principal, Dr. McDonald told *Education World*. Last year, that policy allowed students to bring cell phones to school, but they had to be turned off and in lockers. If a student was found carrying one, the penalty was a three-day in-school suspension. If they had one and it rang, it was a three-day out-of-school suspension.

"We realized that kids needed them after school," said McDonald, adding that most of the 1,700 students in his school have cell phones.

The technology changes and the overwhelming number of student cell phones at St. Elizabeth High School in Wilmington, Delaware, prompted school officials to revise the cell phone policy for this school year, said John Forester, the school's dean of students.

"It seems like every student has one," Forester told *Education World*. "Probably 90 percent of the 420 high school students have phones."

A problem school officials have encountered is students, mostly girls, according to Forester, secretly sending text messages to friends in other schools during class.

The new policy requires that phones be shut off, but students can carry their phones in their lockers, purses, or pockets. If students use a phone during the school day or if one rings during class, the student receives demerits. Camera phones are not forbidden, but the policy states that no cell phone photographs are allowed in the locker rooms or restrooms.

"We haven't heard many complaints," Forester said. "If a parent calls a phone while a student is in class, the student still gets a demerit, and the phone is confiscated for the day. The biggest offense is a phone ringing in class — and it's usually a parent."

What's Next?

Now administrators are bracing for the ramifications of increased cell phone access, even as the technology continues to evolve and reaches younger students.

"Now the issue extends down to the elementary grades," Dr. Scharffe said. "There are first and second graders with cell phones. School districts across the land never thought they would have to deal with elementary students with cell phones."

Law enforcement officials also disagree on the benefits of students having cell phones, Dr. Scharffe added. "It would jam the system if [during an emergency] 250 people tried to call out from a school at one time," he said. "During the siege at Columbine, there were so many cell phone calls going out from the school that it clogged the system." Sheriff's departments in some communities have addressed the safety issue by providing students with pre-programmed cell phones that only can be used to dial 911 and cannot receive calls, Dr. Scharffe noted.

Schools also could lose some control in emergencies, according to Dr. McDonald. "I think this is creating a situation where we all have to deal with things differently," he said. "In the past, we could manage information in an emergency situation. But if students have phones, they will find a way to use them. There could be a lot of misinformation going out there."

Careful monitoring of policies and phone use are solid approaches for most administrators, researchers agreed. "The best you can do is set reasonable policies," Dr. Scharffe added.

Summary Chart

HOW TO WRITE A CRITIQUE

1. **Carefully read and annotate the source text.**
   - *Read and reread the text.*
   - *Identify the author's intent, thesis, and primary assertions or findings.*
   - *Write an informal summary of the piece.*

2. **Analyze and evaluate the reading, breaking it down into its parts and judging the quality of each element.**

   Identify and evaluate the author's logic and reasoning.
   - *Is the thesis clearly stated, and does it direct the development of the text?*
   - *Are the author's primary assertions reasonable and clearly tied to the thesis?*
   - *Are there problems with logical fallacies?*
   - *Are the author's positions or findings logically presented?*

   Identify and evaluate the text's evidence.
   - *Does the author support his or her assertions or findings?*
   - *Is the support offered adequate to convince readers?*
   - *Is the evidence authoritative?*
   - *Is the evidence current?*
   - *Does the author explain how the evidence supports his or her assertions or findings?*
   - *Has the author ignored evidence or alternative hypotheses?*

   Identify and evaluate the text's organization.
   - *Is there a clear connection between the assertions developed in the essay?*
   - *Are the assertions or findings tied to a guiding thesis?*
   - *Does there seem to be a reason for one assertion following another, or do they seem randomly organized?*

   Identify and evaluate the text's style.
   - *Is the author's diction consistently maintained?*
   - *Is the author's word choice clear and effective?*
   - *Is the author's tone consistent and effective?*
   - *Are the author's sentences clear?*

SUMMARY CHART: HOW TO WRITE A CRITIQUE *(CONTINUED)*

3. **Formulate your thesis and choose the criteria you will include in your essay.**
   - *Draft a thesis, a brief statement concerning the overall value or worth of the source text.*
   - *Choose which elements of the reading you will focus on in your critique.*

4. **Write your rough draft.**
   - *Introduce the topic, source text, and your thesis.*
   - *Establish your evaluative criteria and your judgments of them.*
   - *Offer examples to substantiate each of your criteria and judgments.*
   - *Explain your judgments, clarifying how the examples you provide support your assertions.*

5. **Rewrite your critique.**

   Check to make sure your writing is accurate.
   - *Does your writing honestly reflect your judgment?*
   - *Does your writing misrepresent the author?*

   Check to make sure your writing is thorough.
   - *Do you cover all the aspects of the source text you need to cover?*
   - *Do you clearly and thoroughly explain and support your assertions?*

   Check to make sure your writing is organized.
   - *Does your thesis statement guide the development of your essay?*
   - *Have you provided transitional devices to help lead your reader through your work?*

   Check to make sure your writing is clear.
   - *Is your terminology clear?*
   - *Are your sentences clear?*
   - *Are your examples and explanations clear?*

Chapter 7

RHETORICAL ANALYSIS

DEFINITION AND PURPOSE

A rhetorical analysis essay is a special form of critique (see Chapter 6). In a critique essay, you determine a source text's overall value or worth by critically examining a set of relevant criteria; in a rhetorical analysis essay, you determine a source text's rhetorical effectiveness by examining how the author employs language to achieve a particular effect on an audience. Writing a rhetorical analysis of a reading requires you to answer three related questions:

- What response is the author of the reading trying to elicit from his or her readers?
- How does the author employ language to elicit that response?
- How well does the author succeed in achieving this response?

Composing a rhetorical analysis requires you to examine a source text from the perspective of both a reader and a writer, assessing how well an author achieves certain rhetorical goals in a text.

Rhetorical analysis is based on certain assumptions about how writers write and the way writing works. First is the assumption that writing is purposeful, that every text is written by someone who directs it toward some audience to achieve some purpose. To accomplish their ends, writers make a series of strategic choices—they choose this approach to the topic instead of that approach, this set of arguments rather than that set of arguments, this evidence instead of that evidence, this thesis rather than that one, this organizational plan in place of another, this word rather than that word. In a rhetorical analysis essay, you critically examine this series of choices, identifying and critiquing the strategies a writer employs to achieve his or her rhetorical goals.

A second assumption is that text and context are intimately connected, that text is fundamentally influenced by the context in which it is written. Writers work within a set of givens, a rhetorical context or situation that includes their reasons for writing the text, their purpose or aim, their audience's needs or interests, and their knowledge of the topic they are addressing. To be effective, writers must adapt their writing to meet the needs of the given rhetorical situation. If they ignore or misconstrue any element of the rhetorical situation, their writing will be less effective than it might otherwise be. Because writers typically want to produce the most effective text possible, they take particular efforts to ensure that their language suits the text's audience, purpose, message, and occasion. Therefore, to evaluate a text's rhetorical effectiveness, you must understand the context in which it was written.

A final assumption is that no rhetorical analysis is definitive. Readers often disagree about a text's purpose, intended audience, rhetorical strategies, and effectiveness. Because readers always bring their own knowledge, experiences, sensitivities, and biases to a text, they will form unique, individualized responses to even the most fundamental questions concerning how a reading communicates its meaning. Consequently, when you write a rhetorical analysis essay, you must explain your conclusions as clearly as you can, supporting them with thorough explanations and specific references to the source text.

THE RHETORICAL SITUATION

When you write a rhetorical analysis essay, you must examine how an author uses language to achieve a particular response from readers. However, your task is a little more complicated than it might appear at first. You will actually be examining how an author uses language to achieve a particular response from readers *given the specific context in which the writer produced the text*. This "specific context" is called the text's **rhetorical situation**, which includes the author's audience, subject matter, purpose, and occasion for writing. In your paper, you will assess how a writer manipulates language to meet the needs of the rhetorical situation and achieve his or her goals for the text.

A brief example may help explain why understanding the rhetorical situation of a source text is essential to composing an effective rhetorical analysis essay. Suppose your source text is a set of instructions for installing a new hard drive on a computer. Your task is to evaluate how well the instructions achieve their intended purpose: helping readers install that new hard drive on their computers. The first thing you notice is that the instructions are full of undefined technical terms—IDE cables, jumper selectors, drive rails, boot drives. Are the instructions effective? Upon consideration, you would have to conclude that the answer is, "It depends." If the instructions are written for someone who is already well versed in computer technology, they may be fine; if they are written for a novice computer owner, they may not be so effective. Composing an effective rhetorical analysis of the instructions requires that you evaluate the writing in light of its purpose and intended audience, two crucial elements of the text's rhetorical situation.

Because understanding a text's rhetorical situation is so fundamental to writing this type of essay, it is worthwhile to examine each element in isolation. Below are definitions of various elements of a text's rhetorical situation and a series of questions writers frequently ask of each element as they prepare to write a rhetorical analysis essay.

ELEMENTS OF THE RHETORICAL SITUATION

Author—the person or people who wrote the text

- Who wrote the piece?
- What is the author's background in terms of race, sex, education, political affiliation, economic status, or religion?
- What are the author's possible or likely biases?
- What perspective does the author bring to the topic?
- How does the author "sound" on the page—angry, detached, confused, funny?
- What has the author written about the topic in the past?

Topic—what the text is about

- What is the person writing about?
- Is the author addressing a particular aspect of the topic or the topic as a whole?
- Which aspects of the topic receive the most attention and which receive the least?
- What, exactly, is the author stating about the topic?
- What have others said about this subject matter?
- What is the relationship between what others have written about the topic and what the author is writing about it?

Audience—who the writer is addressing

- To whom is the text addressed?
- If the text is not written to a specific person or group of people, what kind of reader did the author seem to have in mind when writing the piece? For example, does the author seem to be assuming he or she is addressing a friendly audience or a hostile audience? An expert audience or a novice audience? An academic audience or a popular audience?
- What is the audience's likely knowledge of or attitude toward the author and/or subject matter?

- What assumptions does the author make about the audience? Are these assumptions accurate?

Purpose or Aim—what the author is trying to accomplish in writing the text

- If the author states a purpose or aim for the piece, what is it? To inform, persuade, entertain, educate, provoke to action, draw attention, ridicule, shock?
- If it is not stated, what is the author's implied purpose or aim for the text?
- Is there more than one purpose or aim for the test? If so, what are they? Does one purpose seem more dominant than the others? Which one?
- How does the author's purpose influence the text's content, structure, or language?

Occasion—what prompted the writer to write the piece

- Why did the author feel compelled to write this text?
- What is the historical context of the piece?
- Is the author adding to a debate over a particular political issue or social question? Is the author responding to another writer or text? Is the author responding to a particular historical event or cultural phenomenon?

Writing a rhetorical analysis essay usually requires you to examine the complex interrelationships that exist among these elements. For example, how does the author's audience influence what she writes about the topic or the language she employs? What is the relationship between a text's purpose and the time or place it was written? How effective is the author in producing a text that is appropriate for both the audience and the occasion?

RHETORICAL STRATEGIES

Once you understand the text's rhetorical situation, you are ready to turn your analysis to the author's rhetorical strategies—the way the author manipulates the text's content, structure, or style to achieve his or her aim. **Content** concerns the material an author includes in the text; **structure** concerns the order in which the author presents that material; and **style** concerns the language and sentence structure an author uses to convey that material. A rhetorical analysis essay is unlikely to address every aspect of a text's content, structure, or style. In fact, it may address just one or two of the author's rhetorical strategies. As the person writing the analysis, you will determine which strategies you wish to examine. They will likely be the ones you think are most essential to the author achieving his or her aim.

CONTENT

When composing a rhetorical analysis essay, most writers analyze a text's content in one or two related ways—by examining its arguments, evidence, and reasoning or by examining its persuasive appeals. Because both approaches are closely related, writers will often examine aspects of each in their essays. Both are discussed below.

Arguments, Evidence, and Reasoning

When analyzing a text's rhetorical strategies in terms of its arguments, evidence, and reasoning, you are primarily concerned in examining the claims or assertions a writer makes, the way that writer supports those claims, and the way he or she explains them. You need to ask yourself, given the text's rhetorical situation, why the writer would choose those particular arguments. Are they the best arguments for the writer to make? Why did the writer choose to support those claims the way he or she did? Again, was this the best choice of evidence? How effective were the writer's decisions? Does the writer explain his or her reasoning in the piece, exploring or defending the link between his or her claims and supporting evidence? Are there certain assumptions or leaps of reasoning the writer leaves unstated? Why might the writer have made that choice? Was it a good decision? Below are some questions that can help you analyze and evaluate a text's rhetorical strategies in terms of its arguments, evidence, and reasoning.

Arguments or assertions

- What arguments or assertions does the author make and how are they related to the rhetorical situation?
- How does the audience, purpose, and occasion of the text influence the author's arguments or assertions?
- Given the audience and purpose of the text, are these the most effective arguments? If so, what makes them effective? If not, why not? What arguments might be more effective?
- What arguments or assertions are emphasized the most? Why did the author decide to emphasize those assertions instead of others?
- What relevant arguments or assertions are ignored or slighted? Why do you think the author chose not to address them?
- How might the intended audience respond to the arguments offered? How well does the author seem to anticipate and perhaps address these likely responses?

Evidence or Examples

- How does the author support his or her assertions? Are they supported by primary or secondary research? By personal experience? By statistics or expert testimony?

- What is the source of the author's evidence for each assertion or argument? Are they particularly effective sources, given the text's rhetorical situation?
- Is the evidence offered appropriate, given the text's rhetorical situation? Does the evidence offered effectively support each claim?
- How might the intended audience respond to the evidence or examples offered? How well does the author seem to anticipate and perhaps address these likely responses?
- Is the presentation balanced or one-sided? In either case, is that choice appropriate given the rhetorical situation?
- How does the author address possible counterarguments or evidence that does not support his or her assertions?
- Are there obvious arguments the author chooses to ignore or gloss over? What are the effects of these omissions? How might they be explained, given the text's rhetorical situation?

Reasoning

- Does the author present a clear and cogent line of reasoning in the text?
- How well does the author move from one assertion to the next?
- How compelling is the connection the author makes among assertions? Between assertions and their supporting evidence?
- Does the text lead logically and convincingly to its conclusion?
- Are there clear connections between the text's thesis and its primary assertions?
- Are there any important assumptions the author leaves unstated? Does leaving them unstated and undefended make the text any less successful?
- Is the reasoning fair and balanced? Should it be, given the text's rhetorical situation?
- Are there any logical fallacies or flaws in reasoning that might hinder the text's effectiveness, given its audience, purpose, and occasion?

Persuasive Appeals

Another set of strategies authors often employ to achieve their rhetorical goals involves appealing to their readers' rationality (logos) or emotions (pathos) or by establishing their own credibility as an authority on the topic (ethos). Though one of the three appeals may dominate a particular reading, most effective persuasive texts use elements of all three. In brief, when authors try to persuade readers by presenting a reasonable series of arguments supported by evidence and examples, they are relying on **logos** to achieve their goal; when they try to persuade readers through emotional language or examples or by appealing to the reader's needs or interests, they are relying on **pathos**; when they try to persuade readers by appearing fair, balanced, and informed or by establishing their own credibility and authority on the subject, they are relying on **ethos**. Below are some questions you can ask about a text's persuasive appeals if you are analyzing its rhetorical effectiveness.

Logos

- How reasonable and appropriate are the author's claims, given the rhetorical situation?
- How clear are the author's claims?
- Are the author's claims broad and sweeping or does the author limit or qualify them?
- How well does the author use facts, statistics, and expert testimony to support his or her claims?
- Are the author's claims adequately explained?
- Does the author avoid lapses in reasoning or logical fallacies?
- Does the author address opposing or alternative viewpoints?
- Are there relevant claims the author fails to address?
- Are the author's claims convincing?

Pathos

- Does the author attempt to convince his or her readers through appeals to their emotions?
- To which emotions is the author appealing? To the reader's personal fears or concerns? To the reader's economic or social self-interests? To the reader's desire for acceptance, love, or beauty? To the reader's sense of justice or social responsibility?
- Does the author appeal to his readers' emotions through his choice of arguments, evidence, language, or some combination of the three?
- How are appeals to emotion balanced with other appeals in the text?
- Does the author try too hard to appeal to readers' emotions? Are the appeals to emotion too clumsy or awkward to be effective?
- Is an appeal to the reader's emotions an effective strategy to employ given the rhetorical situation?

Ethos

- How does the author attempt to establish her credibility or authority?
- What level of expertise does the author demonstrate when writing about the topic of her text?
- Does the author's own experience or expertise lend credibility to the text?
- Does the author demonstrate or document the validity of the source texts used to support her assertions?
- Does the author present a balanced or a one-sided argument? Is that approach appropriate, given the rhetorical situation?
- Does the author demonstrate a sufficient understanding of the topic's complex or controversial nature?

- Does the text's tone or the author's voice contribute to or detract from her credibility?

STRUCTURE

While many rhetorical strategies are related to a text's content, others involve its structure. Once writers decide what information or arguments they will include in their essays, they need to decide the order in which to present them. Structure also involves the way a writer introduces and concludes a text and draws connections among parts of the text. Below are some questions you can ask about a text's structure as you evaluate its rhetorical effectiveness.

- In what order does the author present information or claims?
- What purpose might lie behind this order?
- How might the text's structure influence an audience's response to the author's ideas, findings, or assertions?
- Does the text present a clear and consistent line of reasoning?
- Are there clear connections between the text's stated or implied thesis and its topic sentences?
- Does the text's structure enhance its appeal to logic? Does the author draw clear, logical connections among the text's ideas, findings, or assertions?
- Does the structure of the piece enhance its appeal to emotion, particularly in its introduction or conclusion?
- Does the structure of the piece enhance its appeal to credibility? Does the author seem in control of the writing? Does the text hold together as a whole? Are there any obvious flaws in structure that might damage the author's credibility?

STYLE

Finally, when analyzing an author's rhetorical strategies, consider his or her style. Among other elements of writing, style concerns the text's sentence structure, word choice, punctuation, voice, tone, and diction. Below are some questions that can help you assess how style contributes to a text's rhetorical effectiveness.

- What type of syntax does the author employ? How does the author vary sentence length (long or short) and sentence type (simple, compound, complex, and compound-complex; cumulative, periodic, and balanced)? How is syntax related to the audience, purpose, or occasion of the text?
- What types of figurative language does the author employ (for example, metaphors, similes, or analogies)? Are the choices of figurative language appropriate and effective given the text's rhetorical situation?
- What types of allusions does the author employ? Are they appropriate and effective?

- How appropriate and effective is the author's voice, given the text's rhetorical situation?
- How appropriate and effective is the author's tone, given the text's rhetorical situation?
- How appropriate and effective is the author's diction, given the text's rhetorical situation?

ANALYZING A TEXT'S RHETORICAL STRATEGIES—AN EXAMPLE

To better understand how to analyze a text's rhetorical strategies in terms of its content, structure, and style, carefully read the following speech—Abraham Lincoln's Second Inaugural Address. Lincoln delivered this speech on March 4, 1865, in Washington, D.C. Though the Civil War was not yet over, the struggle had turned in the Union's favor, and the end of the conflict was in sight. In this address, Lincoln acknowledges the price the nation has paid for the war and argues that lasting peace and reconciliation will come only through mercy and forgiveness. Many historians and rhetoricians consider this Lincoln's greatest speech.

Lincoln's Second Inaugural Address

Fellow-Countrymen:

At this second appearing to take the oath of the Presidential office there is less occasion for an extended address than there was at the first. Then a statement somewhat in detail of a course to be pursued seemed fitting and proper. Now, at the expiration of four years, during which public declarations have been constantly called forth on every point and phase of the great contest which still absorbs the attention and engrosses the energies of the nation, little that is new could be presented. The progress of our arms, upon which all else chiefly depends, is as well known to the public as to myself, and it is, I trust, reasonably satisfactory and encouraging to all. With high hope for the future, no prediction in regard to it is ventured.

On the occasion corresponding to this four years ago all thoughts were anxiously directed to an impending civil war. All dreaded it, all sought to avert it. While the inaugural address was being delivered from this place, devoted altogether to *saving* the Union without war, urgent agents were in the city seeking to *destroy* it without war; seeking to dissolve the Union and divide effects by negotiation. Both parties deprecated war, but one of them would *make* war rather than let the nation survive, and the other would *accept* war rather than let it perish, and the war came.

One-eighth of the whole population were colored slaves, not distributed generally over the Union, but localized in the southern part of it. These slaves constituted a peculiar and powerful interest. All knew that this interest was somehow the cause of the war. To strengthen, perpetuate, and extend this interest was the object for which the insurgents would rend the Union even by war, while the Government claimed no right to do more than to restrict the territorial enlargement of it. Neither party expected for the war the magnitude or the duration which it has already attained. Neither anticipated that the *cause* of the conflict might cease with or even before the conflict itself should cease. Each looked for an easier triumph, and a result less fundamental and astounding. Both read the same Bible and pray to the same God, and each invokes His aid against the other. It may seem strange that any men should dare to ask a just God's assistance in wringing their bread from the sweat of other men's faces, but let us judge not, that we be not judged. The prayers of both could not be answered. That of neither has been answered fully. The Almighty has His own purposes. "Woe unto the world because of offenses; for it must needs be that offenses come, but woe to that man by whom the offense cometh." If we shall suppose that American slavery is one of those offenses which, in the providence of God, must needs come, but which, having continued through His appointed time, He now wills to remove, and that He gives to both North and South this terrible war as the woe due to those by whom the offense came, shall we discern therein any departure from those divine attributes which the believers in a living God always ascribe to Him? Fondly do we hope, fervently do we pray, that this mighty scourge of war may speedily pass away. Yet, if God wills that it continue until all the wealth piled by the bondsman's two hundred and fifty years of unrequited toil shall be sunk, and until every drop of blood drawn with the lash shall be paid by another drawn with the sword, as was said three thousand years ago, so still it must be said "the judgments of the Lord are true and righteous altogether."

With malice toward none, with charity for all, with firmness in the right as God gives us to see the right, let us strive on to finish the work we are in, to bind up the nation's wounds, to care for him who shall have borne the battle and for his widow and his orphan, to do all which may achieve and cherish a just and lasting peace among ourselves and with all nations.

A RHETORICAL ANALYSIS OF LINCOLN'S SPEECH

In terms of the speech's content, notice how Lincoln makes several related arguments designed to persuade his audience that after the Civil War ends, the North must treat the South with charity and compassion. He opens his address by asserting that he will not detail a course of action for the country's future—clearly everyone in the nation has been and continues to be consumed by the war. Next, Lincoln asserts that the primary cause of the war was slavery. Four years earlier, the Union sought to halt the spread of slavery peacefully. However, the Confederacy, he asserts, would not accept this position and turned to armed conflict instead. Neither side, though, anticipated the duration and ferocity of the war. While both sides in the conflict call on God for victory, Lincoln questions whether any divine power would support the perpetuation of slavery. Interestingly, he sees *both* sides in the war being chastised for their involvement with slavery and hopes that the suffering all are undergoing can purge their collective guilt and set the stage for a more just nation. Lincoln closes his speech by asserting that reconciliation will only succeed if it is based on mercy, forgiveness, and justice, not revenge and recrimination.

Both Lincoln's position as president and the occasion of the speech lend credibility to his address. However, Lincoln enhances his credibility by articulating the North's perspective on the war's causes, a position most of his audience would presumably endorse. Making numerous references to God and God's will also serves to enhance his ethos but serves as an emotional appeal as well: Lincoln hopes the citizens of the North will be swayed to extend mercy to the South after the war by ascribing such a position to divine will. By speaking mercifully and understandingly about the suffering of the South during the war, Lincoln models the behavior and attitudes he hopes the members of his audience will adopt themselves.

Structurally, Lincoln opens his address by commenting on the previous four years of his presidency and acknowledging the country's current struggle before laying out the North's view of the war's cause. Having articulated a position his audience would accept, Lincoln then changes the direction of the speech. Instead of attacking the Confederacy for its succession from the Union, he speaks about the suffering the war has brought to *all* Americans, how neither side in the conflict accurately anticipated the terrible nature of the war, and how the South has already suffered severely for its actions. Audience members might expect Lincoln to call for revenge against the South; instead, he argues that both sides have suffered enough. At the end of his speech, he urges his audience to treat the South with charity.

Stylistically, the speech is remarkable for its somber tone. Though this is an inaugural speech, Lincoln is not celebrating. Instead, his tone reflects the suffering the nation has endured over the previous four years and the hard work that lies ahead of it. Syntactically, he employs balanced sentences to create memorable phrases—"All dreaded it, all sought to avert it," "Fondly do we hope, fervently do we pray," "With malice toward none, with charity for all"—and to emphasize the balanced view he takes concerning the war's consequences. The North and South have both suffered and reconstruction must be based on an understanding of their shared humanity. Lincoln repeatedly employs language from the Old Testament to emphasize his view of the war as a form of divine judgment against the nation for its past offences. Underlying this argument is the notion that justice lies in the hands of God: if God has scourged the nation for its transgressions, there is no need for humans to further the South's punishment following the war.

This brief rhetorical analysis of Lincoln's speech gives you some idea of how an author can manipulate a text's content, structure, and style to achieve a particular aim.

WRITING A RHETORICAL ANALYSIS ESSAY

STEP 1—CAREFULLY READ THE ASSIGNMENT

As you read the assignment, be sure you understand who *your* audience is for the assignment. What can you assume your reader knows about the source text, its author, or the context in which it was written? How much information do you need to provide so your reader will understand your analysis of the text? Also, what can you assume your reader knows about rhetoric? What terms, if any, will you need to define in your essay?

STEP 2—ESTABLISH THE SOURCE TEXT'S RHETORICAL SITUATION

First, establish the rhetorical situation of the source text (see "Rhetorical Situation" above). Below are some of the questions you should answer either before or as you carefully read the source text:

- Who is the author?
- What is the writer's message?
- Who is the writer addressing?
- What is the writer's purpose or goal?
- Why is the writer composing this text?
- When was the text produced?
- Where was the text published?

To establish the text's rhetorical situation you might need to do a little research, but writing a rhetorical analysis essay requires that you understand the context in which the text was produced.

STEP 3—DETERMINE THE AUTHOR'S GOAL

In a sentence or two, paraphrase what you think the author is trying to accomplish in the text: what effect does she want to have on the audience? Is the author trying to persuade her readers to adopt a particular position? Does the author want to influence what her readers believe? Is the author trying to elicit a particular emotional response from people who read the text? State the author's purpose or goal, as you understand it, as clearly and specifically as you can.

STEP 4—IDENTIFY AND EVALUATE THE TEXT'S RHETORICAL STRATEGIES

Once you have a clear sense of the text's rhetorical situation, read through it again to identify the strategies the author employed to achieve his goal. Examine the text's content, structure, and style in relation to its rhetorical situation. How has the author manipulated various elements of the text to achieve a particular response from his readers? Spend as much time on this step in the process as you need—the ideas and insights you develop now will help you form a thesis for your essay. Remember that in your essay, you will not address every rhetorical strategy the writer employed. Instead, you will focus on the strategies you think most significantly contribute to the text's ability or inability to achieve its rhetorical goal. As you reread the text, make a list of the ways the author employs content, structure, and style to achieve his purpose, noting specific examples of each from the reading. Based on this list, decide which strategies help the writer achieve his goals and which do not, given the text's audience, topic, purpose, and occasion. State in one or two sentences what makes each strategy successful or unsuccessful.

STEP 5—DETERMINE YOUR THESIS

In your thesis, you will state how successful you think the author is in achieving his or her rhetorical goal and indicate which of the author's rhetorical strategies you will examine in your essay. Your thesis may indicate that the author succeeds in achieving his or her rhetorical goals, fails to achieve them, or succeeds in some ways but fails in others. Whatever your assessment, state it clearly in your thesis, along with the rhetorical strategies you will examine to explain and defend your judgment.

Sample Thesis Statement 1: Author succeeds in achieving his or her rhetorical goal

Lincoln's Second Inaugural Address effectively establishes the North's moral imperative for successful Reconstruction by making repeated appeals to authority and emotion.

Sample Thesis Statement 2: Author fails to achieve his or her rhetorical purpose

Lincoln's Second Inaugural Address fails to establish the North's moral imperative for successful Reconstruction because he relies too heavily on religious allusions and does not adequately address the North's desire for revenge after the war.

Sample Thesis Statement 3: Author has mixed success in achieving his or her rhetorical purpose

Lincoln's attempts to establish the North's moral imperative for successful Reconstruction in his Second Inaugural Address are aided by his repeated appeals to authority, but they are hindered by his over reliance on religious allusions.

Whatever stand you assume, your thesis statement should establish the purpose and focus of your essay.

STEP 6—WRITE YOUR ROUGH DRAFT

While every rhetorical analysis essay will be structured a little differently, the following outline may help you determine how to organize your paper.

Introductory Section

- Indicate the topic of the source text.
- Introduce the text you are analyzing or evaluating.
- State your thesis.
- Capture reader interest.

In this part of your paper, you need to indicate the topic of your essay, introduce the source text (provide the author's full name and the title of the reading), and state your thesis. One of the real challenges in writing the introductory section of a rhetorical analysis essay is to capture reader interest as well. You may be able to develop reader interest in your essay by opening with a question raised by the source text, starting with an exciting quotation from the reading or providing some interesting information about the reading's author or historical significance.

Summary of Source Text and Overview of the Rhetorical Situation

- Briefly summarize the source text.
- Explain the source text's rhetorical situation.

In one or two paragraphs, summarize the reading and its rhetorical situation. In addition to stating what the author wrote, explain the audience, purpose, and occasion of the piece. Your analysis will depend on readers understanding the source text's rhetorical situation, so explain it carefully in this part of the paper. You will be making frequent reference back to this information in the body of your essay.

Body Paragraphs

- Examine the text one rhetorical strategy at a time (content, structure, or style).
- Cite specific examples from the source text to support any assertion you make.
- Explain the link between the examples you provide and the assertions you make.

As you draft the body of your rhetorical analysis essay, carefully critique the text one rhetorical strategy at a time, explaining whether employing that strategy helps the author achieve his or her rhetorical goal. You will need to illustrate and support your assertions with specific examples from the source text. Generally, each of your body paragraphs will contain (1) an assertion regarding whether a particular rhetorical strategy helps the author achieve his or her rhetorical goal, (2) examples from the source text that illustrate that particular rhetorical strategy, (3) an explanation of how each example you cite supports your assertion.

Do not make the mistake of thinking that the examples you cite will "speak for themselves," that you do not need to explain how the examples support your assertion because the link will be obvious to anyone who has read the text. Instead, always explain the link between your evidence and your assertion. In fact, the success of your rhetorical analysis essay often depends on the clarity and logic of this explanation: your readers need to understand how the examples you cite support your assertion.

Conclusion

- Wrap up the essay.
- Remind readers of your thesis.
- Maintain reader interest.

In the conclusion of your rhetorical analysis essay, provide your readers with a sense of closure and remind them of your thesis. The conclusion should flow naturally from the body of your essay and recapture your reader's interest. One strategy you might employ is to echo your paper's introduction. For example, if you open your essay with a question, you might want to come back to it in your conclusion; if you open with a quotation, considering concluding your essay with one. This repetition will help give your essay a sense of balance and closure.

STEP 7—REVISE YOUR ESSAY

When revising your rhetorical analysis essay, make sure your work is accurate, developed, organized, clear, and documented.

- *Accurate*—your essay accurately captures your analysis and accurately represents the source text.
- *Developed*—you thoroughly develop and explain your assertions.
- *Organized*—the assertions in your essay are easy to follow and are interconnected.
- *Clear*—you have provided your readers with the information they need to understand your essay and have presented your ideas using clear, accessible language and sentences.
- *Documented*—all quoted and paraphrased material is documented as needed and your readers can easily discern which information comes from the source texts and which information you provide.

Check the Accuracy of Your Assertions and Examples

As you revise, start by checking your essay's content. First, make sure you have covered everything you intended to cover in your paper and that your essay accurately reflects your views. Second, be sure you have not misrepresented the author of the source text—any material you quote or paraphrase from the source text must accurately capture what the author actually wrote. Finally, be sure you fairly and accurately represent the text's rhetorical situation.

Check the Development of Your Essay

All of your assertions need to be fully explained and supported. Because your rhetorical analysis essay will reflect your individual response to and evaluation of the source text, you have to explain all of your assertions thoroughly. Readers need to know not only what you think but also why you think it. Do not expect readers to draw connections between your assertions and evidence on their own.

Check the Organization

First, be sure your thesis statement offers an accurate overview of your essay. The thesis statement should help guide your reader through your rhetorical analysis, previewing assertions you will develop in the body of your essay. Next, check the topic sentences in the body of your essay. Each topic sentence should relate back to the thesis statement, introduce a new idea, and provide a transition from the previous section of your essay. Be sure that you employ effective transitions within your body paragraphs as well, highlighting the logical relationship of one sentence to the next. Finally, check the opening and closing sections of your essay to be sure each accomplishes what it is supposed to accomplish.

Check for Clarity

Are there any terms that need to be defined? Any references drawn from the source text that need to be explained? Any sentences that could be more clear? Check to see that all quoted and paraphrased material will make sense to someone who has not read the source text and that any technical terms that need to be defined are defined.

Check Your Documentation

Because you are working with a source text, be sure that all quoted and paraphrased material is properly documented.

SAMPLE RHETORICAL ANALYSIS ESSAY

The following is a rhetorical analysis of Lincoln's Second Inaugural Address (see pages 125–126).

Rhetorical Analysis of Lincoln's Second Inaugural Address

When President Lincoln stepped up to the podium to deliver his second inaugural address, he knew the Civil War was reaching its end. Though victory was not certain, events on the battlefield suggested that Union forces would soon put down the Southern rebellion and reunite the country. Lincoln knew he would soon be presiding over a deeply divided country, with many in the North demanding revenge against the southern states, including the arrest and execution of the Confederacy's leaders. A close analysis of Lincoln's address makes clear, however, that he envisioned a reconstruction based on mercy and forgiveness rather than vengeance, a message he forcefully conveys though the somber tone of the speech and its many religious allusions.

Since the Union forces were nearing victory after four years of brutal warfare, one might assume that Lincoln would deliver a joyful second inaugural address. Instead, the speech's tone is somber and reserved. While he states that the war's progress has been "reasonably satisfactory and encouraging to all" (125), Lincoln makes no prediction about its final outcome. He asserts that both sides in the conflict "deprecated" (125) war and that neither "expected for the war the magnitude or duration which it has already obtained" (126). Lincoln claims that "American slavery" (126) was the primary cause of the war, and though he states that the South was at fault for maintaining and spreading the practice, Lincoln claims that God "gives to both North and South this terrible war as the woe due to those by whom the offense came . . ." (126). Instead of celebrating the North's impending victory in the war, Lincoln claims that both the North and the South are paying a terrible price for their moral transgressions.

In his speech, Lincoln soberly assesses the causes and consequences of the war and indicates how the nation should proceed once peace comes. The final paragraph of his speech begins with the famous phrase "With malice toward none, with charity for all" (126), summing up Lincoln's message of mercy and forgiveness. The needed course of action now, Lincoln contends, is "to bind up the nation's wounds, to care for him who shall have borne the battle and for his widow and orphan" (126). This statement embraces both sides in the conflict: the nation's obligation is to care for both Yankee and Rebel soldiers, for all widows and orphans. Such mercy is the only way to obtain "a just and lasting peace among ourselves and with all nations" (126). Again, "ourselves" is inclusive: Lincoln is including the people of both the North and South in this statement, pointing the way to a reunited country. Lincoln's reflective, restrained tone in this speech indicates how he would like every citizen of the United States to respond to war's conclusion: with forgiveness, introspection, and understanding.

Lincoln's message of mercy and forgiveness is also furthered by his many religious allusions. Rather than claiming that the North's coming victory in the war has been ordained by God, Lincoln believes that God is neutral in the conflict, that the North and South are united by a common religious heritage: "Both read the same Bible and pray to the same God . . ." (126). Though Lincoln doubts that any deity would support human slavery, he warns his listeners, "judge not, that we be not judged" (126). Lincoln's repeated invocations of God strike a note of humility, reminding his audience that their fate is not in their own hands, that Providence dictates the course of history. The North has no reason to gloat in its victory or to judge the South severely after the war. Both sides have suffered judgment already; now is the time to act "with firmness in the right as God gives us to see the right . . ." (126).

Lincoln's Second Inaugural Address establishes a somber, reflective tone and employs numerous religious allusions to convey successfully his central message that, in victory, the North must act with mercy, forgiveness, and humility during reconstruction. Revenge and retaliation is not the path to reestablishing a peaceful, united, just nation. "With malice toward none, with charity for all," the nation could be reunited. Unfortunately, one of those attending the speech that day was John Wilkes Booth, who would soon assassinate the president at Ford's Theater. Lincoln never had the chance to put his philosophy of merciful reconstruction to the test.

Summary Chart

How to Write a Rhetorical Analysis Essay

1. **Carefully read the assignment.**
    - *Who is your audience?*
    - *What can you assume your audience knows about the source text and rhetoric?*

2. **Establish the source text's rhetorical situation.**
    - *Who is the source text's author?*
    - *What is the source text's topic?*
    - *Who is the source text's audience?*
    - *What is the source text's purpose?*
    - *What was the occasion for writing the source text?*

3. **Determine the author's goal.**
    - *In a sentence or two, state clearly and specifically what you think the author is trying to accomplish in the source text.*

4. **Identify and evaluate the source text's rhetorical strategies.**
    - *Strategies involving the text's content*
    - *Use of arguments, evidence, and reasoning*
    - *Use of logos, pathos, and ethos*
    - *Strategies involving the text's structure*
    - *Strategies involving the text's style*

5. **Determine your thesis.**
    - *State how successful the author is in achieving his or her rhetorical goal.*
    - *State which rhetorical strategies you will examine in your essay.*

6. **Write your rough draft.**
   - *Write the introductory section of your essay, indicating the topic of the source text, its title and author, and your thesis. Capture reader interest as well.*
   - *Summarize the source text and its rhetorical situation.*
   - *Draft the body of your essay, examining one rhetorical strategy at a time and supporting your judgment with specific examples from the source text. Explain how each example you cite supports your claim.*
   - *Write the concluding section of your essay, reminding readers of your thesis and maintaining reader interest.*

7. **Revise your essay.**
   - *Make sure your writing is developed.*
   - *Make sure your essay thoroughly develops and explains your assertions.*
   - *Make sure your writing is organized.*
   - *Make sure the assertions in your essay are easy to follow.*
   - *Make sure the assertions in your essay are connected logically.*
   - *Make sure your essay accurately reflects your thesis.*
   - *Make sure your writing is clear.*
   - *Make sure you have provided your readers with the information they need to understand your essay.*
   - *Make sure you have checked to be sure all of your sentences are clear.*
   - *Make sure your essay accurately represents the source text.*
   - *Make sure your writing is documented.*
   - *Make sure all of the material in your essay that needs to be documented is documented.*
   - *Make sure readers can tell which information in your essay came from your source text and which information comes from you.*

Chapter 8

READING AND WRITING ABOUT VISUAL TEXTS

DEFINITION AND PURPOSE

Consider for a moment the power of images—how photographs, drawings, or graphics affect the way you experience texts. Images can add emotional punch to reading, illustrate an assertion, or make a text more entertaining. Images can even make an argument—sometimes alone or in combination with written text. In our daily lives, we are constantly surrounded by visual images. Which ones grab your attention? How do writers manipulate the visual aspects of a text to achieve their desired effects? By analyzing these images, what lessons can you learn about effectively using visual images in your own texts?

The ability to critically read visual texts is becoming an increasingly important skill. Although visual texts have long been a part of human communication (think about the prehistoric cave drawings found throughout the world), they have become more central to communication over the last century. Since the advent of television, our culture has become more centered on visual images than in the past, and advances in computer technology have made it increasingly possible for students to incorporate visual images in their own texts. In fact, at some schools, visual presentations—films, streaming video, PowerPoint presentations, and posters—have replaced traditional text-based assignments like term papers and reports. In many majors, students are expected to develop the same kind of fluency in manipulating visual images as they are in manipulating the written word.

This chapter offers advice and instruction on how to read, analyze, and interpret the types of visual images that will likely accompany the texts you read in college and perhaps the assignments you write for class. While you may not have much experience thinking about visual texts the way you will be instructed to do in this chapter, remember that the processes you will employ and the types of questions you will ask closely resemble those you commonly use to read, analyze, and interpret written texts.

READING VISUAL TEXTS CRITICALLY

You might find it odd to consider how you "read" visual texts like photographs, drawings, cartoons, or advertisements. People often draw a distinction between written and visual texts: they "read" words, not pictures. However, as discussed in Chapter 1, reading a text—any text—involves understanding, analyzing, and interpreting it. Similar processes apply to both written and visual texts.

Below are a series of questions you can consider to help you read visual texts critically. Answering them will give you a clearer sense of a visual text's content, creator, purpose, and audience as well as your response to the image.

QUESTIONS CONCERNING THE VISUAL TEXT ITSELF

- What image does the visual represent?
- What are the various parts of the visual?
- What written text, if any, accompanies the visual?

As with written texts, start your reading of a visual text by forming a clear understanding of its literal meaning—what is it in and of itself, what are its parts, and what is its relationship to any accompanying written text? Although this first step may sound easy, it can actually be difficult to examine a visual text objectively, to identify its constituent parts, and to find language that accurately describes what you see. Your first step is to summarize and paraphrase the visual text: state in your own words what you think the visual is depicting. At this point, you are not concerned with the visual's intention or purpose, only with its literal meaning. Pay particular attention to the details of the image. Your eye may immediately be drawn to only one or two aspects of the visual text, but don't stop your analysis there. Examine every aspect of the image—note what's in the background and in the foreground, in light and in shadow, in color and in black-and-white.

Next, identify the various parts of the visual text. When analyzing a written text, you may discuss its thesis, claims, examples, explanations, structure, and so forth. When analyzing a visual text, you will focus your attention on elements such as these:

Images: What images are contained in the visual? How many are there in the text? Which ones seem to command the most attention? Are there images of people in the text? If so, who? What are they doing? Are particular objects included in the text? Which ones? What type of setting is depicted in the text: interior or exterior, urban or natural, realistic or fantastic?

Layout: How are the images arranged in the visual? How are they grouped? What aspects of the image are emphasized due to the layout? Which aspects are deemphasized? If there are people in the image, where do they appear in relation to the other images in the text? What appears in the foreground, and what appears in the background? What appears in light and what appears in shadows?

Color: How is color used in the visual text? What colors are used? What is highlighted by the text's use of color, and what is not? If you are examining a black-and-white image, how is shading used to highlight or emphasize particular elements? If there is written text, what color is it? How does color influence the way you respond to the writing?

Appeals: What elements of the visual text are intended to appeal to the reader's emotions, values, or needs? How does the author of the text manipulate its content and/or layout to elicit a particular emotional response from readers? What elements of the text are included to appeal to the reader's intellect or reason? Which elements, if any, are intended to establish the author's credibility or authority?

Note: Carefully examine any written text included in the visual. What does the text say? What is the relationship between the written and visual elements of the text? For example, does the text comment on the images or draw the reader's attention to particular visual elements of the text? How is the writing placed in the text, and where does it appear? Is the placement of the written text significant? Does it impact how you read the visual text?

QUESTIONS CONCERNING THE VISUAL TEXT'S CREATOR OR SOURCE

- Who created the visual text?
- What is the source of the visual text?
- In what publication or website does the visual appear?
- Toward what readership is the publication or website aimed?
- What, generally, is the editorial stance of that publication or website?

Although finding answers to questions might prove difficult, you should try. As with written texts, identifying the authorship of a visual text is central to understanding and evaluating it. Authorial bias can affect visual texts just as it can written texts. If possible, identify who created the visual text. Who was the artist or photographer? What can you learn about that person's previous work and his or her credentials or affiliations? Approach visual texts as skeptically as you would written texts. We tend to trust visual texts more readily than we do written texts. After all, who hasn't heard the saying, "Pictures don't lie." Of course, we know that pictures can lie—visual texts can be manipulated as easily as written texts. Visual texts can communicate truths, untruths, or half-truths. Understanding who created a visual text can help you establish its credibility.

Also consider the visual text's source. In what periodical did it appear? On what website? On what television show? In what film? In what advertisement? You need to understand the agenda of the visual text's source. What is the publication or website attempting to accomplish through its use of this particular visual text? Is its intention to inform, persuade, or entertain readers? What biases or agendas might influence the types of visuals a source employs or how it uses those sources? As noted in the chapter on critical reading (Chapter 1), if you are investigating the topic of abortion rights, it would be important to note whether a visual text you are examining was published by the National Abortion Rights Action League or by Operation Life. Each group has its own agenda on this issue, which may well influence how each designs and employs visual texts in its publications or on its website. Again, the possible bias does not disqualify or discredit a visual text. You simply need to take that bias into account when you read, analyze, or evaluate the text.

To better understand a publication's or website's general editorial stance, read some of the articles it publishes or posts and examine other visual texts it provides. While you may not be able to conclude definitively that the particular visual text you are examining reflects the publication's or website's general editorial stance, you will be in a better position to read that material in context. You will be able to conclude whether the particular visual text you are examining is typical of that publication or website.

QUESTIONS CONCERNING THE VISUAL TEXT'S PURPOSE

- What is the intended purpose of the visual?
- How does the creator attempt to achieve that purpose?

Purpose can be difficult to determine when analyzing a text—visual or written—because any text may be serving multiple purposes. Broadly speaking, a visual text may be attempting to inform, persuade, or entertain readers. Although it may be difficult to determine a visual text's exact intent, making an effort to do so is important. You can misread a visual text if you fail to understand its intended purpose.

For example, imagine an advertisement placed in a news magazine by the Sierra Club, one of the nation's largest environmental groups. The full-page ad consists of a black-and-white picture of a mountainside recently cleared of trees by a logging company. All that's left is a seemingly endless string of stumps, charred tree limbs, and muddy pits. In the lower left-hand corner of the page is a single message, printed in white type against the gray background: "The Sierra Club: *www.sierraclub.org.*" What is the purpose of this advertisement? Is it informative, persuasive, or both? Is it trying to inform readers about the Sierra Club's work, encourage them to find out more about the organization, or persuade them to join? While the picture itself may be striking, is the intention of the advertisement to entertain? How do you know? What if the text were different, that is, what if it read: "Help Us Fight Homelessness, *www.sierraclub.org*"? How would this new text change your interpretation of the advertisement's purpose?

Students sometimes run into problems when they read persuasive visual texts as if the texts were merely informative. We tend to read informative texts as if they were objective and factual; after all, that's what makes them different from persuasive texts. From experience, we know we need to read persuasive texts more skeptically than we do informative texts, because the author is actively attempting to sway our opinion about something or move us to act in a particular way. Our defenses are up when we read texts that we believe are persuasive in ways they are not when we read texts we think are primarily informative. In other words, our interpretation of a text's purpose influences how we read that text, how open we are to its message, and how crucial we are as readers. Clarifying the purpose of the visual texts you read can help you read them more effectively and accurately.

QUESTIONS CONCERNING THE VISUAL TEXT'S AUDIENCE

- What audience is the visual text's creator trying to reach?
- How has the creator manipulated the visual text to successfully reach that audience?
- How does your understanding of the visual text's intended audience influence the way you read that text?

When you read a visual text, consider the type of reader its author or creator is attempting to reach. Sometimes you can base your conclusion on the publication in which the visual text appears: certain publications cater to certain types of readers. The general readership of *Inside Wrestling* magazine is likely different from the general readership of *Opera Aficionado* (although there may well be people who subscribe to both). Consider the interests and backgrounds of the people who would likely read the periodical or visit the website in which the visual text appeared. How might the author's interest in appealing to that type of reader influence the visual text he or she creates?

Another approach to analyzing audience is to consider the elements of the visual text itself: how did the author's view of his or her audience influence the way he or she constructed the visual text? Put another way, if you did not know the publication or website in which the visual text appeared, how can you determine the writer's or creator's sense of audience by carefully analyzing various elements of the text itself? Consider these questions:

- What types of images are included in the text? Would they appeal to a wide range of readers or to just certain types of readers?
- What examples are included in the text? Would they appeal to a popular or to a specialized audience?
- If there are human models in the text, who are they? What types of people are they? Who might identify with these models? Who might not?
- If there is written text, how formal is it? What cultural references does the written text include? What types of figurative language does it employ? What readers would likely understand and appreciate this use of language?

Forming an understanding of the visual text's intended audience is important because it will guide the way you analyze that text. Central to analysis is a deceivingly simple question: Why did the author/creator construct the text this way? Assuming a rhetorical intent for all texts—that they are produced to have a particular effect on a particular audience—identifying the intended audience can guide the way you analyze the text itself. In other words, your analysis of the text will be based on your understanding of its intended audience.

QUESTIONS CONCERNING YOUR RESPONSE TO THE VISUAL TEXT

- What is my response to the visual text?
- Which aspects of the visual text elicit that response?
- What are the sources of my response?
- How does my response influence my understanding of the text?

Authors often incorporate visuals into their texts because they know readers are likely to respond to them in ways they will not respond to words alone. Visuals can stir our imagination, move us to anger or sympathy, attract us or alienate us, and cause us to laugh or to cringe. However, we often don't stop to consider our responses to visual texts: we are so wrapped up in responding to them that we don't consider the nature or cause of the response itself. The first step, then, is to recognize and articulate your reaction to a visual text. How does it make you feel? What is your response? Although it might prove difficult, find language that captures that reaction.

Next, identify which elements of the text evoke those responses. People looking at the same visual text may have very different emotional reactions to it, even if they are focusing on the exact same elements. Likewise, two people may have the same emotional response to a text even if they are focusing on different elements: one may be responding to a particular image included in the text and another to the text's layout. As you consider your response to a visual text, try to identify the specific elements that give rise to it. Encountering that text, you felt a particular way—what was in the text, exactly, that gave rise to that response?

Finally, consider why you respond to particular elements of the text the way you do. What knowledge, experience, or values do you have that cause you to react that way? Examining this link can be difficult, but doing so is extremely important, especially if you are going to discuss your response with someone else. For example, you and a classmate may have similar reactions to the same elements of a visual, but why you respond to those elements a certain way may be very different. Articulating the link between the elements of the text and your responses can help you more fully understand your reactions and how they differ from others'.

READING A VISUAL TEXT: AN EXAMPLE

Below is an advertisement produced by the National Center for Family Literacy and published in the April 2008 edition of *Black Enterprise* magazine. Take a few minutes to carefully study the advertisement, then answer the following questions to get a better sense of how you are reading the visuals and text.

QUESTIONS CONCERNING THE VISUAL TEXT

- What images does the advertisement contain? How would you describe them?
- What do you assume is the relationship between the two people photographed in the advertisement? Why do you assume that? How does the photograph lead you to that conclusion?
- What else does the advertisement contain besides a photograph of the two people? For example, there's copy, but what else is there?
- What does the copy say? What words or ideas stand out in the copy? Why?
- Notice the National Center for Family Literacy name and logo at the bottom of the advertisement. Why are they included? What copy appears below the logo?
- Examine how the images and words on the page are arranged. What purpose might their arrangement serve?
- Notice how the copy employs two colors. What purpose does that alteration serve?
- Which words stand out because they are flush with the margin? Which stand out because they are in dark type?
- Which emotional appeals is the advertisement making? Examine how the people are posed for the picture. What appeal is the photographer making? Read the copy carefully. Point out instances in which particular words or phases are included to appeal to readers in specific ways.

Because I can read,

I can understand. I can write a letter.
I can fill out a job application.
I can finally get off welfare.

Because I can read,

I can learn. I can help my daughter
with her homework.
I can inspire her to be better.
I can be a role model.

Because I can read,

I can succeed, I can
contribute. I can live
my life without fear,
without shame.
I can be whatever
I want to be.

Because I can read.

 National Center for Family Literacy

Literacy can make the difference between poverty and progress.
Visit www.famlit.org to help us write more success stories.

©2005 Photographer: Marvin Young

Source: National Center for Family Literacy

QUESTIONS CONCERNING THE VISUAL TEXT'S CREATOR OR SOURCE

- This advertisement appeared in *Black Enterprise* magazine. What do you assume or know about this publication?
- The advertisement was placed by the National Center for Family Literacy. What do you assume or know about this organization?
- Which types of people are likely to read *Black Enterprise*? What can you assume about their backgrounds and interests?
- How has the National Center for Family Literacy used images and copy to appeal to this type of reader?
- Why does the advertisement include copy like the following:
  - "Because I can read, I can understand. I can write a letter. I can fill out a job application. I can finally get off welfare."
  - "Because I can read, I can succeed, I can contribute."
  - "Literacy can make the difference between poverty and progress."

QUESTIONS CONCERNING THE TEXT'S PURPOSE

- What is the advertisement's intended purpose? How do you know?
- Is the advertisement primarily a call to action ("Visit *www.famlit.org* to help us write more success stories.") or does it serve other purposes as well? If it serves other purposes, what are they?
- How has the National Center for Family Literacy attempted to achieve their purpose with this advertisement? How are their efforts related to the publication in which the advertisement appears?
- If the goal of the advertisement is primarily to inform readers, what does its creators intend for them to learn? How does the advertisement attempt to do this?
- If the advertisement is primarily a call to action, what is the action its creators want readers to take? How do they attempt to convince or move readers to act in this way?

QUESTIONS CONCERNING THE VISUAL TEXT'S AUDIENCE

- What audience is this advertisement attempting to reach?
- If the advertisement is a call to action, who is supposed to act? How do you know?
- How has the National Center for Family Literacy attempted to reach its intended audience? How have they manipulated the elements of the advertisement—for example, images, copy, layout, color—to reach their audience?
- Who do you assume is the speaker in the advertisement? Who is the first-person narrator? How do you know this? Why might the advertisement be written this way?
- What are the race, gender, and ages of the people shown in the advertisement? Why do you think they were chosen as models for this advertisement? How might that choice be related to the intended audience?

QUESTIONS CONCERNING YOUR RESPONSE TO THE VISUAL TEXT

- How do you respond to the advertisement?
- Do you find it interesting? If so, why? If not, why not?
- Are you moved to take any action as a result of reading the advertisement? If so, what action and why? If not, why not?
- Do you respond one way to the photograph of the people and another way to the copy? Why?
- What personal experience or knowledge might influence the way you respond to this advertisement? What is the link between that experience or knowledge and your response?

WRITING AN EVALUATION OF A VISUAL TEXT

Although on occasion you may be asked to write essays in which you describe just visual texts, you will more commonly be required to analyze and evaluate them as well. When you write this type of essay, you will identify how the text's author attempts to achieve a particular rhetorical goal and assess his or her success. In many ways, this type of essay closely resembles a critique (Chapter 6) or a rhetorical analysis (Chapter 7) of a print text. The different is, of course, that you will be analyzing and evaluating images, not just language.

STEP 1—CAREFULLY READ THE ASSIGNMENT

As always, be sure you understand the assignment's intent and requirements. The words *analysis* or *evaluation* may never appear in the assignment. Instead, you might be asked to "assess" or "critique" the text, to decide "how effective" it is, or to argue "how well" it achieves its goal. If you have any questions regarding the goals of the essay you are being asked to write, talk to your teacher.

Also be sure you understand whether you will be evaluating a visual text you locate on your own or if you will be working with an assigned text. If you are free to choose your own visual text for analysis and evaluation, clarify whether there are any restrictions on your choice. For example, does your teacher want you work with a particular type of visual text (i.e., an advertisement, a political cartoon, a photograph, a sign, or a painting)? Are particular types of visual texts excluded from the analysis? Finally, if the choice of source texts is up to you, have your teacher approve your selection before you begin to write your essay.

STEP 2—ANALYZE AND DESCRIBE THE TEXT

Although this step sounds simple, in some ways it is the most difficult. You need to carefully and objectively examine the text, finding language to describe exactly what you see and read. In several chapters, this textbook discusses the issue of bias when it comes to writing and reading texts—readers need to understand and take into account possible authorial bias when they read texts and acknowledge the biases they themselves bring to the texts they read and write. The same concerns hold true for visual texts as well.

While you need to consider the biases that may have influenced the visual text's creation, you also need to be aware of any biases that could cloud or color your reading of it. Bias can lead you to misinterpret a visual image or actually fail to "see" what is on the page or computer screen before you because you are not looking for it. Therefore, when you analyze and describe a visual text, try to put aside as best you can any prejudices or assumptions you have concerning the text's content, message, creator, or source. Just as when you write a summary of a print text, your goal here is to be as objective as possible. Try to describe the visual text as objectively and accurately as you can, using language that is neutral and clear.

STEP 3—ESTABLISH THE TEXT'S RHETORICAL SITUATION

To establish the visual text's rhetorical situation, consider your answers to the following questions:

- Who is the text's author or creator?
- Where was the text published, or where does it appear?
- What is the text's message? If there is more than one message, what are they? Does one message dominate?
- Who is the text's intended audience?
- How does the text want to affect that audience? What is the text's purpose?

If you have a hard time answering any of these questions, consider asking someone else—a classmate, roommate, parent, or friend—to examine the text and discuss it with them. Sometimes talking about a visual text with someone is the best way of determining its rhetorical situation.

STEP 4—DETERMINE HOW THE TEXT ATTEMPTS TO ACHIEVE ITS RHETORICAL GOALS

Once you have determined the text's rhetorical goals, identify how its creator manipulates its images and/or text to achieve that end. Here you would examine how the various elements of the text you identified earlier work separately and together to achieve the text's purpose. Your goal is to find language to describe how the visual text "works," how it communicates its message, and how it accomplishes its goal. The various elements of the text you focus on at this stage in the writing process are the ones you will likely write about in your essay.

STEP 5—DETERMINE YOUR THESIS

Your thesis statement can be either open or closed. An open thesis statement would indicate how successfully you believe the visual text achieved its rhetorical goal. Using the National Center for Family Literacy ad found in Figure 1, an open thesis statement may read something like this:

> **The National Center for Family Literacy produced an advertisement that successfully encourages readers to support their organization.**

This thesis identifies what the writer believes to be the advertisement's goal or purpose (to encourage readers to support the sponsoring organization) and asserts a judgment concerning its success.

A closed thesis statement would indicate both your judgment of how well the visual text achieved its goals and the elements of the text you will examine to support your conclusion. Again, using the ad presented in Figure 1, a closed thesis statement could resemble this:

> **Through its copy and its depiction of a mother and her daughter, the National Center for Family Literacy advertisement successfully encourages readers to support their organization.**

This thesis still indicates the writer's judgment concerning how successfully the advertisement achieves its goal but also indicates how she will support her claim (by examining the advertisement's use of copy and its portrayal of a mother and her daughter).

STEP 6—WRITE A ROUGH DRAFT

Although the content and structure of the essays you write will vary by the type of visual text you are analyzing and evaluating, the following guidelines will help you write an effective rough draft.

Introductory Section
- Introduce the topic of your essay.
- Introduce the source text you will be working with.
- State your thesis.
- Capture reader interest.

You might consider opening your essay by introducing the topic you will be addressing (for example, the topic the visual text addresses), discussing the specific genre of visual text you will be working with (for example, an advertisements or a web page), or paraphrasing the assignment you've been given. Next, introduce the specific visual text you will be working with in your essay, indicating its authorship, source, and perhaps its date of publication. Somewhere in your introduction, you should also include your thesis statement.

Overview of the Visual Text and Overview of the Rhetorical Situation

- Describe the visual text.
- Explain the text's rhetorical situation.

In this section of your essay, describe and summarize the visual text you will be working with. Students sometimes understandably question why this section of the paper is needed, especially if the visual text is going to accompany the essay they write: Why describe the text when readers will have access to it? Keep in mind that your description is preparing your readers for the argument you are going to make concerning the text's effectiveness. Through your description, you will bring to your readers' attention aspects and elements of the text that you will discuss in the body of your essay. You will introduce those aspects and elements in this section of your essay and evaluate them later.

The same advice holds true for explaining the visual text's rhetorical situation. You need to tell your reader where and in what context the visual text appeared, who created it, when it was created, and why it was produced. Identify what you believe to be the text's intended audience and purpose. If you believe your readers might interpret the text's purpose differently than you do in your essay, address those concerns here, acknowledging them and defending your own interpretation. The more clearly you explain the text's rhetorical situation in this part of your essay, the easier it will be to write a convincing argument in the body of your paper.

Body Paragraphs

- Develop your thesis in one criterion or one example at a time.
- Cite specific examples from the visual text to support your assertions.
- Explain how those examples support the assertions you are making.
- Address possible objections or alternatives to your interpretations, as needed.

As you explain and develop the assertion(s) you forward in your thesis, examine one evaluative criterion or example from the visual text at a time. For example, if you are basing your evaluation of a text on its use of color, examine one use of color in the text at a time, explaining how it supports the assertion you are making. Afterward, move on to your next example. If you are basing it on the text's use of color and layout, don't jump back and forth between the two—develop one criterion at a time.

Also, do not assume that the examples you cite speak for themselves, that your readers will understand on their own how the examples you draw from the visual text support the assertion you are making. Instead, carefully explain the link as you see it, and explain how each example lends credibility to your assertion.

Finally, be aware that any conclusions you have reached regarding the visual text are based on your interpretation of that text. Your judgments reflect the way you have interpreted and responded to the images and/or writing. Other readers could legitimately interpret the text differently. As you develop and explain your particular interpretation, when necessary, note likely objections to your assertions or viable alternative interpretations. Acknowledging and addressing these objections or alternatives increases your credibility as a writer and strengthens your assertions.

Conclusion

- Wrap up your essay in an interesting way.
- Remind readers of your thesis.

As with other types of source-based essays, you want to wrap up your analysis/evaluation of a visual text in a way that reminds readers of the primary assertions you've made and that maintains interest. One way to reassert your primary claims is to simply restate your thesis; however, this approach does little to sustain reader interest. Instead, consider closing your essay with an interesting question or provocative assertion, to challenge other readers' interpretations of the visual text, or to predict the future, perhaps speculating on how successful the visual text will be in achieving its desired goals.

STEP 7—REVISE YOUR ESSAY

When revising your analysis/evaluation of a visual text, make sure your writing is clear, developed, and well-organized.

- *Clear*—your readers understand the assertions you are making and the link between your evaluations and the source text.
- *Developed*—you have thoroughly explained your assertions and have examined alternative interpretations when needed.
- *Organized*—your assertions are logically connected, and your evaluation is guided by an overarching thesis.

Check for Clarity

When you revise your essay, at some point try to switch roles: you are no longer the author of your paper but someone reading it for the first time. Are there any assertions a reader might have a difficult time understanding? Are there any terms that need to be more clearly defined? Is the connection between your analysis/evaluation and the source text itself always clear? In other words, would readers understand exactly what aspects or elements of the source text you are analyzing, evaluating, or responding to? Have you explained your assertions thoroughly? Revise your essay as necessary to improve clarity.

Check the Development of Your Essay

Have you supported each of your assertions with references to the source text? Have you explained the connection between your assertions and the source text? Do not expect the examples you cite from the source text to speak for themselves. In other words, do not expect your readers to understand the link between your assertions and the evidence you cite. Instead, clearly explain your reasoning.

Check the Organization

First, check your thesis statement. Does it accurately reflect and predict your essay's content and structure? If not, revise it. Second, check your topic sentences. Does each one introduce a new idea, provide a transition from the previous section of your essay, and, in some way, echo your thesis statement? Check the quality of the opening and closing sections of your essay—do they accomplish their intended goals? Finally, add transitions within paragraphs where needed to help guide your readers through your essay.

SAMPLE EVALUATION OF A VISUAL TEXT

The following sample essay analyzes and evaluates the National Center for Family Literacy advertisement found on page 144.

An Effective Advertisement for Literacy Support

The idea of an organization devoted to the promotion of literacy paying for a magazine advertisement may seem odd. After all, if people can read the ad, they are already literate and have no need of the organization's services. If they are illiterate, they cannot read the ad at all. So what would be the purpose of such an advertisement? Judging by the ad placed by the National Center for Family Literacy in the April 2008 edition of *Black Enterprise* magazine, the purpose would be to garner support for the organization's programs and services. Through its use of copy, layout, and models, the National Center for Family Literacy demonstrates just how effective such an ad can be.

Unlike many other advertisements in *Black Enterprise*, the one sponsored by the National Center for Family Literacy is simple—using shades of black and white rather than color. Most of the ad consists of copy printed on a white background with two models—seemingly a mother and her daughter—appearing in the bottom right-hand corner. The bottom left-hand corner contains the National Center for Family Literacy name and logo, the message "Literacy can make the difference between poverty and progress," and an appeal to "Visit *www.famlit.org* to help us write more success stories."

The copy consists of the phrase "Because I can read" repeated four times in boldface print. Below three of these phrases—which serve as headings—are first-person statements (presumable from the mother in the ad) printed in a lighter type face to finish the sentence. Under the first heading, the copy explains how becoming literate helped her find a job and get off welfare. Under the second heading, the copy focuses on how becoming literate helped her become a better mother and role model for her daughter. Under the third, the copy explains how being able to read has enabled the mother to live without fear and shame, allowing her to achieve economic success.

One reason this advertisement works well is that its copy appeals to the type of person likely to read *Black Enterprise* magazine. *Black Enterprise* is aimed primarily at African American businesspeople, entrepreneurs, and philanthropists, people who have established or work for successful companies, who are looking for business opportunities, or who seek charitable opportunities. Those who read this magazine are aware of how important it is to have a trained, literate workforce and may have a greater understanding of and sympathy for people who must overcome obstacles to succeed.

Consequently, the copy under the first heading reads, "Because I can read, I can understand. I can write a letter. I can fill out a job application. I can finally get off welfare." Many readers of *Black Enterprise* would want to support an organization that helps potential workers learn how to fill out a job application, join the workforce, and move off of welfare. The copy under the second heading appeals to the readers' emotions. Supporting the work of the National Center for Family Literacy will improve the life of the family pictured in the ad—thanks to the organization, the mother can now "help my daughter with her homework," "inspire her to be better," and be a better "role model." Supporting the National Center for Family Literacy is not just in the economic interest of those who read *Black Enterprise*, it is also a humanitarian act.

The copy under the third heading combines elements of the first two. It opens with an echo of the first: "Because I can read, I can succeed. I can contribute." The copy indicates that the National Center for Family Literacy can help women like the one in the advertisement enter the workforce and achieve economic success. The next two statements, however, return to emotional appeals: "I can live my life without fear, without shame. I can be whatever I want to be." The copy is designed to build a bridge between the readers' experiences and the National Center's mission by stressing the need to help people overcome fears and obstacles and by working hard, to succeed.

Also making the National Center for Family Literacy's ad effective is its use of layout—how the copy and visuals are arranged on the page. The phrase "Because I can read," is repeated four times, printed in bold face along the left-hand margin of the page. Due to their placement and appearance, these words catch the reader's eye first. This repeated phrase dominates the ad, leading the reader's eye down the page to the National Center for Family Literacy's logo. The lighter-colored text underneath each heading catches the reader's eye because of its appearance and the repetition of "I": nine of the thirteen lines under the headings begin with "I." The use of first person in these lines makes the advertisement's copy personal, encouraging readers to identify with the mother and daughter pictured in the lower right-hand corner. People are more likely to support a charitable organization if they can identify and empathize with those who will be receiving the aid.

In fact, the depiction of the people in the advertisement also makes it effective. The copy surrounds and frames the two people, a mother and her child. Reading the headings left to right leads the reader's eye directly toward them. The mother is squatting down and her daughter is standing behind her, leaning in, a hand on each of her mother's shoulders. The mother's right hand is on her knee; her left hand rests on top of her daughter's right hand. The mother has a slight, proud grin on her face, while the daughter shows a full-toothed smile. These are average people—the mother appears to be wearing a sweatsuit of some sort and the daughter a polo-shirt. The mother and her daughter are quite ordinary people, people whom the readers of *Black Enterprise* might know or see every day on the street. The message of the ad is clear: the National Center for Family Literacy helps average families like this one.

Finally, the facial expressions and race of the mother and daughter are crucial elements of the advertisement. The daughter seems overjoyed with the fact that her mother can now read, while the mother is brimming with confidence. Who wouldn't want to support an organization that would improve the life of such a cute little girl? Significant, too, is the fact that the mother is white while her daughter is biracial. While *Black Enterprise* magazine primarily attracts African American readers, the advertisement makes clear that the National Center for Family Literacy works to improve the lives of all people, regardless of race.

The National Center for Family Literacy advertisement that appeared in *Black Enterprise* magazine is not aimed at recruiting people who need the center's services. Instead, it is intended to attract possible donors and supporters. Beneath the center's logo at the bottom of the ad is copy that reads, "Literacy can make the difference between poverty and progress," and an appeal to "Visit *www.famlit.org* to help us write more success stories." Readers with a charitable heart may well consider supporting the organization after reading this successful ad.

Summary Chart

HOW TO WRITE AN EVALUATION OF A VISUAL TEXT

1. **Carefully read the assignment.**
   - *Clarify your purpose.*
   - *Clarify the degree of freedom you have to select a visual text to evaluate.*

2. **Analyze and describe the text.**
   - *Examine every aspect of the text.*
   - *Attempt to put aside any biases you bring to the text.*

3. **Establish the text's rhetorical situation.**
   - *Who is the text's author or creator?*
   - *Where was the text published or where does it appear?*
   - *What is the text's message?*
   - *Who is the text's intended audience?*
   - *What is the text's purpose?*

4. **Determine how the text attempts to achieve its rhetorical goals.**
   - *How do the various elements of the text work separately and together to achieve the text's purpose or goal?*

5. **Determine your thesis.**
   - *Identify what you think the text's goal is and assert a judgment concerning how well it succeeds in achieving that goal.*
   - *Decide if you will use an open or closed thesis.*
   - *If you use a closed thesis, indicate which elements of the text you will examine in your essay.*

6. **Write a rough draft.**
   - *Write the introductory section of your essay, indicating the topic of your essay, identifying the source text you will be working with, stating your thesis, and capturing reader interest.*
   - *Provide a brief but thorough description of the text and explain its rhetorical situation.*
   - *Draft the body of your evaluation in a manner that is consistent with your thesis, examining one element at a time of the visual text, citing specific examples from the text to support any assertions you make, explaining how those examples support your claims, and addressing possible objections to or questions concerning your interpretation.*
   - *Write the concluding section of your essay, writing up your evaluation, reminding readers of your thesis, and maintaining reader interest.*

7. **Revise your essay.**
   - *Make sure your writing is clear.*
   - *Make sure your writing is well-developed.*
   - *Make sure your writing is organized.*

Chapter 9

INFORMATIVE SYNTHESIS

DEFINITION AND PURPOSE

In a synthesis, you combine information from two or more readings to support a position of your own. Your aim in the paper can be expository (to convey information) or argumentative (to convince readers that your thesis is correct). In either case, when writing a synthesis, you combine material from two or more readings with your own knowledge and reasoning to explain or support your thesis.

College writing assignments often require you to synthesize material. In some courses the assignment will be direct and clear: "Compare what Author A and Author B have to say about topic X. How are their views alike and how are they different?" Other times the assignment might be more subtle: "Authors A, B, and C all address topic X. Which do you find most convincing?" Completing either assignment would require you to form and defend a thesis by drawing information from two or more readings.

To write a synthesis, you first need to sort through the readings to find information you can use in your paper. Being able to annotate readings thoroughly is essential. Second, you need to find the best way to organize this material around your own thesis and the demands of the assignment. Third, you need to find a place in the essay for your own ideas, findings, or arguments. Composing a synthesis usually involves more than just stringing together quoted and paraphrased material from other writers. Fourth, as you write your paper, you need to keep straight who receives credit for which ideas. Through proper documentation, you need to clarify for your readers when you are drawing on the work of a particular author and when you are developing material yourself. Finally, as you revise your work, you need to keep clearly in mind the rhetorical situation of the assignment. In your efforts to work with other people's ideas, you cannot afford to lose sight of your reader's needs and the purpose of the assignment.

TYPES OF SYNTHESIS ESSAYS

Synthesis essays can assume many different forms in college, some rather specialized and sophisticated. One way to begin sorting through all this variety is to recognize that for the most part the assignments you receive will ask you to compose either an **informative** or an **argumentative** synthesis (see Chapter 10).

The goal of an informative synthesis is to communicate clearly and efficiently information you have gathered from two or more readings. You do not defend a position of your own in this type of paper or critique the source texts. Your primary aim is to summarize the material in the readings and convey the information to your readers in a clear, concise, organized fashion. In contrast, the goal of an argumentative synthesis is to convince your reader to accept your thesis, an argument you are presenting on either the quality of the readings or the topic they address. You use the material in the source texts to support your thesis—sometimes summarizing the readings, sometimes critiquing them.

Either type of synthesis can be organized in a variety of ways. Often writers will choose to employ either a **block** or an **alternating** format. When you use a block format to structure your synthesis, you discuss only one source text at a time. With an alternating format, you switch back and forth between readings as you develop your thesis point by point.

Before examining each type of synthesis in more detail, read the following reviews of the movie *V for Vendetta*. As you read these reviews, consider what they have in common and how they are different: What is the reviewer's opinion of the film? What aspects of the movie does he examine to support his judgment? How convincing is his argument?

Can a Popcorn Movie Also Be Political? This One Can

Richard Corliss

Richard Corliss reviews movies for **Time** magazine.

The first thing a film critic (this one, anyway) should say of *V for Vendetta* is that it's a terrific movie. I love the look and the verve of the thing, the confidence of its epic design, its smart use of half a dozen noted British thesps, lending weight and wit to the supporting roles. Hugo Weaving gives the finest no-face performance since Eric Stoltz in *Mask*, and Natalie Portman, always an eye magnet, does her sharpest film work yet. In her sobbing scenes, when her will must be broken, then forged anew, she comes darn close to acting.

Which is to say, *Vendetta* is up there with the Wachowski brothers' first *Matrix* film, which anybody could see had more on its agenda than aerobatic martial arts. The brothers, who wrote the *Vendetta* script that James McTeigue spiffily directed, are back in top form—not larding political meaning on an action plot but finding a seamless blending of the two. Whether you're mindless or Mensa, you'll find stuff here to challenge and trouble you, the way a good piece of speculative fiction should.

The second thing: yes, it is weird that the original 1980s comic book, an updating of the Guy Fawkes tale ("Remember, remember, the 5th of November"), should so eerily foretell the 2001 bombing of another famous building (Remember, remember, the 11th of September). It's more audacious still that the Wachowskis, rather than scrubbing their script clean of 9/11 references, would emphasize the connection, proposing a dapper quasi-hero who is part *Zorro* (with the fancy swordplay), part *Phantom of the Opera* (but with a jukebox in his underground lair instead of a pipe organ) and just a smidge of Osama bin Laden (but with tastes more aesthetic than ascetic).

That a government should literally poison its citizens, and that a terrorist should be considered a hero, is a pretty nervy premise for a mainstream film. But that's dystopic fiction for you. (In his novel *Winter Kills*, Richard Condon posited that the brains behind the J.F.K. assassination was—Joe Kennedy!) These days, with many millions around the world seeing every evil in Bush and Cheney, a film like *Vendetta* is, at least, timely. And if the villains are the big guys, the hero can be a terrorist—or should we call V an insurgent?

That is surely an apt subject for a movie—even, and especially, a popcorn movie. If a cheapo '50s fantasy called *Invasion of the Body Snatchers* could also be a rich parable of conformist paranoia, and if *The Matrix* could clue kids into mathematics and philosophy, then a film as bold and thoughtful as *V for Vendetta* is allowed to stoke a multiplex debate on the use and abuse of state power. The best works of popular art get to play by their own rules.

Quite the Bomb: *V for Vendetta* Can Blow Away Parliament, but Not Its Audience

Stephen Hunter

Stephen Hunter *is a writer for the* Washington Post.

"V for Vendetta" really should have been called "The Man in the Plastic Mask." Or what about "The Movie With the Plastic Soul?" Or even "Natalie Portman Gets a Haircut."

Really, for all that the film gets out of its putative star, Hugo Weaving (Agent Smith from "The Matrix" movies), it could just as easily star a radio. Weaving is a fruity, stagy voice emanating from a hole in the polyurethane phiz clamped over his real mug. What emotions play across his face, what thoughts flash through his eyes, what joy nurses his mouth into a smile, what rage twists it into a scowl? Is he even acting? We'll never know. What we know is: As a revolutionary dedicated to tearing down the state, he looks like a guy in a comic book. (Wait, he was a guy in a comic book.)

That almost completely ruins the audience's ability to connect with his lonely mission, and the filmmakers know this, so they front-load the regime he despises in order to make up in hatred what they can't create in empathy. The Britain in question in some near future is a dystopian horror: It seems to have been taken over by a liberal's darkest fantasy of the conservative right—a gay-hating, woman-fearing Taliban, puritanical and single-minded, determined to crush human enterprise, creativity and love at every stop.

Of course, others have had a hand at evoking dystopia before and they've done a great deal better: In "1984," George Orwell really worked out the engineering details of such a place and understood its conceptual underpinnings, how the essence of totalitarianism was control of language, education and history. But that was a work of art and genius, where "V for Vendetta" is a piece of pulp claptrap; it has no insights whatsoever into totalitarian psychology and settles always for the cheesiest kinds of demagoguery and harangue as its emblems of evil.

To say that the Wachowski brothers, who made the "Matrix" movies and wrote this picture from the graphic novel that has since been disowned by its creator Alan Moore, are not up to Orwell's level is not to say much. Nobody's Orwell. Nobody writing today has the guts as well as the talent to be Orwell. But they should have come up with better stuff. They say they want a revolution? Then give us a revolution, one that's believable, frightening, heroic, coherent and not a teenager's freaky power trip.

For example: In one foray into disobedience, Weaving's V takes over the national television system, by himself. When the cops show up after he's broadcast his message, they surround the place and send in SWAT team operators. The SWAT team discovers that he has previously shipped hundreds of identical masks to the TV station, he's tied up every one of the several hundred employees (that would take hours itself!) and put masks on all of them (another task that would take hours).

But it never occurs to the filmmakers to think it through: Where would he get hundreds of masks? He'd have to manufacture them, no small task, and certainly one that would leave records, demand payments, receipts, prototypes, the whole ritual industrial fabrication. Then, how would he get them to the delivery service office, and would anyone there think it queer that a fellow is shipping a thousand boxes to a TV network? Clearly, nobody has thought too much about any of this stuff—or any stuff.

One might start the bill of particulars with the mask itself. It's a caricature of Guy Fawkes, who in 1605 tried to blow up King James I and both houses of Parliament and as a consequence is burned in effigy each Nov. 5. It's true, I suppose, that as time has passed, Fawkes's memory has eroded into something warm and cozy. But the real Guy Fawkes was a bit of nasty business, and had he succeeded, it would have been the 9/11 of British history, and his reasons were as spurious as the guys' who took the planes into the buildings: It was religion vs. religion. You'd think that stuff would be gone from the world, but four centuries later it's still around.

Anyway, first-time director (but longtime Wachowski hanger-on) James McTeigue tells the story not from V's point of view, but from that of Evey Hammond, played by the eternally underwhelming American actress Natalie Portman, behind a whisper of a Brit accent that comes and goes at random. Forlorn and mundane throughout, she's set upon in the beginning by a trio of thug/cop/rapists, when V steps out of the darkness and with a samurai's grace, magically disarms and discombobulates them.

Again, in my opinion, bad: He's got daggers, they've got guns. He's faster and better with the daggers than they are with the guns. Oh, yeah? My definition of fool is the man who brings a knife to a gunfight.

That incident sets into motion a variety of plot strands: In one, he continues to seduce her—though not sexually—drawing her to his headquarters full of art and antiques in some London cellar (Batcave, anyone?); in another a decent cop (Stephen Rea) tries to track him down and in so doing, uncovers entirely too much undramatized back story about the origin and nature of the regime; and V continues his war of attrition by dagger and bomb on its elite. It all builds to a celebratory reenactment of Guy Fawkes's deepest dream, and we watch in rapt enthusiasm as Parliament goes up in an apocalyptic gush of flame (you've already seen it a thousand times in the TV ads).

Besides Portman's numb thespianizing, the movie is full of sordid developments. V's dagger-fighting and kung fu moves are entirely too fantastic for belief; they're just an expression of a prepubescent's dark view of total physical mastery of the universe. The villains—John Hurt, Tim Pigott-Smith, Roger Allam—are pudding-faced saliva blasters, too obvious for belief. The movie's most pornographic turn, however, charts Evey's destruction by secret police, complete to the ritual shearing of the hair, as well as the horror of mock drowning. This little ploy turns really sickening when it's revealed who is really torturing her.

Then there's the movie's tasteless celebration of explosive devices taking down famous London landmarks, which it invites us to cheer as another step against the regime. But since we never believed in the regime, we're really celebrating the sheer anarchist spirit of destruction for its own spectacular sake. It's been used too much, but some Canadian comedians on the old SCTV had a riff where they reviewed films entirely in terms of how good they blowed stuff up. "They blowed stuff up real good!" they used to chortle with moronic glee glittering in their piggy little eyes. "V for Vendetta" blows stuff up too good for my taste.

Bombs Trump Big Ideas in Potent *Vendetta*

Ty Burr

Ty Burr *writes for the* Boston Globe.

Something is wrong in the totalitarian state of England. Actually, everything is wrong: minorities, gays, and "radical" protesters have disappeared into death camps, the secret police known as "fingermen" rule the night, and the population has been bludgeoned into sheeplike compliance by wall-to-wall disaster reports in the media. The face of the rabid fascist leader Chancellor Sutler (John Hurt) looms from posters and TV screens, and you can almost taste the spittle from his lips.

"V for Vendetta" wants you to wonder how much of this sounds familiar, and, worse, how much of it might become familiar with a few twists of history's tail. Then it wants you to root for the masked man who plans to blow it all up. Is he a terrorist or a freedom fighter, and what, exactly, defines the difference? The Wachowski brothers think they know. Anyone who gives thought to the matter may respond with one of their screenplay's favorite words: Bollocks.

Still, there's more on this movie's mind than the usual wham-bam-thank-you-ma'am the trailers are promising. In adapting the groundbreaking early-'80s comic book series by writer Alan Moore and illustrator David Lloyd (since collected in paperback; it's well worth the read), Andy and Larry Wachowski of "The Matrix" fame are betting that multiplex audiences are ready for a propulsive Orwellian drama disguised as an action flick. They've made a mainstream provocation at a time when we could use one even a muddled one and for that, they should probably be thanked.

Ever the prickly iconoclast, Moore has had his name removed from the film, but while "V for Vendetta" makes many changes to his story line, it does no essential violence to the work as a whole. A mysterious figure known only as V (Hugo Weaving) still rises from his shadowy lair to visit butt-kicking death upon various minions of the state: a bombastic right-wing TV host (Roger Allam), an archbishop (John Standing) with a thing for young girls.

V still wears a mask that evokes both Guy Fawkes (who plotted to blow up Parliament in 1605) and Edmund Dantes, the count of Monte Cristo. He still takes under his wing a fearful young woman named Evey (Natalie Portman) and teaches her to see the true enemy (he gets her to take the red pill, in other words), and he still talks a mellifluous blue streak that worked better on the page.

There's a good-hearted policeman named Finch (Stephen Rea), who with his loyal assistant (Rupert Graves) works to uncover V's grim back story against the advice of head fingerman Creedy (Tim Pigott-Smith) and Sutler himself. The trail leads to a secret experimental camp and a rueful lady scientist played touchingly by Sinead Cusack. It also leads to images of human bodies steamrollered into pits and covered with quicklime. The Wachowskis are playing with the gloves off.

In point of fact, the brothers have only produced and written "V for Vendetta", handing the directorial reins to "Matrix" assistant director James McTeigue. Regardless of who did what, the movie's a handsome piece of work, dramatically powerful even when it backs into silliness. The strongest sequences are lifted almost intact from the comic: the imprisonment and torture that harden Evey while freeing her soul, a flashback to the sad story of Valerie Banks (Natasha Wightman), movie star and victim of the state.

Even while the movie is set in a post-apocalyptic day after tomorrow, America, we're told, has fallen into chaos after the war it started enveloped the world are its concerns are of the moment. Specifically: What rights might a terrified populace give up in the name of promised safety, and how might a government wield that fear to its advantage? Some will praise or condemn the movie's message as an attack on Bush-ism run amok (Alan Moore was responding to Margaret Thatcher, actually), but that's too easy. The real villain is a cowed and lazy citizenry. Meaning all of us.

Disappointingly, "V for Vendetta" makes this point early and moves on, at some point turning as shallow as what it protests against. (Let's pause to remember, for one thing, that Fawkes wanted to blow up Parliament so he could install a Catholic king on the throne. Freedom for the masses wasn't high on his to-do list.) The film comes close to being the inspired piece of agit-pop it's aiming for, and the performances are first-rate: Portman, both with hair and without, atones for the woodenness of Queen Amidala, and Weaving, well, he gives good voice behind that mask.

In the end, though, the Wachowskis' love of freedom of, in Moore's words, that 1 inch no one can ever take from us is trumped by their love of watching things go boom. Spoiler alert (except to those who've been following news of the movie over the last few months): "V for Vendetta" ends with the destruction of the Houses of Parliament conveniently empty, unlike the London underground trains and buses of July 7, 2005. The movie offers this as an intentionally controversial celebratory sequence, after which the faceless crowds stand revealed at last in their beautiful individuality.

That's a bravura image, yet you're forgiven if you find yourself pondering the individuality of real-life victims. Shortly after the planes smashed into the World Trade towers five years ago after my daughter had come home from her Brooklyn school clutching a burnt memo that had blown across the river, I wrote that I hoped never again to see a movie in which buildings blew up. I was referring to an Arnold Schwarzenegger film, but charges of irresponsibility can apply to a movie of ideas as well, if those ideas are glib. "V for Vendetta" says that terrorism's ok as long as no one really gets hurt, and to believe that, you need the wishful thinking of a child. Unfortunately, the world has grown up since Alan Moore set pen to paper. One wonders if the fan-boys ever will.

INFORMATIVE SYNTHESIS

DEFINITION

Your goal in writing an informative synthesis is to combine material on some topic you have gathered from two or more readings into a clear, organized essay. After finishing your essay, a reader should have a better understanding of the topic and should know the position of the various authors whose work you include. You are not trying to show how one author is correct in what she says and another is wrong. Neither are you trying to advocate a position of your own on the topic. Instead, you are trying to present other people's ideas or findings as clearly and concisely as you can.

For example, if you were writing an informative synthesis of these three *V for Vendetta* reviews, you would want to summarize what each critic had to say about the movie or at least about certain aspects of the film—the acting, the scenery, and the direction, for instance. In fact, a good way to write this paper would be to isolate for examination certain aspects of the film all three critics address—that way you could draw direct comparisons among the reviews. While you point out for your reader any important similarities or differences you see in the various reviews, you would not argue that one critic is correct in his review of the film and that the others are misguided, nor would you comment on the quality of the writing or argument in any particular review.

To compose an informative synthesis, you employ many of the same skills needed to write summaries. As with writing summaries, you may encounter a number of problems when composing an informative synthesis:

1. Because of their content, language, or structure, the source texts themselves might be hard for you to understand. Because you need to form a clear understanding of the readings before you write about them, you need strong critical reading skills to write a successful synthesis.

2. You will often be looking for subtle differences among readings—not just different arguments or findings authors put forward, but slightly different interpretations of data, slightly different uses of terminology, slightly different emphases. Because a synthesis involves multiple source texts, when you examine a reading you plan to use in your paper, you also have to keep in mind the material contained in the readings you have already read. The more readings you are working with, the harder it is to keep track of the material contained in each and the easier it is to overlook the subtle differences between them.

3. You need to stay as objective as possible when examining the source texts and writing your essay. You do not editorialize in an informative synthesis: your goal is *not* to comment on the topic of the readings or on the quality of their writing. Instead, you need to be open-minded when reading them, to pull out from them material relevant to your thesis, and to present that material as clearly, concisely, and fairly as possible. As when you are writing a summary, remaining neutral can be difficult, especially when you feel strongly about a topic and must include in your informative synthesis ideas that disturb or anger you.

4. Organizing an informative synthesis can also be challenging. You need to decide how to construct your thesis so it adequately guides your reader through your work, how to order the information you include in your paper, and how to employ transitions within the body of your essay.

5. Supplying proper documentation in an informative synthesis can be problematic. One paragraph of your paper may contain information you have drawn from several different authors. Learning how to document such passages properly can be trying; remembering to do it is crucial. Improper documentation can lead to problems with clarity and plagiarism.

WRITING AN INFORMATIVE SYNTHESIS

Because writing an informative synthesis can be challenging, it is best to break the process down into a series of more manageable steps:

1. Analyze the assignment.
2. Review and annotate the readings.
3. Formulate a thesis and organizational plan.
4. Write your rough draft.
5. Revise your draft.

Remember that this method of writing a synthesis will not work for everybody. We all have our preferred way of writing papers, which can vary according to the type of essay we are composing and the time we have to complete the assignment. For example, some writers like to complete a rough draft before they write their thesis, while others must have a thesis in hand before they begin to write; some will rewrite a paper several times before they turn it in for a grade, while others revise very little. So use these directions as a rough guide for writing an informative synthesis. The important principle to keep in mind is to complete your paper in a series of steps, no matter the nature or order of those steps.

Step 1—Analyze the Assignment

Read the assignment carefully to make sure your instructor is asking you to write an informative rather than an argumentative synthesis. If you have any doubt, ask your teacher to clarify the assignment. Make sure you understand how many sources you are required to consult when researching the topic or to include when writing your paper. Also, check on the type of source texts your teacher expects you to use if you are required to collect the readings yourself. Some instructors will want you to use only "academic" sources—material written by experts in the field.

Step 2—Review and Annotate the Readings

Once you have assembled the readings that will serve as the basis of your synthesis, read through them several times with your assignment in mind. In most cases, you will look for specific information in each reading, passages that address the topic of your paper. Thoroughly annotate the reading and then summarize it. As you work with the material, remember to be fair and open-minded. Consider how the author's perspective on the topic is similar to or different from what other authors have written and decide whether you think it should be included in your essay.

Step 3—Formulate a Thesis and an Organizational Plan

Your thesis in an informative synthesis serves an important function. More likely than not, it will indicate the topic of your essay and indicate how you will structure your synthesis: what you will discuss and in what order you will discuss it. Always keep in mind the rhetorical function of your thesis statement. When people read your paper, they need to know early on what you will be discussing and will look to your thesis as a guide.

Your thesis for an informative synthesis can be either open or closed. In an open thesis you indicate the topic and general structure of your paper:

> Richard Corliss, Stephen Hunter, and Ty Burr offer widely different appraisals of *V for Vendetta*.

or

> While Richard Corliss offers almost uniform praise of *V for Vendetta* and Stephen Hunter almost uniform criticism, Ty Burr's review is more balanced: he acknowledges the filmmaker's ambitions but believes the movie is fundamentally flawed.

With a closed thesis you list the specific issues you will address in your essay. However, you have to be careful not to put too much information in your thesis—doing so will only lead to cluttered prose. A possible closed thesis statement for the paper described above might read something like this:

> Richard Corliss, Stephen Hunter, and Ty Burr disagree about the quality of *V for Vendetta*, offering conflicting judgments concerning the movie's acting, message, and allusions to the Guy Fawkes conspiracy.

Either type of thesis can be effective, but in general, the longer your paper will be, the more likely you are to use an open thesis.

When writing an informative synthesis, you can employ either a block or alternating format to organize your essay. With a **block** format, you discuss what one author has to say about the topic in relation to your thesis before moving on to what the next author has to say about it. Suppose, for example, that you are writing an essay with the thesis, "Richard Corliss, Stephen Hunter, and Ty Burr offer widely different appraisals of *V for Vendetta*, not all of them positive." In outline form, your paper might look something like this:

Opening Section

Introduce the topic of your essay

Give your thesis

Section on Richard Corliss Review

Summarize Corliss's critique of the film and its relation to the other reviews

Section on Stephen Hunter Review

Summarize Hunter's critique of the film and its relation to the other reviews

Section on Ty Burr Review

Summarize Burr's critique of the film and its relation to the other reviews

Conclusion

You might, though, choose to use an **alternating** format to organize your essay, especially if you use a closed thesis. Remember that with a closed thesis, you list the specific issues you will address in your essay. Using an alternating format allows you to discuss each of these specific issues in order. For example, suppose you are writing an essay with this thesis: "Richard Corliss, Stephen Hunter, and Ty Burr disagree about the quality of *V for Vendetta,* offering offering conflicting judgments concerning the movie's acting, message and allusions to the Guy Fawkes conspiracy." Using an alternating format, your paper might be organized like this:

Opening Section

Introduce the topic of your essay

Give your thesis

Acting in *V for Vendetta*

Corliss's views and their relation to the other reviews

Hunter's views and their relation to the other reviews

Burr's views and their relation to the other reviews

The Message of *V for Vendetta*

Corliss's views and their relation to the other reviews

Hunter's views and their relation to the other reviews

Burr's views and their relation to the other reviews

The Allusions to Guy Fawkes in *V for Vendetta*

Corliss's views and their relation to the other reviews

Hunter's views and their relation to the other reviews

Burr's views and their relation to the other reviews

Conclusion

Of course, you could write the same paper using a block format, if you like. If you did, it might be organized like this:

Opening Section

Introduce the topic of your essay

Give your thesis

Section on Richard Corliss Review

His views on the film's acting and their relation to the other reviews

His views on the film's message and their relation to the other reviews

His views on the film's allusions to Guy Fawkes and their relation to the other reviews

Section on Stephen Hunter Review

His views on the film's acting and their relation to the other reviews

His views on the film's message and their relation to the other reviews

His views on the film's allusions to Guy Fawkes and their relation to the other reviews

Section on Ty Burr Review

His views on the film's acting and their relation to the other reviews

His views on the film's message and their relation to the other reviews

His views on the film's allusions to Guy Fawkes and their relation to the other reviews

Conclusion

Alternating and block formats have their particular strengths and weaknesses. The alternating format allows you to compare and contrast the views of different writers fairly easily. In this paper, for example, you would be able to present each critic's judgments of the film's acting, special effects, and message in its own section. If you were using a block format, you might discuss Corliss's views of the acting on page one of your paper and might not discuss Burr's comments about the acting until page five or six. Your reader would have a hard time remembering Corliss's views by the time you discussed Burr's. Using a block format allows you to give your readers a good sense of the general argument presented by each author. Instead of having the discussion of his opinions spread throughout your paper, each critic's work is developed in a single section of your essay. Using the block format, you give your readers a thorough view of the author's work before you move on to the next source text.

Regardless of the structure you employ, your job in writing an informative synthesis involves more than summarizing what each critic has to say. In writing this paper, you would not be arguing a position of your own concerning *V for*

Vendetta. Instead, you would point out for your readers important similarities and differences among the views advanced by the critics.

Once you have designed your thesis, you need to go back through the readings, consult your annotations, and locate material you want to include in your essay. Preparing an informal outline can be quite helpful at this point. In your outline, indicate the focus for each part of your paper, the material you will draw from the readings to develop that section of the essay, and the ideas you will contribute.

Step 4—Write Your Rough Draft

The introductory section of an informative thesis should, first, capture your reader's interest. You might consider opening your paper with an interesting anecdote, a case history, an important statistic, or a telling quotation from one of the readings. Writing an effective opening gives you the chance to be imaginative and creative. A second goal of the opening section of your synthesis is to introduce the topic of your essay. The title of the synthesis should give your reader some indication of your essay's topic, but you want to be sure to clarify the topic in your opening section. Finally, the introduction to your essay should contain your thesis statement. Whether your thesis is open or closed, you need to include it in your introduction to serve as a guide to the rest of your synthesis.

In the body of your essay, you will follow the structure supplied by your thesis, explaining ideas one author or issue at a time. If you were writing an informative synthesis using the three reviews of *V for Vendetta* as your source texts, in the body of your paper you would summarize, paraphrase, and quote what each critic has to say about the movie, including in your essay material that best captures each critic's views and illustrates your thesis. However, not all the material in your informative synthesis will come from the readings. You have significant contributions to make, too. Besides quoting, paraphrasing, and summarizing what various authors have to say, you will contribute transitions, elaborations, clarifications, and connections.

For example, in one paragraph of your essay, you may introduce the issue to be discussed, introduce a reading by giving the author's name and qualifications as well as the title of the article, quote a relevant passage from the piece, restate the author's ideas in your own words to clarify them, point out how the author's stance differs from the author you discussed in the previous paragraph, and provide a transition to your next paragraph. If you devote a sentence to each of these tasks, your paragraph will be six sentences long, with only one sentence coming directly from the reading. The rest of the material in the paragraph comes from you.

When concluding your informative synthesis, you want to reiterate the main issues or findings you have covered in the body of your essay and give your work a sense of closure. You might want to look back at your opening strategy and reemploy it in your conclusion, if possible. For example, if you opened your paper with a quotation, consider ending it with a quotation. If you began with a question, conclude with the same question, perhaps answering it this time. If you began with a story, come back to the story in your conclusion.

Step 5—Revise Your Draft

Revising a synthesis takes time. In fact, it is probably best to revise your paper in several stages. First, you might check the **content** of your essay. Here you have two concerns. First, reread what you have written to make sure you are being true to your own intentions. You might ask the following questions of your manuscript:

- Does my thesis accurately reflect my understanding of the readings?
- Have I said in my paper what I wanted to say?
- Have I covered all of the material I hoped to cover when annotating the readings?
- Have I covered the ideas I discovered as I wrote the essay, ideas I did not plan on addressing but developed as I wrote?

A related goal is to review the content of your essay in light of the assignment. Here the questions you ask might include:

- Have I met the demands of the assignment?
- Have I adequately covered the ideas contained in the reading?
- Have I avoided editorializing or arguing a particular position?
- Have I kept my reader in mind? Would this essay make sense to someone who knows little or nothing about the readings? Do any ideas need more development or explanation?

Next, you might review the **organization** of your essay. Here you are concerned with the quality of your thesis statement, topic sentences, and transitions. These are some of the questions you should be asking:

- Does my thesis guide the development of the essay? Put another way, does my essay follow the format suggested or outlined by my thesis?
- Do I have clearly stated topic sentences introducing the major sections of my essay? Are these topic sentences tied to the thesis?
- Have I supplied enough transitional devices to guide my reader through my synthesis, especially when I move from discussing one author to discussing another?

Finally, revise with an eye toward **accuracy** and **clarity**. Here your concerns are word choice, sentence structure, and documentation. Again, you need to ask yourself a series of questions as you review your work, making needed changes when any of your answers are no:

- In choosing words, have I remained as fair and objective as possible?
- Have I successfully avoided jargon and highly technical terms when such language would not be appropriate for my audience?

- Are my sentences easy to read?
- Have I varied the type and length of my sentences?
- Have I quoted material accurately and properly?
- Have I paraphrased material accurately, properly, and fairly?
- Have I documented material thoroughly and properly?

You may need to revise your informative synthesis several times to address adequately all of these concerns.

Check Quotations and Documentation

Before you turn in your final draft for a grade, be sure to check the accuracy of your quotations and documentation. Take the time to check any material you quoted against the source text to be sure you have accurately transcribed the information. Pay special attention to any passages where you have added language to or taken language out of a quotation: these changes should not alter the meaning of the source text. Also, check to be sure that you have documented all of the material in your paper that needs to be documented and that you have employed the proper form of documentation in each instance. Remember that all paraphrased and quoted material in your paper should be documented. Because you are combining information from two or more sources in your synthesis, be sure it is always clear to your reader which source text you are referring to in your documentation.

SAMPLE INFORMATIVE SYNTHESIS

Following is a sample informative synthesis of the three reviews of *V for Vendetta*. Notice how the writer structures the essay and employs material from the readings.

A Modern Masterpiece or a Miserable Failure?

Three Reviews of *V for Vendetta*

V for Vendetta was one of the most popular and controversial films of 2006. Written by Andy and Larry Wachowski (who also wrote and directed the Matrix films) and directed by James McTeigue, V for Vendetta presents a dystopian vision of the near future, an England ruled by a tyrannical fascist dictator where civil rights are suspended and people are kept in check by the secret police. (The movie is an adaptation of the graphic novel written by

Alan Moore and illustrated by David Lloyd.) While some viewers may have been drawn to the film's special effects and violence (particularly its scenes of massive explosions), others were attracted by its cast and the themes it explored. Critics were widely split on their view of the film—many acknowledged the dramatic cinematography of the film but questioned other aspects of the work. The range of critical response evoked by V for Vendetta is clearly illustrated by three reviews: "Can a Popcorn Movie Also Be Political? This One Can," by Richard Corliss in *Time*; "Quite the Bomb: 'V for Vendetta' Can Blow Away Parliament, but Not Its Audience," by Stephen Hunter in the *Washington Post*; and "Bombs Trump Big Ideas in Potent Vendetta," by Ty Burr in the *Boston Globe*. While Corliss lauds the film, Hunter and Burr offer sharp criticism, with all three critics focusing their comments on the film's acting, message, and historical allusions.

First, all three critics comment on the acting in *V for Vendetta*, primarily critiquing the work of Hugo Weaving (who plays the title character) and Natalie Portman (who plays V's protégé Evey). Weaving spends the entire film wearing a dark wig and a fiberglass mask depicting Guy Fawkes, a British citizen who was executed in 1605 for plotting to blow up Parliament. Corliss claims that Weaving (who played Agent Smith in the *Matrix* films) "gives the finest no-face performance since Eric Stoltz in *Mask*" (160). Hunter, however, disagrees. He criticizes Weaving for employing "a fruity, stagy voice" and believes that the mask he wears negates Weaving's ability to act: "What emotions play across his face, what thoughts flash through his eyes, what joy nurses his mouth into a smile, what rage twists it into a scowl? Is he even acting? We'll never know" (160). Disagreeing with Hunter, Burr asserts that Weaving "gives good voice behind that mask" (164) but also observes that the his dialogue "worked better on the page" (163) than on the screen, which is more a criticism of the film's writing than on Weaving's acting abilities.

The critics also disagree about the quality of Natalie Portman's acting in the film. Burr claims that the actors' performances are "first-rate" (164), but his comments regarding Portman are mixed—positive but not enthusiastic: "both with hair and without, atones for the woodenness of Queen Amidala" (164). Corliss criticizes Portman's acting with mock praise as well, commenting that Portman, "always an eye magnet, does her sharpest work yet. In her sobbing scenes, when her will must be broken, then forged anew, she comes darn close to acting" (159). Hunter, however, trashes "Portman's numb thespianizing" (162), characterizing her as "the eternally underwhelming American actress" (161) whose British accent "comes and goes at random" in the film (161).

All three critics also disagree in their assessment of the film's message and relevance. Corliss calls *V for Vendetta* "bold and thoughtful" (160), believing it addresses "the use and abuse of state power" (160). Given the fact that we all live in a post 9/11 world, Corliss praises the Wachowski brothers and McTeigue for bringing to multiplex theaters a film that questions whether a hero can be a terrorist (or an "insurgent") (159) and offers a critical look at Bush administration policies. For Corliss, the film succeeds because the director and writers avoided "larding political meaning on an action plot but finding a seamless blending of the two" (159). Although he believes that the film is seriously flawed, Burr, like Corliss, praises the filmmakers' ambition: "They've made a mainstream provocation at a time when we could use one, even a muddled one, and for that, they should probably be thanked" (163). For Burr, the central theme of the film can be summed up in one sentence: "What rights might a terrified populace give up in the name of promised safety, and how might a government wield that fear to its advantage?" (164) Like Corliss, Burr also observes that some will see the film as a critique of the Bush administration, but, in his view, this reading of the movie is "too easy. The real villain is a cowed and lazy citizenry. Meaning all of us" (164). The filmmakers avoid the central ethical dilemma of the movie's final scene by blowing up an empty Parliament building, resulting in a message that Burr rejects: "terrorismis okay as long as no one really gets hurt, and, to believe that, you need the wishful thinking of a child" (164).

Hunter, however, rejects such interpretations of the film, terming its political messages "pulp claptrap" (161). While Corliss and Burr believe the film offers a thoughtful examination important themes, Hunter maintains that *Vendetta* depicts nothing more than "a teenager's freaky power trip" (161). Central to Hunter's critique of the film's message is its depiction of evil and its celebration of violence. The totalitarian figures that V and Evey fight against are too crudely drawn, "a liberal's darkest fantasy of the conservative right" (160). Because the evil characters are "too obvious for belief" (162), the violence at the end of the film has no significance beyond itself; consequently, "we're really celebrating the sheer anarchist spirit of destruction for its own spectacular sake" (162). For Hunter, *V for Vendetta* offers no profound political insights or critiques.

Finally, for all three critics, the film's message is tied to the parallels the filmmakers draw between V and the seventeenth-century English radical Guy Fawkes. With his mask, cape, sword, and explosives, V is a modern-day Fawkes; his goal is to complete the task that Fawkes left unfinished—blow up Parliament. For Hunter, comparing V to Fawkes is completely inappropriate: Fawkes was no freedom fighter, asserting the rights of the individual over an oppressive state. Hunter argues that "the real Guy Fawkes was a bit of nasty business, and had he succeeded, it would have been the 9/11 of British history, and his reasons were as spurious as the guys who took the planes into the buildings: It was religion vs. religion" (161). Fawkes was a Catholic who for religious reasons wanted to kill the Protestant King James I and all of the members of Parliament. Burr agrees with Hunter: "Let's pause to remember," he states, "for one thing, that Fawkes wanted to blow up Parliament so he could install a Catholic king on the throne. Freedom for the masses wasn't high on his to-do list" (164). Corliss, however, disagrees with both critics. He calls *Vendetta* "a terrific movie" (159), remarking how "the 1980s comic book, an updating of the Guy Fawkes tale ('Remember,

remember the 5th of November') should so eerily foretell the 2001 bombing of another famous building (Remember, remember, the 11th of September)" (159).

Is *V for Vendetta* a modern masterpiece or a seriously flawed film? Does it offer a critical examination of the times through the lens of history, or does it clumsily and inappropriately reference the past to support an unsupportable and childish view of the present? While most critics questioned the quality of the film's acting, they were sharply divided on its message and allusions to history. Few dispute the film's ambition or its intention to fuse action with philosophical inquiry and political commentary. How well it succeeds in blending the two, however, remains very much in dispute.

Summary Chart

HOW TO WRITE AN INFORMATIVE SYNTHESIS

1. **Analyze the assignment.**
   - *Determine whether you are being asked to write an informative or argumentative synthesis.*
   - *Determine the number and types of readings you are expected to use in your paper.*

2. **Review and annotate the readings.**
   - *Review the readings with your assignment in mind, looking for and marking information related to the topic of your paper.*
   - *Briefly summarize each reading.*

3. **Formulate a thesis.**
   - *Determine what stance you will assume in your essay.*
   - *Determine whether you will use an open or closed thesis statement.*

4. **Choose an organizational plan.**
   - *Decide how you will order the ideas you will develop in your essay.*
   - *Decide whether you will present your ideas using a block or alternating format.*

5. **Write your rough draft.**
   - *Follow the organization plan implied or stated by your thesis.*
   - *Summarize and combine (synthesize) material from the source text to support your thesis.*
   - *Both paraphrase and quote material as necessary.*
   - *Add transitions, elaborations, clarifications, and connections where needed.*
   - *Include a concluding paragraph.*

6. **Revise your draft.**
   - *Revise to improve the content of your essay.*
   - *Does your thesis accurately reflect your position and intention?*
   - *Have you communicated in your paper what you want to communicate?*
   - *Will your paper give your reader a thorough understanding of the source texts and your thesis?*
   - *Have you avoided editorializing in your paper?*
   - *Would your essay make sense to someone who has not read the source texts?*
   - *Revise to improve the organization of your essay.*
   - *Does your thesis guide the development of your essay?*
   - *Do you provide topic sentences to introduce major sections of your essay?*
   - *Have you provided transitions that help lead your reader through your paper?*
   - *Revise to improve the accuracy and clarity of your essay.*
   - *Have you used language that is as fair and impartial as possible?*
   - *Have you avoided jargon and overly technical language when they would not be appropriate?*
   - *Have you checked for sentence variety and clarity?*
   - *Have you proofread for spelling, punctuation, or usage errors?*

7. **Check your quotations and documentation.**
   - *Have you quoted and paraphrased material properly, accurately, and fairly?*
   - *Have you documented all the material that needs to be documented?*
   - *Have you documented material employing the proper format?*

Chapter 10

ARGUMENTATIVE SYNTHESIS

DEFINITION

In an argumentative synthesis, you use material from various readings to support and illustrate an argument of your own, usually concerning the quality of writing in the source texts or an issue they address. If your argument centers on the quality of the readings, you might argue that one is better written or more convincing than the others. If, however, your teacher asks you to present an argument on the issue the readings address, you will draw on the material in the readings to support your thesis.

For a number of reasons, writing an argumentative synthesis can be challenging:

1. As with the informative synthesis, the sources you consult when gathering information for this type of essay can be difficult to read. They will often present complex arguments themselves or employ terminology or research methodologies new to you. Being able to read this material critically is essential if you hope to write a successful argumentative synthesis.
2. As you read these source texts, you will need to critique them. For example, if you are arguing that one is better written than another, you will have to critique both to determine the relative strengths and weaknesses of each. If you are using the readings to develop an argument of your own on the topic they address, again you will have to critique the source texts

to determine the quality of the arguments and information in each. You want to base your argument on the best available material.

3. When you compose your argumentative synthesis, you have to be concerned, first, with the content and quality of *your* argument. You need to decide if the material you are including in your paper will achieve the desired effect on your reader—will your audience be convinced by your argument? At the same time, since you are working with source texts, you have to pay close attention to the way you are using other people's findings or arguments to be sure you are fairly representing their work.

4. Part of composing an argumentative synthesis is deciding how best to order the claims, evidence, findings, or arguments you present. You need to decide which ideas or arguments you will present in which order and to provide effective transitions between and within the major sections of your argument.

5. In supporting your argument with source material, you will need to be quoting, summarizing, and paraphrasing other people's ideas, arguments, and findings. As a result, documentation becomes a challenge. You will need to be explicit and clear in acknowledging the source of the information you use to support your assertions.

THE ELEMENTS OF ARGUMENT

As you develop, draft, and revise your argumentative synthesis, pay particular attention to the three basic elements of any argument: **claims**, **grounds**, and **warrants**. According to British philosopher Stephen Toulmin in the *Uses of Argument* (1958), every argument involves an assertion (claim) that is supported by evidence (grounds) and rests upon a particular set of assumptions or line of reasoning (warrant). Effective arguments employ clear, limited claims; reliable, appropriate grounds; and fully developed, explicit warrants. Understanding each of these elements can help you compose more effective argumentative synthesis essays.

CLAIMS

A **claim** is an assertion you want your readers to accept. In an argumentative synthesis essay, your thesis statement is a claim, one you will develop and support with other claims in the body of your essay. Suppose, for example, you are writing an argumentative synthesis using the reviews of *V for Vendetta* found in Chapter 9 and decide on the following thesis: "Burr and Hunter both question *V for Vendetta*'s message; however through his use of examples, comparisons, and sarcastic language, Hunter presents a much more convincing argument." Your thesis is a claim: Hunter's review is more effective than Burr's review. You will support this assertion with three other claims or "because" statements: Hunter's review is more effective than Burr's because Hunter uses more effective examples, because he uses better comparisons, and because he uses sarcasm. In the body of your essay you will develop these three claims with valid grounds and warrants if you want readers to accept your thesis.

When you compose an essay from source texts, most of your claims will be based on what you read and can include:

* claims concerning the source text's topic
* claims concerning the source text's content, organization, or style
* claims concerning the quality of the source text's writing
* claims concerning your response or reaction to the source texts

Your teacher may give you several readings to study or require you to collect material on your own outside of class. In either case, you will be expected to critique the readings, form an argumentative thesis or claim, and explain or defend that assertion in your essay.

Well-written claims are **accurate**, **clear**, and **limited**. Any claim you make about a reading should be accurate: you should not misrepresent what an author writes. Claims should also be clear and unambiguous. "There are several good things about Hunter's review" is not a clear claim. What does the writer mean by "good" or by "things"? When forming claims, be as specific as you can, using language that precisely captures the assertion you want to make. Also, avoid broad, unlimited claims because such assertions are usually inaccurate and difficult to support. Claims like "Hunter's review is the best piece of writing ever produced" or "There is absolutely no value at all to Hunter's review" are not sufficiently limited. In writing limited claims, you may find yourself using words like "most" instead of "all," "often" instead of "always," or "likely" instead of "certainly." Limited claims (including limited thesis statements) are easier to explain and defend than unlimited, sweeping claims.

GROUNDS

Grounds is another name for the evidence you use to support a claim. As with claims, when you compose a source-based argumentative synthesis essay, you will draw most of your grounds from readings, though many teachers will allow you to use relevant personal experience to support a claim as well. Source-based grounds can include facts, statistics, testimony, and opinions. Each type of evidence has its own strengths and limitations. When deciding how to employ each in support of a claim, consider the questions that follow. Remember: the quality of your essay often depends on the quality of the grounds you employ to support your claims. If you rely on weak, questionable, or irrelevant grounds to support your claims, your writing is unlikely to convince thoughtful readers.

Facts: information the author of the source text presents as verifiably true

* Is the information up to date?
* Does the information come from a reliable source?
* Is the information documented?

- Is the information clear and unambiguous in its meaning?
- Is the information relevant to the claim you are making?
- Is the information consistent with your understanding, knowledge, or experience?
- Is the information consistent with what other source texts contend?

Examples: illustrations drawn from the source text to support your claim

- Are the examples relevant to the claim you are making?
- How much background information do you need to provide so that your reader will understand the examples you incorporate from the source text?
- Are the examples true or fictional? Is either acceptable given your assignment?
- Do the examples come from a reliable source?
- Are the examples timely?
- Are the examples representative and typical or limited and unique?

Statistics: data the author of the source text employs to support his or her claims

- Do you understand the statistics, what they mean, and their limitations?
- Do the statistics come from a reliable, trustworthy source?
- What are the possible biases of the source text? How might those biases affect the statistics offered in the piece?
- How do the statistics compare with evidence found in other source texts?
- Does the author of the source text acknowledge the limitations of the statistics?
- Are the statistics relevant to the claim you are trying to support in your essay?
- Can you adequately explain the link between the statistics you cite and the claim you are supporting?

Testimony: personal experiences offered by the author of the source text in support of his or her claims

- Does the testimony come from a reliable, qualified source?
- Is the testimony firsthand or secondhand?
- How is the testimony relevant to the claim you are trying to support?
- What background information from the source text will you need to provide so that your reader will understand the meaning and nature of the testimony?
- Does the author of the source text acknowledge the limitations of the testimony?
- How does the testimony complement (or contradict) other grounds provided in the essay?

Opinions: what the author of a source text believes to be true

- Is this the opinion of the source text's author or is the author offering someone else's opinion?
- Is the person sufficiently qualified to offer an opinion worth citing in your essay?
- How will you make clear in the body of your essay that this opinion comes from a reliable source?
- Does the author sufficiently explain and clarify his or her opinion?
- Does the author support that opinion with evidence?
- Is the opinion sufficiently qualified?
- Is the opinion supported by other types of evidence in the source text or by evidence you have gathered from other sources?

Whatever grounds you employ in your essay, be sure they are **relevant**, **reliable**, and **appropriate**. As you defend or illustrate a claim, first be sure the evidence you use is relevant to the assertion you are making. Writing an argumentative synthesis can be confusing because you are working with multiple texts and multiple claims. As you select the grounds you will use to support a particular claim, be sure they clearly relate to that claim and not to some other assertion you are making in your essay. Also, be sure the grounds are reliable—examine the credentials and possible biases of the source text's author, the publication's or Web site's credibility, and the date of publication. Finally, be sure your grounds are appropriate for the assignment and audience. As you write papers in classes across the curriculum, you will discover that what counts as valid grounds in one class may not count as valid grounds in another. Learning what grounds are appropriate for arguments in a field of study is part of learning how to reason like a member of that discipline. Analyze the texts you read in class to determine the kinds of evidence successful authors in that field of study utilize in their arguments and ask your instructor for help if you have doubts about the appropriateness of evidence you plan to use in any essay.

One final note about grounds. Most writers know that they can support a claim in an argumentative synthesis essay by quoting, paraphrasing, or otherwise alluding to the work of authors who agree with the position you are advancing. Citing authorities who support the claims you make improves your work's credibility. However, there are other ways to use source material to support an argument. For example, consider citing authorities who *disagree* with the claim you are making. Incorporating counterexamples into your argumentative synthesis can be effective if you employ them correctly. First, acknowledging alternative positions increases your credibility as a writer. It demonstrates your knowledge of the subject matter, your fairness, and the confidence you have in your own position. However, just citing counterexamples alone will not help you achieve these benefits; instead, you must integrate them into your essay by refuting them, conceding to them, or accommodating them.

When you **refute** counterexamples, you offer a fair summary of the opposing view, then demonstrate how that position is wrong, problematic, or otherwise flawed. You can then explain how your position is better. When you **concede** to an opposing view, you acknowledge how and when the opposition might be right in its assertions. However, you then demonstrate how that fact does not seriously damage your own position or thesis. Finally, when you **accommodate** an opposing view, you explain how that position and your own may be equally correct and how, by combining them, one might gain a better, more comprehensive understanding of the issue. In short, be imaginative in your use of source material as grounds in an argumentative synthesis. Just be sure the grounds you use are linked to your claims with strong warrants.

WARRANTS

Warrants are a little harder to understand than claims or grounds because they tend to be more abstract. Simply stated, though, a warrant is a line of reasoning, set of assumptions, or explanation that links a claim to its grounds. When writing an argumentative synthesis, remember that in most cases the grounds will not speak for themselves: you need to explain how they support the claim you are making. For instance, suppose you wrote the following passage, a claim supported by an example:

> Stephen Hunter's review of *V for Vendetta* is better than Ty Burr's review of the film because Hunter effectively uses sarcasm. For example, in his review, Hunter characterizes the film's critique of totalitarianism as "a teenager's freaky power trip" (161).

Are you ready to move on to your next claim now? Have you sufficiently supported your claim by citing an example from the text? No. What's missing here is your warrant—before you move on to your next claim, you have to explain how language, like "a teenager's freaky power trip" (your grounds), makes Hunter's writing better than Burr's writing (your claim). As you do this, you will probably find that citing only one example is insufficient. You may have to examine a few more passages from Hunter's review to prove your point, comparing them to the language found in Burr's essay. In each case, you will need to explain exactly how the examples you cite support your claim. You will need to provide warrants for your argument.

As you draft and revise your argumentative synthesis, you need to ask yourself a series of questions concerning the nature and effectiveness of your warrants.

1. *Is my warrant stated or unstated? If unstated, will the link between my claims and my grounds be sufficiently clear for my readers?*

   In everyday conversation, many warrants go unstated: the link between a claim and its grounds is so clear or so readily accepted that no warrant is needed. In academic writing, however, warrants usually need to be stated and explained. The aim of an academic argument is to let your reader know where you stand on an issue (your claim), to convince your reader to accept this position as reasonable or correct by supporting it with evidence (your grounds), and to explain how this evidence makes the case for the claim (your warrant). Two writers may make the same assertion in their papers and may even support those assertions with similar evidence, but how they explain the link they see between the evidence and the claim will likely differ. In academic writing, warrants can help make your essay distinctive. Therefore, examine your essay for any unstated warrants and decide whether they need to be made explicit. If you think there is any chance your readers may question the link between a claim and its grounds, state your warrant.

2. *Is my warrant logical and reasonable?*

How *do* the grounds you employ actually support your claim? What assumptions are you making about the link between your grounds and claims? Are you assuming that your readers will recognize and accept the connection you see between your claims and grounds? Is the connection you see between them logical and reasonable? Will your readers see the connection as logical and reasonable?

3. *Is my warrant clear, fully explained, and supported?*

Underdeveloped warrants are a common problem with argumentative synthesis essays: writers, understanding that they need to state their warrants, simply fail to explain them adequately. Clear, well-developed warrants are crucial to successful arguments, especially if you believe your audience will question the validity of your claim or grounds. In these cases, you may need to explain your warrant at length, perhaps even acknowledging alternative readings of your grounds as you clarify your own interpretation. Determining whether your warrants are sufficiently explained and supported can be difficult, which is why you should have other people read and critique drafts of your writing. Specifically ask them to read your essay skeptically; to question the validity of your claims, grounds, and warrants; and to indicate any weaknesses they note or questions they have. Sometimes the warrants you employ themselves rest upon unstated assumptions that need to be explained and defended.

ARGUMENT AND PERSUASION

Rhetoricians often draw a distinction between argument and persuasion. Argument, they maintain, involves demonstrating the credibility of a position; persuasion involves moving readers to accept or act on that position. The most commonly acknowledged agents of persuasion are logos (logic), pathos (emotion), and ethos (character): writers can often persuade readers to accept or act on an argument by appealing to the readers' logic or emotions or by sufficiently establishing their own credibility or character (see Chapter 7 for a further discussion of logos, pathos, and ethos).

APPEALS BASED ON REASON

In an argumentative synthesis, successful appeals to **logos** largely depend on the quality of your claims, grounds, and warrants. Clear, qualified claims supported by valid grounds and clear, reasonable warrants will go a long way toward persuading a reader that your position is reasonable enough to accept and act on. Such writing, however, rarely happens by accident. It results from careful, critical drafting and revision. Here are a few steps you can take to improve the logical appeal of your argumentative synthesis essay:

1. **Make clear, limited claims.**

    Be sure all of your claims are clear, reasonable, and limited. Vague claims will not be convincing and neither will unreasonable assertions or sweeping generalizations. The claims you make—including your thesis—form the framework around which you will build your argumentative synthesis. If your claims are unclear, unreasonable, or unconnected to one another, the logical appeal of your essay will be diminished.

2. **Employ grounds that are relevant, credible, and timely.**

    As you decide what evidence or examples to offer in support of a claim, choose the material that is most relevant to your assertion. First, avoid using grounds that are only tangentially related to your claim. Second, be sure the grounds you employ come from credible sources. If you use reliable sources in your essay, readers are more likely to see your assertions as reasonable. Basing your paper on material drawn from questionable sources will bring into question the legitimacy of your own assertions. Finally, be sure the material you use in your paper is timely. As a rule, draw on the most recent research you can find when writing your paper—employing out-of-date source texts may hamper your efforts to sway readers' opinions.

3. **Explain your reasoning process.**

    One of the best ways to improve the logical appeal of your essay is to explain your reasoning process on the page. Lay bare for your readers the reasoning process that led you to your conclusions: elaborate on the meaning of your claims, explain connections among your assertions, explore alternative arguments, discuss the links you see between your claims and their grounds. Most academic audiences will expect to find this type of discussion and explanation in your essay.

APPEALS BASED ON EMOTION

Successful persuasive appeals to **pathos** can be difficult to achieve but can also be very effective. Employing pathos to persuade a reader is tricky because it can have the opposite effect if used incorrectly or clumsily. Pathos can quickly turn into bathos, or unintentionally comic appeals to emotion. However, when used sparingly and appropriately, emotionally charged grounds or language can prove very persuasive. Here are a few suggestions on how to employ pathos effectively in an argumentative synthesis essay.

1. **Include in your essay material that might appeal to your reader's interests.**

    While it is often difficult to know with any degree of certainty what material might appeal to your reader's interests, it may be possible to make some educated guesses. For example, what might interest them given their economic, political, educational, or religious backgrounds? What can you assume they know or may want to know about the topic of your essay? What aspects of the topic interest you? How similar are you to your audience—can you assume they might have similar interests? Though it is very difficult to make completely accurate assessments of what material might interest your readers, the closer you come to hitting the mark, the more likely you are to obtain a positive emotional response to your writing.

2. **Include in your essay material that might appeal to your reader's needs or fears.**

    As you consider what material to include in your argumentative synthesis, can you identify examples, arguments, testimonials, statistics, or other material that might appeal to your reader's needs or address concerns? Your goal is not to play on your reader's emotions. Instead, you want to connect emotionally with readers, to construct a bridge between your essay and reader needs or concerns, thus helping them see the relevancy of your essay to their lives. Is there material, for example, that might appeal to your reader's concerns about his or her physical, psychological, or financial safety; need for self-affirmation; or desires for joy or happiness? Successfully employing this type of material in your argumentative synthesis greatly increases the chances that readers will find your essay persuasive.

3. **Employ language that is evocative or captivating.**

    Another way to improve the emotional appeal of your argumentative synthesis is to use especially evocative or captivating language. Words have both denotative (literal) and connotative (emotional) meanings. You will often face instances when you can choose among words that have roughly the same denotative meaning but vary widely in their connotative implications. In these cases, consider using language that more effectively appeals to your reader's emotions. Also consider your use of figurative language. While most academic writers employ extended metaphors sparingly, the use of analogies, allusions, and other figurative language is more common. Your goal is not to produce flowery prose. Instead, your aim is to employ language that persuades readers to accept or act on your arguments by developing in them an emotional understanding of your topic.

Appeals Based on Character and Credibility

In one sense, **ethos** is closely linked to logos because it has to do with the credibility of the claims, grounds, and warrants you employ in your essay. Ethos involves trust and character: do you demonstrate through the quality of the claims, grounds, and warrants you employ in your writing that you are a trustworthy, knowledgeable, fair-minded individual? If you do, then you may persuade some readers to accept your position through your own ethos as a writer. Ethos, though, also has to do with the quality of your own prose. Even if you compose a synthesis with strong claims, grounds, and warrants, you will lose credibility if your prose is marred by misspellings, grammatical problems, typos, or other surface errors. Readers may feel that they cannot trust authors who are careless with their writing; if an author is so sloppy with word choice, syntax, spelling, or punctuation, how sloppy has the author been with his or her research, reasoning, and documentation? Persuasion depends on trust, and you may lose the trust of your readers—and your credibility as a writer—if your writing is full of easily correctable errors. Here are a few steps you can take to improve ethos in your argumentative synthesis:

1. **Present informed, balanced arguments.**

   You will enhance your credibility as a writer if you present a balanced argument in your essay, examining the strengths and weaknesses of your assertions and exploring alternative points of view. Presenting a balanced argument requires you to research and consider a range of perspectives on your essay's topic. Examining this range of perspectives in your essay increases the likelihood of readers seeing you as a knowledgeable, fair-minded writer, and readers are more likely to consider and perhaps adopt arguments presented by writers they perceive as informed and fair.

2. **Demonstrate the credibility of your source texts.**

   Another way to enhance your ethos is by demonstrating the credibility of the source texts you use in your essay. Readers are more likely to accept or act on your arguments if they perceive that your claims are supported by authoritative sources. In-text documentation is one way to demonstrate that your arguments are supported by credible sources. You can also establish the authority of your source texts by including in your essay the full name of the person who wrote the text and a summary of his or her credentials whenever you quote or paraphrase material.

3. **Employ fair, balanced language.**

   Just as you want the content of your argumentative synthesis to be fair and balanced, you also want to avoid language that might make you appear narrow-minded or uninformed. While on occasion you will want to employ emotionally evocative language (see discussion of "pathos" above), consistently employing words that make you sound shrill, sarcastic, or hostile will usually hinder your efforts to persuade readers to consider or accept your arguments, especially if you are addressing a neutral or possibly antagonistic audience. In these cases, you might be better served using language that is more judicious and fair.

4. **Proofread your work carefully.**

Finally, remember that the quality of your own prose influences whether your readers perceive you as a credible authority. Argumentative synthesis essays that are full of surface-level errors are unlikely to persuade many readers. Rightly or wrongly, most readers will judge the quality of your argument by the quality of your prose: in their minds, error-laden writing is likely to reflect error-laden thinking. You can help ensure that your writing is persuasive simply by proofreading your essay thoroughly before you submit your final draft for review.

WRITING AN ARGUMENTATIVE SYNTHESIS

Because argumentative syntheses are so complex, writing them in a number of steps or stages is often helpful. Here are some of the steps you might consider following when writing an argumentative synthesis:

1. Analyze the assignment.
2. Annotate and critique the readings.
3. Formulate a thesis and organizational plan.
4. Write your rough draft.
5. Revise your draft.

STEP 1—ANALYZE THE ASSIGNMENT

Some teachers will not specify the type of argument they want you to present in your synthesis. If this is the case, you will need to decide for yourself whether you want to focus on the quality of the writing in the readings or on the issue they address. However, if a teacher specifically asks you to focus your argument on the quality of the source texts, his assignment might include directions such as these:

> Review the readings in Chapter 6 of the textbook. Which author do you believe presents the most convincing case? Why?

* * * * *

> Review the readings in Chapter 6 of the textbook. Which piece is better written? How so?

In the first assignment, the teacher wants you to analyze, evaluate, then compare the **arguments** presented by the various writers, arguing that one presents the best case. In the second assignment, the teacher wants you to analyze, evaluate, then compare the **styles** of the various writers, arguing that one produces the best-written text.

However, when a teacher wants you to take a stand on the topic the readings address, her directions may read something like this:

> Review the readings in Chapter 6 of the textbook. Where do you stand on the issue? Present an argument in favor of your position using the readings for support.

Here the teacher wants you to read the articles, think about the arguments presented by each author, reflect on your own knowledge and feelings concerning the topic, then present an argument in which you assume and defend a position of your own on the issue.

Once you have determined the type of argument the teacher wants you to write, check the assignment to determine the number and types of sources the teacher wants you to use in your paper. Sometimes instructors specify a certain number of readings you must use in your paper, asking you, for example, to base your paper on four to six sources. Other times teachers specify the types of readings you have to use: those provided in class, those you find on your own in the library, academic sources only, and so on. If you have any questions about the number or type of readings you need to use in your synthesis, be sure to check with your instructor.

STEP 2—ANNOTATE AND CRITIQUE THE READINGS

As you begin to collect the readings you plan to use when writing your argumentative synthesis, you need to annotate and critique them (see Chapter 6 for advice on critiquing readings). First, annotate each reading, identifying its thesis, primary assertions, and evidence. Next, analyze and critique the content and structure of each reading. If you base your argument on other authors' faulty writing or reasoning, your essay will likely reflect their weaknesses; likewise, if you base your argument on solid, well-written sources, your argument will likely be stronger. The questions you want to ask of a reading include:

- What, exactly, is the main point of this reading?
- How has the author supported his ideas, arguments, or findings?
- How well has the author explained or supported his ideas, arguments, or findings?
- Do I find the reading convincing? Why or why not?
- How have the structure and tone of the piece influenced my reaction?
- What is the quality of the writing?
- How do the author's ideas, arguments, or findings compare with those found in the other sources I have read?

Place your annotations in the margins of the reading, on sheets of paper, or on index cards. If you use paper or index cards, be sure you copy all the bibliographic information you will need to complete a reference list entry on the source, in case you use any of that material in your paper. In an argumentative synthesis, all quoted, paraphrased, or summarized material needs to be documented.

STEP 3—FORMULATE A THESIS

Formulating a clear thesis statement is an essential step in writing a successful argumentative synthesis. Your thesis statement tells your reader the position you plan on advancing in your paper and will likely indicate the structure of your essay. Put another way, your thesis statement establishes in your readers' minds certain expectations concerning the content and form of your paper. When you satisfy those expectations, your reader will have an easier time following your argument; if you do not, however, readers may feel your work is confusing and disorganized. So you need to spend some time forming and refining your thesis statement.

In an argumentative synthesis you advance a position of your own, on either the quality or the topic of the readings. If you are focusing on the quality of the readings themselves, you can assume a number of different positions. For example, suppose you are writing an argumentative synthesis using the reviews of *V for Vendetta* found in Chapter 9 (159–164). You may argue that one author is most convincing:

> While Corliss, Hunter, and Burr each presents an insightful critique of *V for Vendetta*, Corliss alone offers a convincing argument explaining why the film became so popular.

Or you may argue that one author's work is better written than another's:

> While Hunter and Burr both criticize *V for Vendetta* for its portrayal of violence, Hunter presents a much better argument supporting his interpretation.

In either case, the thesis sets out the position you will be developing in your paper.

As with other types of essays, thesis statements for argumentative syntheses can be either open or closed. While both of the examples above are open thesis statements, they could easily be modified to give the reader a better indication of what exactly will be covered in the paper:

> While Corliss, Hunter, and Burr each presents an insightful critique of *V for Vendetta*, through his clear examination of the film's cinematography, Corliss alone offers a convincing argument explaining why the movie became so popular.

* * * * *

> While Hunter and Burr both criticize *V for Vendetta* for its portrayal of violence, Hunter presents a much better argument supporting his interpretation by examining specific scenes from the movie.

If, however, your goal in composing an argumentative synthesis is to argue a position of your own on the topic of the readings, your thesis will read a little differently, something like this (employing an open thesis):

> Although reviewers seem divided in their judgments concerning *V for Vendetta*, it is an important modern film.

Or, perhaps this (employing a closed thesis):

Although reviewers seem divided in their judgments concerning *V for Vendetta*, its special effects and message make it an important modern film.

STEP 4—CHOOSE AN ORGANIZATIONAL PLAN

If you use a **block format** to organize your essay, you would critique in turn what each reviewer has to say about the film's importance, then advance your own argument, focusing on the movie's special effects and message. You would need to critique what each reviewer has to say about the film's importance, then present your own position, referring back to the reviewers to bolster your argument. In outline form, your paper might look like this:

Argumentative Synthesis—Block Format

Opening Section

Capture reader interest

Introduce the topic

Introduce the film

Give your thesis

Summary of the Film (optional)

Discussion of Richard Corliss Review

Introduce the review—title, author, place of publication

Summarize the review—what Corliss says about the film's importance

Critique the review—how Corliss is or is not correct in his assertions

Tie criticisms to specific passages in the review

Fully explain or defend your criticism

Discussion of Stephen Hunter Review

Introduce the review—title, author, place of publication

Summarize the review—what Hunter says about the film's importance

Critique the review—how Hunter is or is not correct in his assertions

Tie criticisms to specific passages in the review

Fully explain or defend your criticism

Discussion of Ty Burr Review

Introduce the review—title, author, place of publication

Summarize the review—what Burr says about the film's importance

Critique the review—how Burr is or is not correct in his assertions

Tie criticisms to specific passages in the review

Fully explain or defend your criticisms

Your Argument Concerning the Film's Importance

How the film's special effects make it an important modern film

Tie argument to specific examples from the film

Fully explain and defend your assertions

Refer back to the reviewers' opinions to bolster your position

How the film's message makes it an important modern film

Tie argument to specific examples from the film

Fully explain and defend your assertions

Refer back to the reviewers' opinions to bolster your position

Conclusion

In the opening section of your paper, you would introduce the topic of the essay, introduce the film you will be discussing, and offer your thesis in a way that captures your readers' interest. In the body of the paper, you would critique the reviews of all three movie critics, focusing your attention on their judgments concerning the importance of *V for Vendetta*. You would *first* summarize and then critique what each has to say about the film's significance, advancing your position through your criticisms of the reviewers' positions. Finally, you would present your own argument, supporting your position with specific references to the film and to the reviewers' opinions.

If you prefer, you could organize the same paper using an **alternating format**, structuring your essay around the elements of the film you have chosen to focus on (special effects and message) rather than around the critics' reviews. In this case, your paper might be organized like this:

Argumentative Synthesis—Alternating Format

Opening Section

Capture reader interest

Introduce the topic

Introduce the film

Give your thesis

Summary of the Film (optional)

Discussion of Why Special Effects Make the Film Important

Describe the special effects—specific examples from the film

Argue why special effects make the film important

> Present your argument

> Support your argument with material from the reviews

> Critique the reviewers' positions when necessary

Discussion of Why Message Makes the Film Important

Examine the message—specific examples from the film

Argue why the message makes the film important

> Present your argument

> Support your argument with material from the reviews

> Critique the reviewers' positions when necessary

Conclusion

In the opening of your paper, you would again introduce the topic of the essay, give the title of the film, and offer your thesis, trying at the same time to capture your readers' attention and interest. In the body of your essay, you would argue, first, that *V for Vendetta*'s special effects make it an important modern film, then, second, that its message does as well. In developing your essay, you would refer to specific examples from the film, explain how those examples support your thesis, and examine what the three reviewers have to say about the matter. If any of the reviewers agrees with your position, you can use their views to bolster your argument; if any of them disagree with your position, you will need to address that disagreement by explaining why your position is more sound than the reviewer's position.

Once you have drafted at least a preliminary thesis for your paper and have some sense of the assertions that will serve as the focus of your synthesis, you will need to return to the readings to locate material to include in your essay. Remember that the focus of an argumentative synthesis should be the argument you are advancing, not the material from the readings. In other words, your first responsibility is to develop a sound argument—the source material serves to illustrate or support *your* assertions.

STEP 5—WRITE YOUR ROUGH DRAFT

When you feel you are ready to begin writing your rough draft, be sure you have in front of you all of your source texts and notes. Some students like to begin writing immediately—they need to see some of their ideas in writing before they can decide on a final thesis or organize their paper. Other students have to begin with a clear thesis and outline in hand. Follow the method of composing that is most comfortable and successful for you.

When writing your essay, you will support your argument with material from the readings. You can use source material to give your readers background information on the topic (quote or paraphrase material you think your reader needs to know to understand your argument), to support your assertions (quote or paraphrase material that substantiates or illustrates your claims), or to acknowledge opposing views (quote or paraphrase material that calls into question your assertions; you then must decide whether to refute, accommodate, or concede to these different perspectives).

STEP 6—REVISE YOUR DRAFT

Revising your argumentative synthesis to make it ready for others to read is a time-consuming process again best approached in a series of steps. First, revise to improve the **content** of your paper, focusing on the quality and clarity of the argument you are advancing. Here are some questions you might ask about your draft as you revise to improve its content:

- Have I clearly indicated the point I want to prove?
- Have I clearly indicated the reasons I believe others should accept my position?
- Have I supported each of those reasons with expert testimony, statistics, or some other means of support as well as with clear explanations?
- Have I acknowledged opposing views in my paper when necessary? Have I found ways of refuting, acknowledging, or conceding to them?

Next, review the **organization** of your essay, asking these questions:

- Is the thesis statement clearly worded, and does it control the structure of the essay?
- Have I provided clear transitions between the major sections of my essay?
- Are there clear connections between the material I draw from the readings and my own elaborations and explanations?

Finally, when checking the **accuracy** and **clarity** of your work, ask yourself:

- Have I chosen words that are clear yet contribute to the effect I wanted to elicit from my readers?
- Are my sentences clearly structured with adequate variety?
- Have I quoted and paraphrased material accurately and properly?
- When incorporating quoted or paraphrased material in my synthesis, have I supplied enough background information on the source text so the material makes sense to my readers?
- Have I defined all the terms I need to define?
- Have I documented all the material that needs to be documented?

CHECK QUOTATIONS AND DOCUMENTATION

Before you turn in your final draft for a grade, set aside time to check the accuracy of your quotations and documentation. First, make sure that you have quoted material accurately by comparing your text against the source text. Second, be sure that you have documented all of the material in your paper that needs to be documented, including all paraphrased information. Because you are combining information from several source texts in your synthesis and presenting your own argument as well, be sure your readers can always tell through your documentation the source of the material you include in your paper.

SAMPLE ARGUMENTATIVE SYNTHESES

Below are two argumentative synthesis essays drawing on the three reviews of *V for Vendetta* found in Chapter 9. The first essay focuses on the quality of the arguments presented in the reviews; the second presents the writer's own argument concerning the film, using the reviews to support or clarify the writer's thesis. As you read the essays, consider how each is structured and how each uses material from the source texts to give readers a better understanding of the film, the critics' views, and the writer's thesis.

SAMPLE ARGUMENTATIVE SYNTHESIS (FOCUSING ON THE QUALITY OF THE READINGS)

The Message of *V for Vendetta?*

Director James McTeigue's *V for Vendetta* proved to be one of the most popular—and controversial—films of 2006. Written by the creators of the *Matrix* series, Andy and Larry Wachowski, *V for Vendetta* presents a dystopic vision of England under the control of a fascist dictator, Chancellor Sutler (John Hurt). Sutler and his secret police control every aspect of society and culture by manipulating the media and brutally repressing any resistance. However, resistance does arise in the form of V (Hugo Weaving), a masked fighter who plots to overthrow the government and blow up Parliament, bringing to fruition the plot of his seventeenth-century inspiration, Guy Fawkes. Although many critics praised the film's look and cinematography, most considered it an artistic failure, hampered by an implausible plot and weak acting. Several critics also raised serious questions about the film's message, including Ty Burr who wrote "Bombs Trump Big Ideas in Potent 'Vendetta,'" for the *Boston Globe* and Stephen Hunter who wrote "Quite the Bomb: 'V for Vendetta' Can Blow Away Parliament, but Not Its Audience" for the *Washington Post*. Although Burr and Hunter both question *V for Vendetta*'s message, through his use of examples, comparisons, and sarcastic language, Hunter presents a much more convincing critique.

On the whole, Burr offers a balanced review of *V for Vendetta*, matching his criticism of the movie's message with praise for other aspects of the film, calling it "a handsome piece of work" (163) and "dramatically powerful" (163). Burr points out for special notice the scenes in which V's protégé Evey (Natalie Portman) is imprisoned and tortured and flashbacks that tell the story of an earlier victim of Sutler's government, movie star Valerie Banks (Natasha Wightman). In fact, Burr asserts that as actors, Portman and Weaving are "first-rate" (164).

However, Burr is far less enthusiastic about the film's message, an aspect of the movie he devotes the bulk of his review discussing. First, Burr credits McTeigue and the Wachowski brothers for their ambition, stating "there's more on this movie's mind than the usual wham-bam-thank-you-ma'am the trailers are promising" (163), characterizing it as "a propulsive Orwellian drama disguised as an action flick. They've made a mainstream provocation at a time when we could use one, even a muddled one and for that, they should probably be thanked" (163). Burr believes *V for Vendetta* raises provocative questions about state power and freedom which it fails to pursue vigorously or seriously, preferring instead to focus on the movie's violence and special effects: "In the end . . . the Wachowskis' love of freedom . . . is trumped by their love of watching things go boom" (164). Burr finds the film's violence oddly unconnected to real victims: crowds of people watch as V blows up a *deserted* Parliament building. At a time when the movie-going population watched real terrorists blew up all-too-populated buildings on September 11, the film's attempt to serve as an allegory on the human spirit's desire for freedom falls flat. The film's message is too "glib" (164): terrorism is okay as long as no one really gets hurt, and to believe that, you need the wishful thinking of a child" (164).

Stephen Hunter's critique of the film is much more critical than Burr's. For example, while Burr praised the film's acting, Hunter ridicules it. Weaving, he asserts, employs a "fruity, stagy voice" and the mask he wears makes it impossible for the audience to understand what he is feeling as he converts Evey to his cause: "What emotions play across his face, what thought flash through his eyes, what joy nurses his mouth into a smile, what rage twists it into a scowl? Is he even acting? We'll never know" (160). Hunter is even harder on Portman, mocking her "whisper of a Brit accent that comes and goes at random" (161) and criticizing her "numb thespianizing" (162).

Like Burr, though, Hunter focuses most of his criticism on the film's message. However, whereas Burr critiques the message in terms of its relevance to recent history, Hunter criticizes how the movie develops its key themes and presents V's adversaries. Hunter compares McTeigue's dystopic vision *V for Vendetta* with George Orwell's in *1984*, concluding that next to Orwell's "work of art and genius" (161), *V for Vendetta* "is a piece of pulp claptrap; it has no insights whatsoever into totalitarian psychology and settles always for the cheesiest kinds of demagoguery and harangue as its emblems of evil" (161). Instead of presenting a credible, moving, insightful examination of resistance to totalitarianism, McTeigue offers "a teenager's freaky power trip" (161). To support these claims, Hunter closely examines several incredible incidences in the plot, ridiculing the idea, for example, that V could single-handedly commandeer the nation's television network, generate thousands of Guy Fawkes masks for people to wear, and overpower gun-wielding police with nothing but his daggers. In the end, the revolution V foments is simply not believable or moving. Neither, according to Hunter, is the film's depiction of evil in the form of Chancellor Sutler and his minions. McTeigue's portrayal of the totalitarian government is over the top, "a liberal's darkest fantasy of the conservative right—a gay-hating, woman-fearing Talilban, puritanical and single-minded, determined to crush human enterprise, creativity and love at every stop" (160). The film presents the villains as "puddling-faced saliva blasters, too obvious for belief" (162). Because *V for Vendetta* fails to present a credible revolution against a believable enemy, in the end the film is only about blowing things up—its message endorses anarchism: "since we never believed in the regime, we're really celebrating the sheer anarchist spirit of destruction for its own spectacular sake" (162). For all of their ambitions, McTeigue and the Wachowskis have succeeded only in producing a special effects movie with a silly plot and bad acting, not a thoughtful examination of totalitarianism, revolution, and the human spirit.

Although both Burr and Hunter criticize *V for Vendetta*, Hunter's critique of the film is much more effective because of the examples and comparisons he uses to support his assertions and his often sarcastic tone. The main weakness both reviewers focus on is the movie's message. To support his contention that the film's themes are ineffectively presented for a post-9/11 audience, Burr alludes to his personal experiences of the attack on the World Trade Center and his own revulsion toward violent movies (". . . I hoped never again to see a movie in which buildings blew up" (164)). However, to support his view that the film's message is poorly conceived and presented, Hunter provides numerous examples from the movie itself: implausible plot devices, unconvincing villains, and poor writing. Hunter's argument is more effective than Burr's because it is supported by examples drawn from the film, which all readers can evaluate on their own when weighing his opinions. Hunter does not rely on personal experience to support his views; instead, he uses actual scenes from the film, making his opinions more open to scrutiny and, in the end, more convincing.

Likewise, both authors assert that *V for Vendetta*'s politics and moral philosophies are too simplistic. However, Hunter compares *Vendetta*'s dystopic vision to Orwell's in *1984*, a work likely familiar to many readers. As Hunter points out, *V for Vendetta* and *1984* examine similar themes, and his contention that *Vendetta* pales in comparison is a convincing argument. People familiar with both works will likely agree with Hunter's assertions: McTeigue's vision of the future is not as sophisticated or insightful as Orwell's. On its own, without comparison to other nightmare visions of the future, *V for Vendetta* might appear novel, moving, and convincing, but when Hunter rightly places it in the context of similar creative works, it clearly pales in comparison. By comparing *Vendetta* with *1984*, Hunter adds depth and context to his review of the film, making his critique much more effective than Burr's.

Finally, Hunter's critique of the film is more effective than Burr's because of Hunter's often sarcastic tone. Hunter's sarcasm adds humor to his review, starting with his opening paragraph: "'V for Vendetta' really should have been called 'The Man in the Plastic Mask.' Or what about 'The Movie With the Plastic Soul'? Or even 'Natalie Portman Gets a Haircut'!" (160). When mocking the ridiculous fight scenes in the movie, Hunter observes of V, "He's faster and better with the daggers than they are with the guns. Oh, yeah? My definition of fool is the man who brings a knife to a gunfight" (161). Hunter's humor and sarcasm makes it difficult to defend the film—his observations, though caustic, are insightful and truthful. *V for Vendetta* takes itself seriously: McTeigue and the Wachowski brothers present a cautionary tale they want viewers to find convincing and moving. Nothing cuts the legs out from under a movie like this better than ridicule. Instead of taking the film seriously, Hunter mocks it, and his sarcasm leads his readers to do the same. Once you laugh at a film like *V for Vendetta*, you can't again take it seriously. Hunter's sarcastic tone makes his critique of the movie much more effective than Burr's.

Audiences may find *V for Vendetta* an interesting film with dramatically choreographed fight scenes and beautiful cinematography, but, after reading Burr's and Hunter's reviews, they may have a hard time accepting the film's message. While both writers find this to be the movie's primary weakness, Hunter offers a more effective critique of the film through his use of examples, comparisons, and sarcasm. Even people who initially loved the film and considered its message to be deep, thoughtful, or provocative may be moved to reconsider their previous judgments after reading Hunter's review.

SAMPLE ARGUMENTATIVE SYNTHESIS
(FOCUSING ON THE TOPIC OF THE READINGS)

The Message of *V for Vendetta*: Substance or Silliness?

For a while in 2006, popular media outlets seemed to be obsessed with James McTeigue's controversial film, *V for Vendetta*. Stories about the movie appeared on the evening newscasts, pundits discussed the film on political talk shows, and posters of the film sprung up everywhere, from billboards to building sites to dorm rooms. The public appeared fascinated by the film's brooding look and feel, the violence and eloquence of its masked anti-hero, and its spectacular special effects. Some viewers may have been drawn to the film because it was written by Andy and Larry Wachowski, creators of the popular *Matrix* films. As they did with those earlier films, when writing *V for Vendetta*, the Wachowski brothers attempted to create a "serious" action film, a popcorn movie that blends philosophical inquiry and action. However, where the original *Matrix* examines the definition of humanity, *V for Vendetta* takes up the issues of freedom and political resistance. While critics generally praised *V* for its special effects and action sequences, many correctly raised serious questions about the film's ultimate meaning or message. Beneath all of the explosions and eloquence, the message of *V for Vendetta* is clear: vengeance-based violence is an acceptable expression of political resistance and an effective response to political oppression. However, for a number of reasons the film fails to present a convincing argument for this position.

Despite the film's popularity, the critical response to *V for Vendetta* was mixed. A few critics found the film's message not only interesting but also compelling. For example, writing in *Time* magazine, Richard Corliss calls the film "bold and thoughtful" (160), identifying as its central theme, "the use and abuse of state power" (159). Likewise, in his *Boston Globe* review, critic Ty Burr believes the film raises important questions about the consequences people face when they give up their rights to a government that promises to keep them safe (164). While Burr believes the film is fundamentally flawed, he acknowledges and praises the director's and screenwriters' intention: "They've made a mainstream provocation at a time when we could use one, even a muddled one, and for that, they should probably be thanked" (163).

Both Corliss and Burr are correct; two of the primary themes in *V for Vendetta* are the use and abuse of state power and the willingness of people to sacrifice civil rights for security. However, the film's primary concern and central message involve the title character's response to the state's actions: both what he does and why he does it. In the movie, V is a freedom fighter, a terrorist, or a vigilante (depending on one's perspective), who years earlier was victimized by state-sanctioned experiments that left him permanently disfigured. Throughout the film, he wears a mask bearing the caricatured visage of Guy Fawkes, a seventeenth-century religious zealot who attempted to blow up Parliament and kill King James I. Like Fawkes, V intends to bring down the government by blowing up its central symbol—the Houses of Parliament. Audiences must consider the morality of V's actions: Is he justified in rebelling against the government? Does he do so for the right reasons? Do his motives matter? If his cause is just, are his methods? While these are all important questions, the film ultimately fails to take them seriously— McTeigue and the Wachowski brothers undercut their message of individual resistance to a corrupt government by drawing on the wrong historical figure and inadequately developing V's motives.

First, there is the question of V's role model, Guy Fawkes. As several critics have noted, Fawkes was far from a champion of freedom and individual rights. Richard Corliss believes the link to Guy Fawkes works well in the film, making it relevant to a post-9/11 audience: ". . . it is weird that . . . an updating of the Guy Fawkes tale ('Remember, remember, the 5th of November'), should so eerily foretell the 2001 bombing of another famous building ('Remember, remember, the 11th of September)'" (159). Ty Burr asserts that in developing the character of V, the Wachowski brothers actually drew on two inspirations, one real and one fictitious: "V wears a mask that evokes both Guy Fawkes . . . and Edmund Dantes, the count of Monte Cristo" (163). However, to equate V with both Fawkes (a religious zealot and terrorist) and Dantes (a victim of state injustice who seeks both justice and his own salvation) is at best strained. Critic Stephen Hunter makes this point well in his *Washington Post* review of the film. Hunter, who believes the movie evidences little serious thought, begins his argument by examining the V's relationship to Fawkes:

> One might start the bill of particulars with the mask itself. It's a caricature of Guy Fawkes, who in 1605 tried to blow up Kind James I and both houses of Parliament and as a consequence is burned in effigy each November 5. It's true, I suppose, that as time has passed, Fawkes's memory has eroded into something warm and cozy. But the real Guy Fawkes was a bit of nasty business, and had he succeeded, it would have been the 9/11 of British history, and his reasons were as spurious as the guys' who took planes into the buildings: It was religion vs. religion. You'd think that stuff would be gone from the world, but four centuries later it's still around. (161)

Likewise, Ty Burr points out that "Fawkes wanted to blow up Parliament so he could install a Catholic king on the throne. Freedom for the masses wasn't high on his to-do list" (164). Fawkes was a religious zealot who believed he could further his goals by blowing up a symbol of repression and killing as many people as possible. Wearing the Fawkes mask actually makes V more of an Osama bin Laden than an Edmund Dantes, completely undercutting the film's intention.

Another problem with the film involves the motives behind V's vendetta: Is he seeking freedom for the masses, personal vengeance, or some combination of the two? The answer to this question matters because it helps determine the morality of the film's message. V's violence might be easier to justify if it is aimed at achieving a greater social good (freedom for all) rather than settling a personal grudge. Again, while the film's intention might be to portray V as a freedom fighter, the way McTeigue and the Wachowskis portray his antagonists undercuts that goal. In its dystopic vision of the future, *V for Vendetta* offers an over-the-top, totally unbelievable portrayal of the fascist government that V opposes. Several critics have noted that the film can be read as a critique of Bush administration policies: "Some will praise or condemn the movie's message as an attack on Bush-ism run amok . . ." (Burr 164).

However, Hunter maintains that what has actually run amok in the film is its depiction of V's enemies. The filmmakers' own political biases have caused them to oversimplify and caricature the fascist government that it appears comic rather than threatening: "The Britain in question in some near future is a dystopian horror: It seems to have been taken over by a liberal's darkest fantasy of the conservative right—a gay-hating, woman-fearing Taliban, puritanical and single-minded, determined to crush human enterprise, creativity and love at every stop" (160). As a result, the film "settles always for the cheesiest kinds of demagoguery and harangue as its emblems of evil" (161).

Such a depiction of the government and its officials has real consequences for the film and the audience's understanding of V's motives. If audience members cannot take seriously the oppressive government portrayed in the film—if they can't believe that such a clownish set of villains actually poses a threat to the people—then they justify the film's violence as anything but a zealot's personal vengeance. Hunter believes that, in the end, the film merely celebrates anarchic violence because the oppressive government depicted in the movie can't be taken seriously. When Parliament is destroyed at the end of the film, ". . . since we never believed in the regime, we're really celebrating the sheer anarchist spirit of destruction for its own spectacular sake" (162).

Toward the end of his review of *V for Vendetta*, Burr characterizes the film's message as "glib" (164). Hunter is less charitable, calling it "pulp claptrap" (161). While *Vendetta* attempts to blend an action movie and a film of ideas, it ultimately fails because the filmmakers undercut their own intentions. Because they draw the wrong historical analogy and oversimplify the movie's antagonists, the filmmakers end up portraying V as less of a freedom fighter than a madman out to right his own personal wrongs, regardless of the death and destruction that ensue. In a post-9/11 world, such a message is irresponsible and naïve.

College Prep: Adapting to College Life in an Era of Heightened Stress

Glenn C. Altschuler

Glenn C. Altschuler is Dean of the School of Continuing Education and Summer Sessions and the Thomas and Dorothy Litwin Professor of American Studies at Cornell University.

The first week of her freshman year at Cornell University, Kate Wilkinson of Plymouth, Mass., made a big mistake. She agreed to play Trivial Pursuit with several other students in her dormitory. Kate was embarrassed that she did not know what element was converted to plutonium in the first nuclear reactor, what onetime Yugoslav republic is shaped like a boomerang or even the longest American war. Far worse, everyone else did (or seemed to).

Kate called her mother and, between sobs, gave voice to her fear that she was not smart enough to succeed at the university.

While some first-year students experience little or no anxiety, most freshmen have a stress story like Kate's, be it academic or personal—about family or financial responsibilities, inadequate high school preparation or pressure to do well in today's increasingly competitive environment.

In a 1999 survey of 683 colleges and universities conducted in the first days of school by the University of California at Los Angeles, 30.2 percent of freshmen acknowledged that they frequently felt overwhelmed, almost double the rate in 1985.

The number of appointments at Cornell's counseling and psychological services has risen by 29 percent in the last four years. More than 40 percent of first-year students at Johns Hopkins University visit its counseling center.

According to Dr. Samuel Parrish, medical director of the Student Health and Wellness Center at Johns Hopkins, better recordkeeping, greater awareness of on-campus services and additional staff and office hours account for some of the increase. And, he said, now "there is no stigma in asking for help."

Mental health professionals say that young adults today appear to be under much more stress than past generations were. Many of them have fewer "stabilizing forces in their lives," said Dr. David Fassler, chair of the American Psychiatric Association's Council on Children, Adolescents and Their Families and author of "Help Me, I'm Sad" (Viking, 1997).

"Many live far away from their extended family, or they've moved a lot of times so they're less connected to their neighborhoods," he said.

At the extreme end of the continuum, more students may be arriving on campus with diagnosed psychological problems. After documenting a rising incidence of depression among students, Harvard University issued a report last year recommending, among other steps, that more psychologists be hired, that residence assistants and tutors receive instruction on mental problems and that two rooms be set aside in every living unit for students experiencing emotional crises.

While academic pressure may not cause mental illness, it can act as a trigger. "Some kids have a genetic predisposition for depression, and are more likely than others to get depressed," said Dr. Fassler, ticking off the warning signs—"sadness, decreased energy and appetite, loss of interest in usual activities, decreased interest in sex, any thoughts of suicide."

The vast majority of students, of course, are not clinically depressed but are experiencing the self-doubt and anxiety typically associated with the critical transition from high school and home to college, and will adjust. Ms. Wilkinson, for example, has made that transition and is now doing well.

In an attempt to minimize the trauma of freshman year, most colleges and universities supply peer counselors, residence hall advisers, faculty advisers, an academic advising center, a mental health clinic and suicide prevention services. At Cornell, students can call the Empathy, Assistance and Referral Service (EARS); at the State University of New York at Albany, the Middle Earth Peer Assistance Program sponsors a telephone line, a campus radio talk show, a weekly advice column and peer theater performances about student problems.

Even the traditional organized activities of freshman year—ice cream socials, Wilderness Reflection weekends, wrestling parties in kiddie swimming pools filled with yogurt—have therapeutic undercurrents to help students let off steam and face the seemingly monumental task ahead.

Noting that students who accept stress as normal and even beneficial tend to respond more creatively to its demands, therapists, counselors and faculty members offer a variety of advice for coping with freshman year.

In "Beating the College Blues" (Checkmark Books, 1999), Paul A. Grayson and Philip Meilman advise students who are frequently irritable, anxious or angry, or have difficulty sleeping, to try relaxation techniques: warm baths, slow, deep breathing, meditation, guitar playing, a long walk.

Dr. Grayson and Dr. Meilman, who direct counseling services at New York University and Cornell, also recommend making an inventory of commitments (say, a five-course load, 20-hour-a-week job, crew team practice at 6 a.m., a steady girlfriend); personal habits (procrastinating or partying too much?) as well as impressions of college life. That exercise helps students determine whether to drop a course or change study habits. A reality check by peers and parents can also identify flawed thinking ("I'm the only person here who has not chosen a major").

Students tend to waste time between classes, then try to read and to write papers at night, when they are tired and are tempted to socialize. It is better to complete three to four hours of course-related work, six days a week, before dinner.

Students who get eight hours of sleep, get up early and study during the day, starting with the first week of classes, do not have to scramble as the assignments pile up. (This schedule has another advantage: the first person up in the morning gets immediate access to the bathroom and a hot shower.)

Freshmen should get to know at least one adult on campus fairly well, starting with a faculty adviser. Alas, many students stand at the adviser's door with a hand on the knob, seeking a signature and speedy get-away, afraid to interrupt a Nobel Prize-winning experiment.

More often than not, those who plant themselves in a chair ready to discuss their backgrounds, their academic and professional aspirations and uncertainties and their personal interests will get a warm response. Students who take the initiative to meet with advisers and visit professors' offices—not only after doing poorly on an exam but also to discuss a required text or ask how a professor became interested in a subject—learn that many teach better in private than in a large lecture hall. And the college, whatever its size, begins to seem far less impersonal.

In the midst of the forced social interaction that characterizes college life, it takes time and many false starts to make a real friend. Roommates do not have to be best friends, but they can be a freshman's first friend. Eating dinner with a roommate, even if she is only "just O.K.," and meeting others in the dormitory and in class will help students get through those sometimes lonely first weeks.

Participating in an extracurricular activity during the first semester provides contact with students who share interests. With their regular practice schedules, the marching band or rugby team may inspire discipline and efficiency.

Noting that Henry David Thoreau went to the woods because he wanted to live deliberately, Prof. Allan Emery, who teaches English at Bowling Green State University in Bowling Green, Ohio, reminds his freshmen students to pause at least once a day to examine their lives.

Too often, as students drive through day after busy day, waiting to vegetate, lubricate or unleash a primal scream on the weekend, college resembles anything but Walden Pond.

"Seize opportunities to reflect on life—your life and the lives of others," Professor Emery suggests, "and you will be far less likely to lose your equilibrium. That's what those well-stocked libraries, tree-lined avenues and peaceful quadrangles are for."

More in College Seek Help For Psychological Problems

Erica Goode

Erica Goode writes for the **New York Times.**

A study of college students seeking psychological counseling has found that their emotional difficulties are far more complex and more severe than those seen in the past.

From 1989 to 2001, the percentage of students treated for depression doubled. So did the percentage of suicidal students, according to the study, conducted at the counseling center at Kansas State University. More than twice the percentage of students were taking some type of psychiatric medication, even though the absolute number of students seen by the center remained stable.

Problems related to stress, anxiety, learning disabilities like attention deficit disorder, family issues, grief and sexual assault also rose. The study also found accompanying increases in more traditional college complaints like trouble in separating from parents, romantic relationships or the choice of careers.

"What we're seeing is people with multiple problems, and some of those are significantly more serious," said Dr. Sherry A. Benton, the assistant director of training at the counseling center in Manhattan, Kan., and the lead author of the report, which appears today in the journal Professional Psychology: Research and Practice. The study was based on forms filled out by therapists after treating more than 13,000 students seen at the center between 1989 and 2001.

Mental health professionals at other college counseling services said the study, the largest of its kind and the first to look at specific categories of problems, confirmed their impressions that students are now struggling with more serious forms of distress.

In a 2002 national survey, more than 80 percent of 274 directors of counseling centers said they thought the number of students with severe psychological disorders had increased over the previous five years.

What lies behind the increase is not clear. A greater awareness of mental illness and the easing of the stigma attached to seeking psychiatric help may play a role. But experts also cite the pressures on students to succeed academically and the breakdown of family support systems as factors.

"People just don't seem to have the resources to draw upon emotionally to the degree that they used to," said Dr. Robert Portnoy, the director of counseling and psychological services at the University of Nebraska. "What would once have been a difficult patch for someone in the past is now a full-blown crisis."

Doris Bertocci, a social worker at Columbia University's counseling center, said about the Kansas State study, "If anything, the conclusion understates the gravity of the problem."

Columbia last year reported a 40 percent increase in the use of the counseling center since the 1994–95 academic year and has nearly doubled its staff, extended its hours and set up offices in dormitories. A spokeswoman said the number of students using the center had risen further in the last year. Other colleges have registered similar growth in demand.

Ms. Bertocci said many clients coming to the center suffered from depression, manic depression, panic attacks and eating disorders or were dealing with family issues, including physical or sexual abuse. Some, she said, were "chronically suicidal."

"Our impression," she added, "has been that by the time students get to Columbia, many of them have had their emotional needs neglected by a lack of access to adequate mental health services."

In the Kansas State study, the percentages of students with eating disorders, chronic mental disorders or who abused drugs or alcohol was not significantly higher in 2001 than in 1989. The percentage of students dealing with sexual or physical abuse from childhood increased sharply in the mid-1990's but then declined.

The prevalence of psychiatric problems on campus and the question of how much responsibility colleges have for the mental health of their students received wide attention two years ago, after highly publicized suicides at several institutions, including the Massachusetts Institute of Technology.

Many campuses have had sharp increases in psychiatric hospitalizations. For example, Dr. Portnoy said 15 to 20 students at Nebraska were now hospitalized each semester, up from 3 or 4 a decade ago. In the vast majority of those cases, he said, suicidal thoughts or actions precipitate the hospitalization.

In the 2002 national survey, the counseling service directors reported a total of 116 suicides at 55 colleges. Only 20 of those students, the survey respondents said, had been seen by college counseling centers before the suicides.

Dr. Benton, at Kansas State, said addressing the needs of suicidal students was one of the most taxing responsibilities that counseling center staff members have. In 2002, she said, her center dealt with 96 students who were contemplating suicide or had made suicidal gestures or attempts.

"The amount of time and energy and resources that it takes is unbelievably high," Dr. Benton said. "I've had a mother say about her occasionally suicidal son, 'I'm counting on you to keep him alive.' That's a lot of pressure."

Ms. Bertocci, of Columbia, said that many of the students she sees require antidepressants or other psychiatric medication but cannot afford to pay for it and do not have insurance to cover the cost. Dr. Benton said that only about 30 percent of the students at Kansas State had health insurance. About 15 percent of college counseling centers charge students for individual counseling sessions.

Lindsay Gangwish, 23, saw a counselor at the University of Nebraska counseling center once a week during her four years at the university. She paid $20 per session for the first 25 sessions, she said, then $45 per session after that.

Ms. Gangwish, who graduated in December, said she sought counseling in her freshman year after having panic attacks and mood swings.

Eventually, bipolar disorder was diagnosed. She said the illness runs in her family. But she added that the pressures of college had contributed to her difficulties. "There's a lot of stress," she said. "You hear a lot of people talking about the stress."

Complex Set of Ills Spurs Rising Teen Suicide Rate

Jessica Portner

Jessica Portner *writes for* Education Week.

Two teenagers burst into their Colorado high school one year ago this month and gunned down 13 people. But nearly lost in the avalanche of reaction to the shootings at Columbine High School was the fact that the young men were also on a suicide mission.

The high school seniors had meticulously planned their own deaths—down to the last bullet and explosive—for nearly a year. They fashioned homemade pipe bombs and attached them to their bodies, apparently intending to blow themselves up along with the school. But instead, after shooting their victims, they turned their weapons on themselves, punching bullets into their own heads.

"They wanted to do as much damage as they possibly could and then go out in flames," John Stone, the Jefferson County, Colo., sheriff, said that day.

By committing mass murder, Dylan Harris, 18, and Eric Klebold, 17, joined a small group of other American teenagers. In their suicides, however, they had plenty of company.

For every adolescent who opened fire at schools from West Paducah, Ky., to Springfield, Ore., in the past few years, thousands more shot themselves, slit their wrists, or gulped down pills in suicides or attempts.

In the 1998–99 school year, eight students committed homicides in schools, and 26 students died in violent incidents on school grounds. That same year, an estimated 2,700 young people ages 10 to 19 took their own lives.

While suicide rates among adults have steadied or even declined over the past few decades, teenage suicide rates have tripled. In 1960, the suicide rate among 15- to 19-year-olds was 3.6 per 100,000. But by 1990, 11.1 out of every 100,000 teenagers 15 and older committed suicide, according to the U.S. Centers for Disease Control and Prevention.

In 1997, more than 30,000 suicides were recorded in the United States; about 9 percent of those were committed by people age 19 or younger. "Where it used to be your grandfather, now it's your son," said Tom Simon, a suicide researcher at the CDC. He added that more Americans under age 19 now die each year from suicide than from cancer, heart disease, AIDS, pneumonia, lung disease, and birth defects combined.

Likely Victims

Which teenagers are most likely to take their own lives? Federal statisticians say the surge in suicides among the nation's youths is fueled by unprecedented increases in such deaths in certain populations. For example, suicide rates among 10- to 14-year-olds have nearly doubled in the past few decades. And black teenagers are now more than twice as likely to kill themselves as they were just 20 years ago. But white teenagers, particularly boys, still tower over their peers in their rates of self-destructiveness.

For every teenager who commits suicide, 100 more will try. Every year, one in 13 high school students attempts suicide, a 1997 federally funded Youth Risk Behavior Survey found. Half of all high school students report they have "seriously considered" suicide by the time they graduate, the survey says. That's an estimated 700,000 American high school students annually who attempt to kill themselves, and millions who say they have contemplated doing so.

According to a report released last fall by the U.S. Department of Education, *Indicators of School Crime and Safety, 1999*, a quarter of the deaths that occur on school grounds are actually suicides. Students who kill themselves on school property tend to do so in highly public venues—such as their classrooms or the school parking lot. Of the 34 students who died violently at school in the 1997–98 school year—the year of the multiple killings in Springfield and West Paducah—nine were suicides.

Teenage girls attempt suicide three times as often as boys do, but males are four times more likely to finish the job. This gender gap, reported in the 1997 survey, reflects the fact that boys tend to employ more lethal means, such as firearms and hanging; girls favor more survivable methods, such as overdosing on pills.

Girls attempt suicide more than boys, experts say, because their act is an effort at communicating their desperation. Boys tend to keep their emotions hidden. "Girls cry out for help, while boys are taught to be tough and never to act like a 'girl,'" said Dr. William Pollack, a professor of psychiatry at Harvard University and an expert on adolescent mental health. As a result, Dr. Pollack said, "boys are so ashamed of their feelings they figure they'd be better off dead" than express their pain.

A small percentage of the increase in teenage suicide rates could reflect improvements in reporting over the past few decades, according to Lloyd Potter, an epidemiologist and suicide expert at the CDC. But, Mr. Potter said, rates have been and continue to be artificially low because suicides are often masked or misclassified.

A child's suicide is often camouflaged by parents who rearrange the site of the death or hide suicide notes. And some medical examiners classify a death as a suicide only when a note is found, something that occurs in less than a third of all cases.

"There's no doubt there are families who don't want it to appear on the death certificate, and the coroner obliges them," said Dr. Tom Shires, a trauma surgeon with the National Suicide Prevention Institute in Las Vegas. In some states, Dr. Shires added, the person designated to determine the cause of death may be a lawyer or a justice of the peace with no medical training who is ill-equipped to investigate such cases.

Dr. Shires, who is compiling a comprehensive database on suicide attempts among people of all ages, added that police are often complicit in the undercount of suicides. Law-enforcement officers across the country so consistently record single-car collisions—even those showing no skid marks on the pavement—as accidents that doctors have coined a term for them: autocides. Such misclassification disproportionately affects youth suicide rates because the category of "unintentional injuries," primarily from automobile accidents, represents the leading cause of death for 15- to 19-year-olds in the United States.

Another way suicide is hidden from the record books, say experts who study gangs, is that some teenagers who want to escape gang life but see no way out choose to die the "honorable" way by provoking police to fire at them.

"We call that 'suicide by cop,'" said Gloria Grenados, a psychiatric social worker at Bell High School in Los Angeles, a school whose students are nearly all affiliated with a gang, she said. "There are kids [that survived] who literally tell me they ran to meet the bullets because they so much wanted to die."

Taking note of such subterfuges, U.S. Surgeon General David Satcher recently called suicide "the nation's hidden epidemic." Suicide, Dr. Satcher said as he launched a suicide-prevention campaign last fall, must be destigmatized and addressed as a public-health problem.

Impulsive Youths

Young people are more vulnerable than adults to thoughts of suicide, experts say, because they often don't comprehend in a rational sense that death is final. Suicide notes collected by researchers show children fantasizing about what they will do when they are dead. Young people often see suicide as the end of their problems, not their existence. "The developmental stage of adolescence is consistent with not thinking of the long- or short-term consequences of behavior," said Mr. Simon of the CDC.

Another tenet of child development is that adolescents are risk-takers by nature who change friends, clothing styles, and attitudes constantly and for no apparent reason. Such impulsivity still rules when teenagers want to chuck more than their wardrobes. But those traits are most often coupled with environmental stresses before a young person decides to commit suicide.

The impetus for inner turmoil in the hearts of American adolescents in recent years cannot be gleaned from superficial clues such as whether a teenager plays violent video games, listens to Marilyn Manson CDs, or dons black trench coats, school psychologists say. Young people, they say, rarely wear their angst so conveniently on their sleeves.

In his 1991 book, *The Enigma of Suicide*, journalist George Howe Colt writes that searching for a single cause for suicide is as futile as "trying to pinpoint what causes us to fall in love or what causes war."

Finding an answer to the riddle of self-murder is not like tracing the origins of a disease to a single genetic marker. Suicide is more akin to a multicolored tapestry whose yarn must be unraveled strand by strand.

Looking for Reasons

Sociologists and mental-health experts point to a tangle of cultural, psychological, and medical factors that have in the past 30 years fueled teenagers' heightened self-destructiveness: a higher divorce rate, parental abuse, poor impulse control stemming from exposure to television, the availability of handguns, lack of access to mental-health services, and a general sense of isolation and alienation from caring adults both at home and at school.

Some experts argue that the leading reason why young people are more at risk for suicide now than they were a generation or two ago is the decline of the traditional family unit. The teenage suicide rate began its climb just as the divorce rate started to surge upward in the 1970s. Half of U.S. marriages now end in divorce, compared with 28 percent in the 1960s; 70 percent of children who attempt suicide have parents who are divorced. In addition, the percentage of children living with two parents declined from 85 percent in 1970 to 68 percent in 1996, federal statistics show.

The dissolution of a two-parent family, whether from divorce, desertion, or the death of a parent, makes children more vulnerable, experts say. Ultimately, though, it's the quality of the parenting, not the constitution of the family unit, that matters most, children's advocates say. Whether married, divorced, or single, most parents are now working more than in the past and, as a result, have far less free time to spend with their children.

"We are benefitting in this society from everyone working, women working, the gross-national-product productivity per dollar increasing," said Kevin Dwyer, the president of the National Association of School Psychologists. "But now kids are growing up without the supports they had in the past." The term "latchkey kid," for children left to fend for themselves at home after school, was coined in the 1980s.

To fill the parenting void and the decreasing ratio of caring adults to children, television increasingly has become children's stalwart companion after school. Parents spend an average of just two minutes a day communicating with their child, while the TV set spends an average of 3½ hours a day with that child, Mr. Colt writes in his book.

Studies are mixed on how exposure to media images of murders and assaults affects children's behavior, though many youth advocates are convinced that violent television shows, movies, and computer games inflame destructive tendencies. More than 86 percent of television shows and movies depict characters who solve interpersonal problems with violence, according to NASP.

By the end of elementary school, the average child will have witnessed more than 100,000 acts of violence on television, including 8,000 murders, according to the Center for Media Education in Washington.

Served the common fare of shootouts and knifings on TV, children come to believe that violence is an appropriate solution to problems, Mr. Dwyer said.

In today's media-saturated, high-velocity society, youths with poor impulse control are given the message that it's only natural that they should want everything yesterday.

While the video-game industry rejects the idea that some of its games are virtual training classes for potential gunmen, some recent, controversial studies contend that playing violent video games helps youths' dexterity with real firearms and desensitizes them to the visceral realities of violence. In one recent study, high school students interviewed after suicide attempts expressed surprise that their actions were so painful because it didn't look that way on TV.

The Media Factor

Some research suggests that the news media may foster children's self-destructive and violent behavior simply by reporting horrific events.

A 1986 study by Madelyn Gould, a professor of psychiatry at Columbia University who examined media coverage of suicides, found that the suicide of a person reported either on television or in newspapers makes at-risk individuals who are exposed to the coverage feel that suicide is a "reasonable, and even appealing, decision."

After last year's shootings at Columbine High School, which touched off weeks of intensive coverage by the national news media, there was a spike in teenage suicides across the nation, according to several experts. In Los Angeles County alone, six students killed themselves within six weeks of the shootings. In the four of those cases in which notes were left, three mentioned Columbine as an inspiration. "If you plaster their face up on the news for 20 minutes, that's going to make the difference," said Dr. Pollack of Harvard. Media coverage of suicides isn't the reason for a child's decision to kill himself, Dr. Pollack said, but it's a contributing factor.

"These things open the floodgate," he said of news accounts. "But to flood, the waters have to already be at a high level."

Keeping afloat emotionally is challenging for many young people because the violence they're exposed to is not just on their television screens. Not surprisingly, children who suffer chronic physical or emotional abuse at home or who witness domestic violence are much more likely to kill themselves than their peers who do not witness such violence.

"A child doesn't just wake up suicidal," said Richard Lieberman, a school psychologist with the suicide-prevention unit of the Los Angeles public schools who handles distress calls from school officials 24 hours a day. "Kids are dealing with more loss. Families are under more stress."

In all areas of the country—poor, rich, urban, suburban, and rural—reports of child abuse have accelerated dramatically in the past few decades. Though a small portion of the increase is attributable to better reporting, the bulk represents a real and disturbing trend, according to federal health officials. In 1997, 42 out of every 1,000 children in the United States were reported as victims of child abuse, a 320 percent leap from 10 per 1,000 children in 1976, figures from the U.S. Department of Health and Human Services show. Newspapers regularly report stories that were once rare: children locked in basements without food; battered and bruised toddlers entering shelters; teenage girls sexually assaulted by their fathers.

Changing School Climate

While home environments in general seem to have become more hazardous, so in large part have schools, say researchers who monitor school climate. Apart from the increasing rates of assaults and shootings since the 1970s, garden-variety bullying behavior is rampant, says Dorothy Espelage, a professor of educational psychology at the University of Illinois at Urbana-Champaign. In a study published last fall, Ms. Espelage found that 80 percent of the 558 Illinois middle school students surveyed reported they had been "threatened, ridiculed, or been physically aggressive" with at least one classmate in the past 30 days.

Other experts suggest that the increased emphasis on raising academic standards and student-achievement levels adds pressure to the mix.

"We have become so focused on raising standards and testing students, and we are paying very little attention that this is working against creating a motivating environment for kids to come to school," said Howard Adelman, a professor of psychology at the University of California, Los Angeles, who runs a project to promote mental health in schools.

Of course, not every student who feels pressured at school, is harassed, or even has a chaotic home life becomes suicidal.

A suicidal teenager is often fundamentally unstable, mental-health experts say.

Currently in the United States, they note, an estimated 11 percent of children ages 9 to 17—or 4 million children—have a diagnosable mental disorder, ranging from obsessive-compulsive disorders to major depression.

The rate of depression has been rising among the young, researchers say, in part because the average age of puberty has declined, and depressive illness tends to emerge after puberty.

Clinically depressed adolescents are five times more likely to attempt suicide than their nondepressed peers, according to a 15-year study that tracked 73 depressed adolescents and compared them with peers who were not clinically depressed.

Psychiatrists who have been enlisted to analyze the motivation of the Columbine shooters point to the fact that Mr. Harris was being treated with an anti-depressant.

In a new book, *Night Falls Fast: Understanding Suicide*, Dr. Kay Redfield Jamison, a professor of psychiatry at Johns Hopkins University, says clinical depression is quite distinguishable from common adolescent angst. "In its severe forms, depression paralyzes all of the otherwise vital forces that make us human, leaving instead a bleak, fatiguing, deadened state," she writes.

In *Darkness Visible*, the author William Styron describes his own severe depression as "a hurricane of the mind." And five years before killing herself, poet Sylvia Plath said of her depressive moods: "I felt as if I were smothering. As if a great muscular owl were sitting on my chest, its talons clenching and constricting my heart."

A growing number of children are now being treated for mood disorders. In 1996, 600,000 children under age 18 with clinical depression were prescribed the antidepressants Prozac, Paxil, and Zoloft, according to IMS America, a research group in New York City. Because no long-term studies on the use of antidepressants by children have been conducted, it is difficult to determine whether such medicinal remedies can lift the suffocating darkness that Dr. Jamison describes.

Whatever the effect, the upsurge in prescribing psychiatric medications has occurred mainly in middle- and upper-class populations, in which children have more access to health care. For millions of teenagers, the last trip to any kind of doctor was for childhood inoculations.

A study released last fall by the University of North Carolina at Chapel Hill found that one-fifth of teenagers said they had had no health care in the past six months, even though they had a condition that warranted a medical visit. That situation represents a lost opportunity, suicide experts say, because family doctors can detect sudden changes in mood, sleeping patterns, and eating habits—indicators of depression.

Some depressed teenagers, who are either embarrassed to seek help or can't afford it, eschew traditional medical care in favor of illicit drugs to elevate their moods. There is a strong link between the use of illegal drugs and suicide; alcohol and certain drugs are depressants and can often have the effect of deepening one's mood. And, because they knock down inhibitions, teenagers feel freer to act on their suicidal fantasies.

Autopsies of adolescent suicide victims show that one-third to one-half of the teenagers were under the influence of drugs or alcohol shortly before they killed themselves, according to HHS statistics. The rate of overall teenage drug use has fluctuated over the past three decades, peaking in the 1970s and then receding somewhat in the 1980s. Use of marijuana and alcohol—both depressants—surged in the 1990s.

Teenagers haven't been gravitating much toward church for comfort. Religious affiliation as a buffer against the harsh realities of the world has a solid grounding in research. For example, studies have shown that elderly people who participate in church-based activities—such as social events and bingo games—have a decreased risk of mortality. That finding, researchers say, could be due as much to the balm of faith as to the fact that attending places of worship decreases isolation.

But while teenage attendance at religious services rose in the late 1990s, far fewer adolescents attend than did 20 years ago.

Means and Reasons

The burgeoning numbers of isolated, despondent teenagers now more than ever have lethal means at their fingertips.

The federal Bureau of Alcohol, Tobacco, and Firearms reports that in 1960, 90 million guns were in circulation; today, there are an estimated 200 million firearms in private hands. That's enough weaponry, if distributed among the U.S. population, for three out of four Americans to be armed. Despite state and federal laws banning possession of handguns by anyone under 18, for many young people, finding a firearm is no more complicated than pilfering from a parent's closet. Other teenagers know where to buy guns illegally on the streets.

Guns are the method of choice for suicidal youths: More than 67 percent of boys and nearly 52 percent of girls ages 10 to 19 who kill themselves use a firearm. Hanging or suffocation follows far behind—the choice of roughly 23 percent of both male and female suicide victims. Smaller percentages die by overdosing on drugs, drowning, in falls, or by slitting their wrists.

Before a youth pulls the trigger, experts say, some event usually has to set him or her off. A recent survey of 15- to 19-year-old students in Oregon who had attempted suicide found that the top three things that spurred them to act—while none was the sole reason—were conflict with parents, relationship problems, or difficulties at school.

Whatever the eventual catalyst, every suicidal youth's life story has a uniquely tragic plot. More often than not, it's a circuitous route that leads him or her toward suicide. The profiles of three youths that follow show how a particular combination of character traits, circumstances, and events conspired to usher each of them to an early death.

Suicide and Depression Among College Students: A Decade Later

Susan R. Furr, John S. Westefeld, Gaye N. McConnell, and J. Marshall Jenkins

Susan R. Furr is a faculty member of the Department of Counseling, Special Education, and Child Development at the University of North Carolina, Chapel Hill.
John S. Westefeld teaches counseling psychology at the University of Iowa.
Gaye N. McConnell is the director of student life at Rowan-Cabarrus Community College.
J. Marshall Jenkins is the director of the counseling center at Berry College.

Psychologists practicing on college campuses today are often perplexed as to the best way to deal with suicidal college students. This is because suicide among college and university students is a problem of complex dimensions that impacts many people: clients, survivors, and psychologists alike. Over the years, various researchers have examined college student suicide from several perspectives. For example, researchers have examined the causes of suicide among college students and have identified a variety of causes, including social problems (e.g., Bernard & Bernard, 1982), hopelessness (Schwartz & Whitaker, 1990; Westefeld, Whitchard, & Range, 1990), inadequate reasons for living (Westefeld, Cardin, & Deaton, 1992), academic problems (Bernard & Bernard, 1982; Schotte & Clum, 1982), and interactive factors (Bonner & Rich, 1988).

One of the most extensive analyses of suicide prevalence rates among college students was published by Schwartz and Whitaker (1990), who examined the research on college student suicide rates over a 60-year period (1928–1988) at 12 colleges and universities. From this research, they concluded that the suicide rate among college students was approximately half that of the nonstudent group. However, some professionals working in college counseling center settings have reported an increase in the severity of presenting problems (Heppner et al., 1994), which suggests that depression and suicide might be becoming increasingly prevalent on college campuses.

The authors conducted a study in 1987 that was designed to examine a variety of issues related to college student suicide (Westefeld & Furr, 1987). A total of 962 students from three institutions were surveyed about their experiences with depression and suicide. Results indicated that 81% of the respondents experienced what they identified as "depression" while in college, with grade problems, relationship problems, loneliness, and money problems cited most frequently as the contributing factors. Thirty-two percent of the students stated that they had thought of committing suicide, with 1% reporting having made a suicide attempt while in college. Attempters were significantly more likely to report hopelessness, helplessness, loneliness, and depression.

Survey of Suicide and Depression on College Campuses

Survey participants in the current study were 1,455 college students at four different colleges and universities, including a major research university located in the Midwest with 28,000 students (Institution A); a southeastern state university with 16,700 students that has a majority of commuter students (Institution B); a southeastern community college that offers both technical and college preparatory programs with an enrollment of 4,000 students (Institution C); and a small, private liberal arts college with 1,800 students (Institution D) in the southeast.

Students in academic classes were asked to complete a brief questionnaire. Characteristics of the student participants included 35% male and 65% female with 82% of the students in the traditional age of college students (18–24 years of age). Thirty-two percent of the participants were freshman, 25% were sophomores, 22% were juniors, 16% were seniors, and 5% were graduate students. Respondents were asked a number of questions related to (a) whether they had experienced depression since coming to college, and if so, the reasons for that depression; (b) whether they had thought about or attempted suicide since coming to college, and if so, why; (c) what kind of counseling they had sought if depressed or suicidal, and if so, whether it was helpful; and (d) how their college or university could more effectively deal with the problem. Because help-seeking behavior often is based on a self-assessment of the problem, we left the definition of depression open to the students' self-definition rather than providing a formal assessment.

If the respondent indicated that he or she had experienced depression, the respondent then was asked to check the contributing factors from the following list: "money problems," "parental problems," "grade problems," "loneliness," "hopelessness," "legal problems," "helplessness," "relationship problems with boyfriend/girlfriend," "other," and "don't know." A similar format was followed for the question, "Have you ever thought about committing suicide since coming to college?" The factor of "general, undefined depression" was added to the list of contributing factors for this question.

Of the 1,455 students surveyed, 53% indicated that they had experienced what they would label as depression since beginning college (55% from Institution A, 59% from Institution B, 44% from Institution C, and 46% from Institution D). When asked the question, "Have you ever thought about committing suicide since coming to college?" 9% of all respondents answered "yes." In response to the question, "Have you ever attempted suicide while at college," approximately 1% of the students responded "yes."

The most frequently cited causes of depression among the students who reported that they had experienced depression since coming to college were grade problems (cited by 53% of the depressed students), loneliness (51%), money problems (50%), and relationship problems with boyfriend/girlfriend (48%). Other contributing factors included hopelessness (26%), parental problems (25%), helplessness (17%), other (13%), don't know (5%), and legal problems (5%).

Hopelessness was cited most frequently (49%) as a contributing factor to suicidal ideation or behavior by those students who identified themselves as having suicidal thoughts, followed by loneliness (47%) and helplessness (37%). Additional factors identified as contributing to suicidal ideation or behavior included relationship (girlfriend or boyfriend) problems (27%); general, undefined depression (26%); money problems (26%); and parental problems (20%). It is interesting to note that the grade-problems factor was ranked seventh out of nine items in contributing to suicidal ideation or behavior, whereas it was ranked first in contributing to depression.

The self-labeling of depression in this survey was 53%, compared with 81% in the last survey (Westefeld & Furr, 1987). The percentage of students indicating suicidal ideation in this survey was 8.5%, compared with 32% in the 1987 survey. The rates of self-reported suicide attempts were basically the same in the two surveys. Additionally, the causes of depression were very similar in the two studies.

When asked if they had sought any type of counseling to assist them when they were in a depressed state, 17% of the students who reported experiencing depression indicated that they had sought counseling. (Sixty-eight percent of these students reported that counseling had been helpful.) The most frequently cited reasons for why counseling was helpful were that the student (a) had someone to talk to (24%), (b) received medication (18%), (c) was helped to explore options (16%), and (d) developed new ways to look at things (13%).

Twenty-five students (20%) out of the 125 who indicated suicidal ideation reported that they had sought counseling. (Forty-eight percent of those students reported that counseling had been helpful.) Reasons for helpfulness included that the student (a) had someone to talk to (27%), (b) felt empowered (13%), (c) developed new ways to look at things (13%), and (d) was helped to sort through things (13%).

Comparison of Suicide Attempters and Nonattempters

To develop a profile of a student who moves from depression to suicidal thoughts to suicidal behavior, we made the following comparisons.

Suicide attempters in comparison with persons who indicated that they had experienced depression. Compared with individuals who only reported depression, suicide attempters (n = 14) experienced significantly more hopelessness and helplessness.

Suicide attempters in comparison with persons who indicated that they had experienced suicidal thoughts. There were no significant differences.

Persons who had experienced suicidal thoughts in comparison with persons who indicated that they had experienced depression. In comparing students who had suicidal thoughts with students who experienced depression, several significant differences were found. Students who experienced suicidal thoughts were more likely to indicate helplessness, hopelessness, loneliness, problems with parents, and "don't know" as contributing factors to depression. These students were also more likely to report that they had sought counseling.

Although severity of depression was not assessed, the number of contributing factors indicated by students did differ slightly. Students who reported that they had attempted suicide checked an average of 4.6 factors, whereas students who reported depression checked an average of 3.6 factors. Students who experienced suicidal ideation but who did not attempt suicide checked an average of 4.0 factors.

Students also were asked whether they felt depression was a serious problem at their particular institution. Even though 53% of the respondents indicated that they had experienced depression, only 37% believed it to be a serious problem on their campus. Of those students who reported that they had experienced depression since coming to college, only 47% believed it to be a serious problem. When asked how their institution could more effectively deal with the problem, 19% of the students suggested a possible strategy. Of the 278 students who offered suggestions, 78 students believed that it was critical to make students more aware of the services available, and 56 students stated that the institution should make services more accessible. In addition, 27 students believed it was important to educate people about depression, and 16 students believed it was important to provide supportive activities for students.

Comparisons Among Institutions

Students at the two larger institutions were more likely to have experienced depression since coming to college and to list grade problems as a contributing factor to depression.

Students from the community college were less likely to cite loneliness as a factor in depression. When the institution had a large commuter population (comprehensive university and community college), money was more frequently cited as a contributing factor to depression. Students at the community college were more likely to have a local support network because the vast majority of these students lived in the local community and did not have to relocate to attend college. Being a part of the community may be a mitigating factor against depression. The small college in the sample is a religiously affiliated institution. Students may be attracted to this institution because of the opportunities for fellowship, service, and spiritual growth. Research (Stack, 1998) has found a relationship between low religiosity and increased suicide acceptability. Consequently, students who choose a college with a religious atmosphere may be more inclined to view suicide as less acceptable.

Implications for Education and Practice

Clearly, according to the data, only a small proportion of those who are depressed ever seek counseling services, and this is a phenomenon that needs to be addressed. Even though college students on these campuses have access to free services, why do they not seek assistance? Turner and Quinn (1999) found in their sample that 62% of the college students stated they would seek help for depression and 90% stated they would consult a mental health professional if experiencing suicidal feelings. Although these factors are generally well known on campuses, administrators may need to rethink the strategies for service availability and implementation. Public service announcements through a wide variety of campus information channels that are created by students may be more effective in normalizing help-seeking behavior among the student population. Turner and Quinn (1999) provided some excellent suggestions for developing campus-based publicity. Because more students are connected to computer networks, campus Web sites need to be used to link students to services. In today's college population, high value is placed on getting instant access to services. When counseling services involve a waiting period for an appointment, students may not persist in seeking assistance. Reexamining the traditional counseling center models is imperative if the accessibility of counseling services is to be increased. Specifically, waiting times and waiting lists need to be reduced to whatever extent possible, and counseling centers need to be accessible.

Hopelessness and depression have been cited in the literature as key factors in suicidal behavior (Beautrais, Joyce, & Mulder, 1999; Hawton, Kingsbury, Steinhardt, James, & Fagg, 1999), and these variables need to be carefully assessed since these factors increase the likelihood of subsequent suicidal ideation and attempts. This can be done using depression and suicide paper-and-pencil tests and by verbally inventorying students concerning their feelings of depression and hopelessness at intake. In these situations, an evaluation for medication, hospitalization, or both is often needed. In terms of the variable of helplessness, campus personnel need to work with individual students to assist them with increasing their social and psychological resources; they also need to work to increase the support systems on campus. Resident assistants, extracurricular activities, and the provision of social networks are all examples of what may be helpful.

Perhaps students are looking for instant relief, a view that receives some support from the number of students who indicated that counseling was helpful because of receiving medication. How do practitioners move away from models involving extensive intake interviews and move toward more action-oriented models that give students a feeling of empowerment and movement? Although psychologists' theoretical orientations may value building relationships and addressing underlying dynamics, the realities of counseling are that practitioners generally only have a few sessions with the majority of people who seek their services. Researchers must continue to evolve models of brief intervention and assess the effectiveness of these services. It may be that in some situations the use of medications and psychotherapy is the treatment of choice, as it has been shown to be in many settings.

For some campuses, loneliness is a major issue, and counseling centers need to work with other student affairs offices to design opportunities for students to become more engaged with the entire community. This includes student activities, fraternities and sororities, clubs, and living-learning centers, to name but a few examples. If grade pressures are extreme in some majors, environmental assessments should be developed to determine what the appropriate demands and pressures for that particular field are. Faculty in those departments may need more guidance in making referrals, or workshops can be developed to strengthen students' abilities to cope with the demands. Rather than remaining in a reactive or remedial mode, counseling centers need to provide guidance in the development of prevention programs. These prevention programs, as discussed above, can take a variety of formats. An effective suicide prevention program on a college campus should focus on three areas: (a) warning signs, (b) what to do if one is concerned about someone, and (c) discussion and identification of local resources. It is crucial for psychologists on college campuses to be proactive—as well as reactive—in addressing this important mental health phenomenon.

References

Beautrais, A., Joyce. P., & Mulder, R. (1999). Personality traits and cognitive styles as risk factors for serious suicide attempts among young people. *Suicide and Life-Threatening Behavior, 29,* 37–47.

Bernard, J. L., & Bernard, M. L. (1982). Factors related to suicidal behavior among college students and the impact of institutional response. *Journal of College Student Personnel, 23,* 409–413.

Bonner, R. L., & Rich, A. R. (1988). A prospective investigation of suicidal ideation in college students: A test of a model. *Suicide and Life-Threatening Behavior, 18,* 245–258.

Hawton, K., Kingsbury, S. T., Steinhardt, K., James. A., & Fagg, J. (1999). Repetition of deliberate self-harm by adolescents: The role of psychological factors. *Journal of Adolescence, 22,* 369–378.

Heppner, P. P., Kivlighan, D. M., Good, G. E., Roehlke, H. J., Hills, H. I., & Ashby, J. S. (1994). Presenting problems of university counseling center clients: A snapshot and multivariate classification scheme. *Journal of Counseling Psychology, 41,* 315–324.

Schotte. D. E., & Clum, G. A. (1982). Suicide ideation in a college population: A test of a model. *Journal of Consulting and Clinical Psychology, 50,* 690–698.

Schwartz, A. I., & Whitaker, L. C. (1990). Suicide among college students: Assessment, treatment, and intervention. In S. J. Blumenthal & D. J. Kupfer (Eds.), *Suicide over the life cycle: Risk factors, assessment, and treatment of suicidal patients.* Washington, DC: American Psychiatric Press.

Stack, S. (1998). Heavy metal, religiosity, and suicide acceptability. *Suicide and Life Threatening Behavior, 28,* 388–394.

Turner, A., & Quinn, K. (1999). College students' perceptions of the value of psychological services: A comparison with APA's public education research. *Professional Psychology: Research and Practice, 30,* 368–371.

Westefeld, J. S., Cardin, D., & Deaton. W. L. (1992). Development of the College Student Reasons for Living Inventory. *Suicide and Life. Threatening Behavior, 22,* 442–452.

Westefeld, J. S., & Furr, S. R. (1987). Suicide and depression among college students. *Professional Psychology: Research and Practice, 18,* 119–123.

Westefeld, J. S., & Pattillo, C. M. (1987). College students' suicide: The case for a national clearinghouse. *Journal of College Student Personnel, 28,* 34–38.

Westefeld, J. S., Whitchard, K. A., & Range, L. M. (1990). College and university student suicide: trends and implications. *The Counseling Psychologist, 3,* 464–476.

Summary Chart

HOW TO WRITE AN ARGUMENTATIVE SYNTHESIS

1. **Analyze the assignment.**
   - *Determine whether you are being asked to write an informative or argumentative synthesis.*
   - *Determine the number and types of readings you are expected to use in your paper.*

2. **Review and annotate the readings.**
   - *Review the readings with your assignment in mind, looking for and marking information related to the topic of your paper.*
   - *Briefly summarize and critique each reading.*

3. **Formulate a thesis.**
   - *Determine what stance you will assume in your essay.*
   - *Determine whether you will use an open or closed thesis statement.*

4. **Choose an organizational plan.**
   - *Decide how you will order the ideas you will develop in your essay.*
   - *Decide whether you will present your ideas using a block or alternating format.*

5. **Write your rough draft.**
   - *Follow the organization plan implied or stated by your thesis.*
   - *Combine your insights, ideas, arguments, and findings with material in the source texts to develop and support your thesis.*
   - *Both paraphrase and quote material as necessary.*
   - *Add transitions, elaborations, clarifications, and connections where needed.*
   - *Include a concluding paragraph.*

6. **Revise your draft.**
   - *Revise to improve the content of your essay.*
   - *Have you clearly indicated the point you want to prove?*
   - *Have you clearly indicated the reasons you believe others should accept your position?*
   - *Have you supported each of those reasons with expert testimony, statistics, or some other means of support as well as with clear explanations?*
   - *Have you acknowledged opposing views in your paper when necessary? Have you found ways of refuting, accommodating, or refuting them?*
   - *Revise to improve the organization of your essay.*
   - *Is the thesis statement clearly worded, and does it control the structure of the essay?*
   - *Have you provided clear transitions between the major sections of your essay?*
   - *Are there clear connections between the material drawn from the readings and your own elaborations and explanations?*
   - *Revise to improve the accuracy and clarity of your essay.*
   - *Have you chosen words that are clear and contribute to the effect you want to elicit from your readers?*
   - *Are your sentences clearly structured with adequate variety?*
   - *Have you defined all the terms you need to define?*
   - *Have you proofread for spelling, punctuation, or usage errors?*

7. **Check your quotations and documentation.**
   - *Have you quoted and paraphrased material properly, accurately, and fairly?*
   - *When incorporating quoted or paraphrased material in your synthesis, have you supplied enough background information on the source text so that the material makes sense to your readers?*
   - *Have you documented all the material that needs to be documented?*
   - *Have you documented material employing the proper format?*

Chapter 11

PLAGIARISM

DEFINITION

Plagiarism occurs when writers take credit for work that is not really theirs. Because it encompasses a wide range of errors in academic writing, from improper citation to calculated fraud, plagiarism is an especially common problem for writers unfamiliar with the conventions of source-based writing. These writers often do not realize that any material they quote or paraphrase from a reading must be documented to avoid plagiarism.

Penalties for plagiarism vary from school to school, department to department, even instructor to instructor. They can range from a warning, to a failing grade on a paper, to a failing grade for a course, to expulsion from school. The academic community takes plagiarism seriously, but with care and honesty you can avoid problems and give the authors of the readings you use the credit they deserve for their work.

FORMS OF PLAGIARISM

Plagiarism is a difficult problem to address because it can assume so many different forms and involves so many different types of errors, some more serious than others. Understanding the various forms that plagiarism can assume will help you avoid problems.

PURCHASING A PAPER

Sometimes students will decide to purchase a paper rather than write one themselves. Whether you buy one from a fellow student or from a commercial vendor, purchasing a paper and turning it in as if it were your own is clearly a form of plagiarism. You are purposely taking credit for work that is not truly yours. Your teachers expect you to do your own work. Sometimes they may ask you to work with other students to write an essay, but even then you will be expected to do your own work in the group. Purchasing a paper—or even part of a paper—from someone and turning it in as if were your own is never acceptable.

TURNING IN A PAPER SOMEONE ELSE HAS WRITTEN FOR YOU

This form of plagiarism, related to the first, occurs when two students decide to let one take credit for work the other has actually completed—a student may ask his roommate to write a paper for him then turn it in for a grade. If caught, both students may face some sort of penalty for plagiarism. In other cases, roommates taking different sections of the same class may hand in the same paper to their instructors without permission. In this case, both students have committed plagiarism. Finally there are instances where a student retrieves a paper from the "fraternity" or "sorority" file, collections of papers written for various courses kept for students to copy and turn in (high tech versions of this file are the collections of student papers kept on university computer systems). These papers may have been written by people the student has never known; however, if the student represents it as her own work, that student is guilty of plagiarism.

TURNING IN ANOTHER STUDENT'S WORK WITHOUT THAT STUDENT'S KNOWLEDGE

This form of plagiarism has increased over the past few years as more and more students write their papers on computers. Here a student searches another student's computer files for a paper, copies the paper, then turns it in as if it were his own work. Most students and instructors would likely consider this action to be a form of theft and fraud. It is clearly a form of plagiarism.

IMPROPER COLLABORATION

More and more teachers are asking students to work together on class projects. If a teacher asks you to collaborate with others on a project, be sure to clarify exactly what she expects you to do individually when preparing the final essay. Sometimes a teacher will want a group of students to produce a single paper. The members of the group decide among themselves how they will divide the labor, and all group members get equal credit for the final essay. Though the group members should help each other complete the essay, if you are asked to complete a certain task as part of the larger project, make sure you give credit to others, when appropriate, for any material that was not originally your own. Other times a teacher will want the members of the group to work individually on their own papers; the other group members serve as each other's consultants and peer editors rather than as coauthors. In this case, you should acknowledge at the beginning of your essay or through documentation in the body of your paper any ideas or material you did not develop yourself.

COPYING A PAPER FROM A SOURCE TEXT WITHOUT PROPER ACKNOWLEDGMENT

This form of plagiarism occurs when a student consults an encyclopedia, book, or journal article, copies the information directly from the reading into his paper, puts his name on the essay, and turns it in for a grade. Sometimes a student will compose an entire essay this way; sometimes he will copy only part of his paper directly from a source. In either case, copying from a reading without proper quotation and documentation is a form of plagiarism. So is copying material directly from a computerized encyclopedia. Even though your computer may come with an encyclopedia on CD, you cannot copy material from it and turn it in as your own work without proper documentation and acknowledgment.

COPYING MATERIAL FROM A SOURCE TEXT, SUPPLYING PROPER DOCUMENTATION, BUT LEAVING OUT QUOTATION MARKS

Many students have a hard time understanding this form of plagiarism. The student has copied material directly from a source and has supplied proper documentation. However, if the student does not properly quote the passage, the student is guilty of plagiarism. The documentation a student provides acknowledges the writer's debt to another for the ideas she has used in the paper, but by failing to supply quotation marks, the writer is claiming credit for the language of the passage, language originally employed by the author of the source text. To properly credit the author for both the ideas and the language of the source text, the student needs to supply both proper quotation marks and proper documentation.

PARAPHRASING MATERIAL FROM A READING WITHOUT PROPER DOCUMENTATION

Suppose a student takes material from a source, paraphrases it, and includes it in his paper. Has this student committed an act of plagiarism? The student has if he fails to document the passage properly. The language is the student's own, but the original ideas were not. Adding proper documentation ensures that the author of the source text will receive proper credit for his ideas.

Few other important concepts in writing are as poorly defined as is plagiarism. Sometimes plagiarism results from premeditated fraud—a student purposely attempts to deceive her readers. Other times it results from sloppy note taking or poor proofreading—the student simply forgets to place quotation marks around a passage or fails to supply needed documentation.

HOW TO AVOID PLAGIARISM

DO YOUR OWN WORK

Obviously, the first way to avoid plagiarism is to do your own work when composing papers—do your own research and write your own essay. This suggestion does not mean, however, that collaborating with others when you write or getting needed help from your teacher, tutor, or classmates is wrong. Many instructors will suggest or even require you to work with others on some writing projects—classmates, writing center tutors, friends. Just be sure the paper you turn in fairly and accurately represents, acknowledges, and documents the efforts you and others have put into the essay. If you get help on a paper you are writing, make sure that you can honestly take credit for the unacknowledged ideas and language it contains. If important or substantial ideas or words in the paper came from someone else, be sure to document those contributions properly. When you turn in a paper with your name on the title page, you are taking credit for the material in the essay. You are also, though, taking responsibility for that material—you are, in effect, telling your reader that you compiled this information, developed these arguments, or produced these findings and will stand behind what you have written. Taking that responsibility seriously, doing the hard work of writing yourself and composing papers that represent your best efforts, can help you avoid problems with plagiarism.

TAKE GOOD NOTES

One common source of unintentional plagiarism is poor note taking. Here is what can happen: a student goes to the library and looks up an article she thinks will help her write her paper. She reads the piece and, taking notes, copies down information and passages she thinks she might use in her essay. However, if she is not careful to put quotation marks around passages she takes word-for-word from the source, she can be in trouble when she writes her essay. If she later consults her notes when drafting her paper, she may not remember that the passage in her notes should be quoted in her paper—she may believe she paraphrased the material when taking notes. If she copies the passage exactly as she has it written in her notes and fails to place it in quotation marks in her paper, she has plagiarized the material, even if she documents it. Remember, to avoid plagiarism, passages taken word-for-word from a source must be quoted *and* documented. Therefore, be very careful when taking notes to place quotation marks around material you are copying directly from a reading. If you later incorporate that material in your essay, you will know to place the passage in quotation marks and document it.

PARAPHRASE PROPERLY

Another source of unintentional plagiarism is improper paraphrasing. When you paraphrase material, you have to be sure to change substantially the language of the source passage (see Chapter 3 for guidelines on paraphrasing material). If you do not do a good job paraphrasing a passage, you can be guilty of plagiarism even if you document the material. If in your paraphrase there are phrases or clauses that should be quoted (because they appear in your paper exactly as they appear in the source), you will be guilty of plagiarism if you do not place quotation marks around them, even if the whole passage is properly documented.

SUPPLY PROPER DOCUMENTATION

When you proofread a source-based essay, set aside time to look for problems involving documentation before you turn it in. Problems like these can be hard to detect; you need to pay close attention to finding them as you review your work. Make sure everything that should be documented is properly cited. If you ever have any questions about whether to document a particular passage or word, see your instructor. Because instructors know the documentation conventions of their particular fields of study, they can often give you the best advice. If you have a question about whether to document a passage and you cannot reach your teacher for advice, you should probably err on the side of documentation. When responding to your work, your teacher can indicate whether the documentation was absolutely necessary.

Remember, whenever you quote *or* paraphrase material, you need to supply proper documentation, indicating the source of those words or ideas. Most students remember to document quotations. Remembering to document paraphrased material can be more problematic, especially if you have been told *not* to document "common knowledge." Though this may appear to be a fairly simple guideline, in practice it can be confusing and vague. What is **common knowledge**? What qualifies as common knowledge varies from discipline to discipline in college and from audience to audience. Information that does not need to be documented in a history research paper may need to be documented in a philosophy research paper—the information is common knowledge for readers in history but not for readers in philosophy. Among one group of readers, certain facts, references, statistics, claims, or interpretations may be well known and generally accepted; among other readers, the same material may be new or controversial. For the first group of readers, documentation may not be necessary; for the second, it probably is. Again, if you ever have a question concerning whether something should or should not be documented, ask your instructor, who has expert knowledge about the discipline.

Many students express dismay over this guideline because it means that if they are writing a paper on a topic relatively new to them, they will have to document almost everything. When you are writing certain kinds of papers in certain classes, there may be no way to avoid having documented material in almost every paragraph. However, this situation is not "bad"; in fact, it is to be expected when you are writing on a subject new to you. There are ways to consolidate your documentation so the citations do not take up too much space in your essay (see the three "Consolidating References" sections in Chapter 12).

CLARIFY COLLABORATION GUIDELINES

If you are asked to collaborate with others on a project, be sure to clarify the guidelines your teacher wants you to follow. You want to be sure you know what your teacher expects of each student in the group. Are the individual members of the group supposed to work together to produce a single essay? Are the group members supposed to help each individual member of the group write his or her own paper? How much help is acceptable? Can another student supply you with the material or arguments you will use in your essay? Can others help you with the organization, perhaps suggesting how you should structure your work? Can other students write part of your paper for you? Can others revise your paper for you, changing the language when needed? Be sure you know what your teacher expects before you begin work on a collaborative project, and be sure to ask your teacher to clarify how she expects you to acknowledge and document the help you receive from others.

Summary Chart

PLAGIARISM

1. **Forms of Plagiarism**

   Purchasing a paper.

   Turning in a paper someone else has written for you.

   Turning in another student's work without that student's knowledge.

   Improper collaboration.

   Copying a paper from a source text without proper acknowledgment.

   Copying material from a reading, supplying proper documentation, but leaving out quotation marks.

   Paraphrasing material from a reading without proper documentation.

2. **How to Avoid Plagiarism**

   Do your own work.

   Take good notes.

   Paraphrase properly.

   Supply proper documentation.

   Clarify collaboration guidelines.

Chapter 12

DOCUMENTATION

DEFINITION AND PURPOSE

Proper documentation for your papers serves several functions. First, it allows your readers to know exactly where to find specific information if they want to check the accuracy of what you have written or if they want to learn more about the subject. When combined with a reference list or bibliography, proper documentation enables readers to locate information easily and efficiently. Second, documentation gives credit to others for their ideas, arguments, findings, or language. When you write from readings, you are joining an ongoing conversation—people have likely written on the topic before you began your research and will likely write on it after you have finished your essay. With documentation, you acknowledge the work of those previous authors and locate your work clearly in that conversation. Finally, as a practical matter, proper documentation helps you avoid plagiarism. Many instances of unintentional plagiarism result from improper documentation. You can avoid these problems if you take a few minutes to check the accuracy of your documentation before you turn your papers in for a grade.

TYPES OF DOCUMENTATION

In college, you will encounter two primary methods of documentation: (1) in-text parenthetical documentation and (2) footnotes or endnotes. When you use in-text parenthetical documentation, right after the quoted or paraphrased material you indicate in parentheses where that information can be found in the original source. With footnotes or endnotes, you place a raised (super-script) number after the quoted or paraphrased material, then indicate where in the source text that information can be found, either at the bottom of your page (in a footnote) or at the end of your paper (in an endnote). Over the past few years, parenthetical methods of documentation have largely replaced footnotes and endnotes. You may still find professors, though, who prefer those older forms of documentation. Always check with your teacher if you have any questions about the type of documentation you should be using in a class.

PRIMARY ACADEMIC STYLE MANUALS

The biggest problem you will face when documenting papers in college is lack of uniform practice—styles of documentation will vary from class to class. When you write papers in college, your teacher will expect you to follow the guidelines set out in the style manual commonly used in that field of study, a set of directions writers in that discipline follow when composing and documenting papers.

Fortunately, only a few style manuals are commonly used in college. Teachers in humanities classes (English, history, philosophy, art) often follow the guidelines established by the Modern Language Association (MLA), as published in the *MLA Style Manual and Guide to Scholarly Publishing*. Teachers in the social sciences (sociology, anthropology, psychology, criminal justice) tend to follow the rules set by the American Psychological Association (APA), which appear in *Publication Manual of the American Psychological Association*. Teachers in the natural sciences (biology, geology, chemistry) frequently follow the guidelines set out by the Council of Science Editors (CSE), whose guide is entitled *Scientific Style and Format: The CSE Manual for Authors, Editors, and Publishers*.

However, you may have a class with a sociology teacher who prefers that you follow MLA rules or a philosophy teacher who wants you to use APA style. Also, teachers within a given field may want their students to follow different style manuals. During the same term, for example, you may be taking two education courses, with one teacher asking you to use MLA documentation and the other wanting you to follow APA guidelines. If teachers do not specify the format they want you to follow, always ask them which style manual they want you to use when writing your paper. If a teacher voices no preference, then choose one format and follow it consistently.

The APA, CSE, and MLA style manuals agree that writers should employ in-text parenthetical documentation and explanatory footnotes; however, they disagree over the exact form this documentation should assume. Though differences among the formats dictated by these style manuals may seem minor, knowing how to properly document your work helps mark you as a member of a particular academic or research community. Not knowing how may mark you as a novice or outsider.

The following are guidelines for using APA, CSE, and MLA styles of documentation. The examples offered are not comprehensive. They may be sufficient for some of the papers you write, but you may have to use types of source texts not covered below. If you do, you can find each of the major style manuals in your college library; consult them if the following examples do not answer your questions.

APA GUIDELINES

IN-TEXT DOCUMENTATION

The APA recommends an author-date-page method of in-text documentation. When you quote material, note parenthetically the last name of the author whose work you are using, the year that work was published, and the page number in the reading where that material can be found. When you paraphrase material, you need to note the last name of the author whose work you are using and the year that work was published, but you do not need to include a specific page number in the documentation. What you include in a parenthetical citation can change, though, depending on the information you have already included in the body of your paper. For example, if the author's name has already been used to introduce the material, you do not repeat the name in the parenthetical citation.

Source with One Author

When you quote a passage from a source that has only one author, place the author's last name in parentheses, followed by the year the work was published and the page number where the passage can be found in the source text, all separated by commas. Precede the page reference with "p." if the passage is located on one page in the source text ("p. 12") and with "pp." if the passage runs on more than one page ("pp. 12–13"):

Example 1

> "Drug-using women may be in a position to capitalize most on the advantages of women-inspired prevention methods, and be hindered the least by the disadvantages, as compared with other groups of at-risk women" (Gollub, 2008, p. 108).

If you were to paraphrase that passage, following APA guidelines, you would not include in the documentation a specific page number, only the author and year of publication:

Example 2 Paraphrase

> Prevention methods designed and inspired by women may offer more help to drug-using women than to other similar at-risk groups (Gollub, 2008, p. 108).

Note the space between the end of the quoted or paraphrased passage and the parenthetical citation. Also, the period for the sentence follows the documentation (which is not the case with block quotations). Also, remember not to repeat information in your parenthetical citation that is included in the body of your essay. For example, if you mention the author's name to introduce a quotation or paraphrase, cite the year of publication parenthetically right after the author's name and the page number right after any quoted source material:

Example 3

> According to Erica L. Gollub (2008), "Drug-using women may be in a position to capitalize most on the advantages of women-inspired prevention methods, and be hindered the least by the disadvantages, as compared with other groups of at-risk women" (p. 108).

Source with Two Authors

If a work has two authors, cite the last names of both authors when you refer to their work. Separate the names with an ampersand (&) if you are citing them parenthetically, with "and" if they appear in the body of your text:

Example 4

> "At the beginning of the AIDS epidemic, the large size of high-risk groups, and their lack of organization around public health issues virtually guaranteed that high levels of collective action to combat AIDS would be extremely low" (Broadhead & Heckathorn, 1994, p. 475).

Example 5 Paraphrase

> According to Broadhead and Heckathorn (1994), because the group of people most likely to be affected by AIDS was so large and tended not to focus on health issues, a poor response to the epidemic was almost certain.

Source with Three to Five Authors

The first time you refer to work from a source with three to five authors, list the last names of all the authors in the order in which they appear in the source. Again, use an ampersand before the last name when citing the authors parenthetically. In subsequent references to the work, cite the last name of the first author followed by "et al." (which means "and others"):

Example 6

> A recent study has shown that people who are infected with the HIV virus live longer and healthier lives when they receive various combinations of antiretroviral treatments (Kalichman, Eaton, Cain, Cherry, & Pope, 2006).

Example 7

> A recent study by Kalichman, Eaton, Cain, Cherry, Pope, & Kalichman (2006) has shown that people who are infected with the HIV virus live longer and healthier lives when they receive various combinations of antiretroviral treatments.

Example 8

> Kalichman et al. (2006) found that . . .

If shortening a citation through the use of "et al." will cause any confusion (that is, if two or more citations become identical when shortened), include all the authors' names every time you refer to their works.

Source with Six or More Authors

If a work has six or more authors, cite only the last name of the first author followed by "et al." and the year of publication:

Example 9

> A recent study in Africa confirms that among sexually active people, regular condom use helps prevent the spread of HIV and AIDS (Laga et al., 1994).

Example 10

> A recent study in Africa by Laga et al. (1994) confirms that among sexually active people, regular condom use helps prevent the spread of HIV and AIDS.

If shortening a citation through the use of "et al." will cause any confusion (if two or more citations become identical), list as many authors' last names as needed to differentiate the works, and then replace the remaining names with "et al."

Source with No Author

When a work has no author, cite the first two or three words of the title and the year of publication. If the source text is a journal article or book chapter, the shortened title will appear in quotation marks; if the work is a pamphlet or a book, the shortened title should be underlined:

Example 11

> "The world has recognized that an adult with AIDS in Zambia has as much right to treatment as one in Norway. Children should not be left to die simply because they cannot pay" ("Children," 2005, p. 16).

Example 12

> In "Children and AIDS" (2005), the editors of the *New York Times* argue, "The world has recognized that an adult with AIDS in Zambia has as much right to treatment as one in Norway. Children should not be left to die simply because they cannot pay" (p. 16).

Because the title of the article is used to introduce the quotation in Example 12, it is not repeated in the parenthetical citation.

Sources Whose Authors Have the Same Last Name

If two authors have the same last name, differentiate them by their first initials:

Example 13

> Surveys have found that many people avoid discussing AIDS because they feel they know too little about the topic (J. Brown, 1991); consequently, a number of companies are beginning to develop programs to educate their workers (L. Brown, 1991).

Two or More Sources by the Same Author

If you are referring to two or more works by the same author, differentiate them by date of publication separated by commas. If both are included in the same parenthetical citation, order them by year of publication:

Example 14

> Because AZT has proved to be ineffective in controlling the effects of AIDS (Brown, 1993), scientists have been working hard to develop a vaccine against the virus, especially in Third World countries where the epidemic is spreading quickly (Brown, 1994).

Example 15

> A series of articles in *New Scientist* by Phillida Brown (1993, 1994) traces efforts to develop adequate treatments to combat AIDS.

Two or More Sources by the Same Author Published the Same Year

If you are referring to two or more works by the same author published in the same year, differentiate them by adding lowercase letters after the dates:

Example 16

> Two recent articles (Brown, 1994a, 1994b) trace the efforts to improve AIDS treatment in Third World countries.

The "a" article would appear first in the reference list, the "b" second, and so on.

Electronic Sources of Information

If you refer to the work as a whole, include the author's last name and the year of publication. If, instead, you are citing specific information in the source text, include the author's last name, the year of publication, and the page number. If the pages are not numbered, include the paragraph or section number in the source text where the material can be found preceded by the paragraph symbol (¶) or by "para.":

Example 17

> According to one expert, AIDS has killed 14 million people over the past 20 years (Underwood, 1999, para. 1).

As always, do not repeat information in the citation that is already present in your essay.

Consolidating APA-Style References

If you want to include references to two or more sources in one parenthetical citation, arrange them alphabetically by the last name of the authors and separate them with semicolons:

Example 18

> Many recent studies have examined the best treatment options for women who suffer from HIV infection (Gollub, 2008; Kalichman et al., 2006; Wanjama, Kimani, & Lodiaga, 2007).

FOOTNOTES AND ENDNOTES

Some style manuals still advocate using footnotes or endnotes as the primary means of documenting source-based essays, but the APA suggests they be used sparingly, only to supply commentary or information you do not want to include in the body of your paper. These notes are numbered consecutively in the text with superscript numerals.

Example 19

> A survey of recent articles published on AIDS shows a growing interest in developing reliable research methods to test high-risk groups, such as drug abusers and prostitutes.[1]

The notes then appear on a separate page at the end of the paper with the word "Footnotes" centered at the top. The footnotes are double spaced in numerical order, preceded by superscript numerals. The first line of every note is indented five to seven spaces.

CSE GUIDELINES

IN-TEXT DOCUMENTATION

The documentation practices suggested by the CSE are much less uniform than those suggested by the APA or MLA, though in the sixth edition of its style manual, the CSE sets as one of its goals greater standardization of documentation forms. The CSE recommends that when you are preparing a manuscript for publication you consult previous issues of the journal you hope will publish your work to determine the form of documentation it employs. Periodicals in the natural sciences will likely employ, with slight variations, one of two documentation systems: the name-year system or the citation-sequence system.

The Name-Year System

This system closely resembles APA documentation. When you document material, note parenthetically the last name of the author and the year the work was published. The CSE style manual is much less explicit, though, in its guidelines for adapting parenthetical citations to suit the nature of the material being documented.

Source with One Author

When you quote material from a source, include the last name of the author, the year of publication, and the page number where the passage can be found in the reading preceded by "p" for both single- and multiple-page references:

Example 20

> "Drug-using women may be in a position to capitalize most on the advantages of women-inspired prevention methods, and be hindered the least by the disadvantages, as compared with other groups of at-risk women" (Gollub 2008, p 108).

Note that there is no comma between the name of the author and the year of publication. Include a comma between the year of publication and the page reference. The "p" denoting "page" is not followed by a period. Also note the placement of the period following the documentation. (In a block quotation, the period precedes the documentation.)

When you paraphrase a passage, generally you will refer not to specific page numbers but only to the author and year of publication:

Example 21 Paraphrase

> Prevention methods designed and inspired by women may offer more help to drug-using women than to other similar at-risk groups (Gollub 2008).

Source with Two Authors

When a work is written by two authors, cite the last names of both separated by "and":

Example 22

> "At the beginning of the AIDS epidemic, the large size of high-risk groups, and their lack of organization around public health issues virtually guaranteed that high levels of collective action to combat AIDS would be extremely low" (Broadhead and Heckathorn 1994, p 475).

Example 22 Paraphrase

> According to Broadhead and Heckathorn (1994), because the group of people most likely to be affected by AIDS was so large and tended not to focus on health issues, a poor response to the epidemic was almost certain.

Source with Three or More Authors

If a source has three or more authors, give the last name of the first author followed by "and others":

Example 24

> A recent study in Africa confirms that among sexually active people, regular condom use does help prevent the spread of HIV and AIDS (Laga and others 1994).

Example 25

> A recent study in Africa by Laga and others (1994) confirms that among sexually active people, regular condom use does help prevent the spread of HIV and AIDS.

Source with No Author

When the author's name is not given in the source, use the term "Anonymous," followed by the year of publication:

Example 26

> "The world has recognized that an adult with AIDS in Zambia has as much right to treatment as one in Norway. Children should not be left to die simply because they cannot pay" (Anonymous 2005, p 16).

Example 27

> In "Children and AIDS" (Anonymous 2005), the editors of the *New York Times* argue, "The world has recognized that an adult with AIDS in Zambia has as much right to treatment as one in Norway. Children should not be left to die simply because they cannot pay" (p 16).

Sources Whose Authors Have the Same Last Name

When you are working with sources written by people who have the same last name, give their initials as well:

Example 28

> Surveys have found that many people avoid discussing AIDS because they feel they know too little about the topic (Brown WJ 1991); consequently, a number of companies are beginning to develop programs to educate their workers (Brown LL 1991).

Note the punctuation: do not include periods between or after the initials.

Two or More Sources by the Same Author

If you are referring to two or more works by the same author, differentiate them in your documentation by adding the date of publication separated by commas if needed.

Example 29

> Because AZT has proved to be ineffective in controlling the effects of AIDS (Brown 1993) scientists have been working hard to develop a vaccine against the virus, especially in Third World countries where the epidemic is spreading quickly (Brown 1994).

Example 30

> A series of articles in *New Scientist* by Phillida Brown (1993, 1994) traces efforts to develop adequate treatments to combat AIDS.

Two or More Sources by the Same Author Published the Same Year

If you are citing two or more works written by the same author published in the same year, differentiate them in your documentation by adding lowercase letters after the dates:

Example 31

> Two recent articles (Brown 1994a, 1994b) trace the efforts to improve AIDS treatment in Third World countries.

Electronic Sources of Information

If you are citing the work as a whole, include the author's name and the year of publication. If, however, you are citing only a portion of the source text, include the page number or numbers as well. If the pages in the source text are not numbered, include the paragraph number where that information can be found.

Example 32

> According to one expert, AIDS has killed 14 million people over the past 20 years (Underwood 1999, par 1).

Consolidating CSE Name-Year References

If you want to include references to two or more sources in one parenthetical citation, arrange them alphabetically by the authors' last names and separate them with semicolons.

Example 33

> Many recent studies have examined the best treatment options for women who suffer from HIV infection (Gollub 2008; Kalichman and others 2006; Wanjama, Kimani, Lodiaga, 2007).

The Citation-Sequence System

This system numbers references consecutively as they occur in your text. The first source you use you number "1," the second source "2," and so on. Usually, the number is a superscript placed after the quoted or paraphrased material. The next time you refer to that source, you repeat the same number it was first given. The superscript numbers should be one or two points smaller than the type used in the body of your paper. Some journals prefer you cite the number of the reference parenthetically:

Example 34

Most of the scientists investigating HIV believe it causes AIDS and seriously damages a person's immune system even before that person comes down with the disease[1].

Example 35

Most of the scientists investigating HIV believe it causes AIDS and seriously damages a person's immune system even before that person comes down with the disease (1).

Pay attention to the placement of the period at the end of the sentence: the period always follows the citation number. Also, if you refer to the authors in the body of your essay, the citation number comes right after their names, before a comma or other punctuation mark:

Example 36

According to Broadhead and Heckathorn[1], because the group of people most likely to be affected by AIDS was so large and tended not to focus on health issues, a poor response to the epidemic was almost certain.

Referring to a Specific Page

The CSE style manual does not suggest how to refer to a specific page number of a source text when using superscript numbers. When citing sources parenthetically, however, common practice among scientific journals suggests that in your citation you list the source number followed by the page number. Precede the page number with "p" when referring to material found on one or more pages in the source (if the pages are not numbered, as is commonly the case with electronic sources of information, include the paragraph number preceded by "par"). Separate the source number from the page or paragraph number with a comma:

Example 37

"Drug-using women may be in a position to capitalize most on the advantages of women-inspired prevention methods, and be hindered the least by the disadvantages, as compared with other groups of at-risk women" (1, p 108).

Example 38

"Few things in life are more satisfying than solving a mystery—especially if it involves 14 million deaths that have stumped the world for nearly 20 years" (2, par 1).

Consolidating CSE Citation-Sequence References

If you want to include references to two or more works in one citation, list them in numerical order, separated by commas:

Example 39

> A survey of recent articles published on AIDS[1,3,7] shows a growing interest in developing reliable research methods to test high-risk groups, such as drug abusers and prostitutes.

Example 40

> A survey of recent articles published on AIDS (1,3,7) shows a growing interest in developing reliable research methods to test high-risk groups, such as drug abusers and prostitutes.

If you refer to several sources listed consecutively in the reference list, include only the first and last numbers, joined by a hyphen (for example, "1-3,7,11-13").

FOOTNOTES AND ENDNOTES

The CSE style manual discourages the use of footnotes. It suggests that if you use endnotes, designate them sequentially in the text with superscript lower-case letters, "a," "b," "c," and so on:

Example 41

> A survey of recent articles published on AIDS shows a growing interest in developing reliable research methods to test high-risk groups, such as drug abusers and prostitutes[a].

The notes then appear on a separate page at the end of the paper under a heading such as "Notes." The endnotes may be single- or double-spaced. Precede each note with the appropriate lowercase letter (*not* a superscript), a period, and a space:

Notes

a. See, for example, the articles by . . .

MLA GUIDELINES

IN-TEXT DOCUMENTATION

MLA style uses an author-page system of in-text documentation. When you quote or paraphrase material, you tell your reader parenthetically the name of the author whose work you are using and where in that reading the passage or information can be found. If your reader wants more information on this source text (for instance, whether it is a book or an article, when it was published, or what journal it appeared in), she will refer to the works cited list at the end of your paper, where you provide this information.

The exact form of the parenthetical documentation—what information goes into the parentheses and in what order—varies depending on the type of source you are referring to and what you have already mentioned about the source in the body of your essay.

Source with One Author

When you quote or paraphrase information from a reading that has just one author, place the author's last name in parentheses, leave a space, and then indicate the page number or numbers in the source where the passage or information can be found. Whether you are quoting or paraphrasing material, the period follows the parentheses. In the following examples, pay particular attention to spacing and the proper placement of quotation marks:

Example 42

> "Drug-using women may be in a position to capitalize most on the advantages of women-inspired prevention methods, and be hindered the least by the disadvantages, as compared with other groups of at-risk women" (Gollub 108).

Example 43 Paraphrase

> Prevention methods designed and inspired by women may offer more help to drug-using women than to other similar at-risk groups (Gollub 108).

When using the MLA format, do *not* include "p." or "pp." before the page number or numbers. Again, notice that the final period is placed *after* the documentation. The only exception to this punctuation rule occurs when you block quote information, in which case the period comes before the parenthetical documentation.

Do not repeat in the parentheses information that is already included in the text itself. For example, if you mention the author's name leading up to the quotation or believe your reader will know who the author is from the context of the quotation, you do not need to repeat the author's name in parentheses:

Example 44

> According to Erica L. Gollub, "Drug-using women may be in a position to capitalize most on the advantages of women-inspired prevention methods, and be hindered the least by the disadvantages, as compared with other groups of at-risk women" (108).

MLA style requires you to record specific page references for material directly quoted or paraphrased. If you are quoting or paraphrasing a passage that runs longer than one page in a reading, indicate all the page numbers where that information can be found:

Example 45

According to Gollbub, many recent studies have investigated the sexual practices of drug users who are infected with the HIV virus (107–108).

Source with Two Authors

If a work has two authors, list the last names of the authors in the order they appear in the source, joined by "and." If you mention the authors in the body of your essay, include only the page number or numbers in parentheses:

Example 46

"At the beginning of the AIDS epidemic, the large size of high-risk groups, and their lack of organization around public health issues virtually guaranteed that high levels of collective action to combat AIDS would be extremely low" (Broadhead and Heckathorn 475).

Example 47 Paraphrase

According to Broadhead and Heckathorn, because the group of people most likely to be affected by AIDS was so large and tended not to focus on health issues, a poor response to the epidemic was almost certain (475).

Source with Three Authors

If a work has three authors, list the last names of the authors in the order they appear in the source, separated by commas, with "and" before the last name:

Example 48

Recently, researchers have begun to examine the AIDS epidemic by combing a wide range of scientific and social perspectives and methodologies (Fan, Conner, and Villarreal).

- Since this citation refers to the entire work, no specific page reference is provided.

Source with More Than Three Authors

If a source has more than three authors, include the last name of the first author followed by "et al.":

Example 49

A recent study has shown that people who are infected with the HIV virus live longer and healthier lives when they receive various combinations of antiretroviral treatments (Kalichman et al. 401).

Source with No Author

If a work has no author, parenthetically cite the first word or two of the title. If the work is a journal article or book chapter, the shortened title will appear in quotation marks. If the work is longer, the shortened title should be italicized. If you mention the title of the work in the body of your essay, you will need to include only the page number or numbers in parentheses:

Example 50

> "The world has recognized that an adult with AIDS in Zambia has as much right to treatment as one in Norway. Children should not be left to die simply because they cannot pay" ("Children" 16).

Example 51

> In "Children and AIDS," the editors of the *New York Times* argue, "The world has recognized that an adult with AIDS in Zambia has as much right to treatment as one in Norway. Children should not be left to die simply because they cannot pay" (16).

Sources Whose Authors Have the Same Last Name

If two different authors have the same last name, differentiate them in your documentation by including their first initials:

Example 52

> Surveys have found that many people avoid discussing AIDS because they feel they know too little about the topic (J. Brown 675); consequently, a number of companies are beginning to develop programs to educate their workers (L. Brown 64).

Two or More Sources by the Same Author

If you are referring to two or more works by the same author, differentiate them in your documentation by putting a comma after the last name of the author and adding a shortened version of the title before citing the specific page reference:

Example 53

> Because AZT has proved to be ineffective in controlling the effects of AIDS (Brown, "Drug" 4), scientists have been working hard to develop a vaccine against the virus, especially in Third World countries where the epidemic is spreading quickly (Brown, "AIDS" 10).

Again, the shortened title of an article or chapter is placed in quotation marks; the shortened title of a longer work would be italicized.

Electronic Sources of Information

If the pages in the electronic source text are numbered, include the author's last name and the page number. If, instead, the paragraphs or sections in the source text are numbered, include the author's last name and the paragraph or section number or numbers (use "par." for one paragraph, "pars." for more than one paragraph). *Separate the author's last name and the paragraph numbers with a comma.* If the source text does not number pages, paragraphs, or sections, include only the author's last name.

Consolidating MLA-Style References

Many times in papers, you will include in one paragraph information you gathered from several different sources. When you document this passage, arrange the references alphabetically by the last names of the authors and separate them with semicolons:

Example 54

> Many recent studies have examined the best treatment options for women who suffer from HIV infection (Gollub; Kalichman et al.; Wanjama, Kimani, and Lodiaga).

No page numbers are included here because the passage refers to the general topic of the articles, not to specific information in them.

FOOTNOTES AND ENDNOTES

The MLA suggests that footnotes or endnotes be used only to supply commentary or information you do not want to include in the body of your paper. Whether you are adding content notes (explanations of or elaborations on ideas you have discussed in the body of your paper) or bibliographic notes (a list of sources your readers might want to consult if they are interested in learning more about the topic you are discussing), try to keep them to a minimum because they are distracting.

Number footnotes and endnotes consecutively in the body of your essay with superscript numerals:

Example 54

> A survey of recent articles published on AIDS shows a growing interest in developing reliable research methods to test high-risk groups, such as drug abusers and prostitutes.[1]

If you are using footnotes, the citation appears at the bottom of the page on which the corresponding number appears. These notes are placed four lines below the text on the page and are single-spaced. Leave one blank line after each note. If a note carries over to the next page, place a solid typed line across the second page, two lines below the text; then continue the note two lines below that. Begin each note with the proper superscript number and indent the first line of each note five spaces or one-half inch from the left margin.

If you are using endnotes, all the citations appear in numerical order at the end of your paper on a separate page with the heading "Notes" centered one inch from the top margin. Double-space after typing this heading; then begin the citations. All the citations are double-spaced and begin with the corresponding superscript number followed by a space. Indent the first line of each note five spaces or one-half inch from the left margin.

Chapter 13

REFERENCE LISTS AND WORKS CITED ENTRIES

DEFINITION AND PURPOSE

A reference or works cited list comes at the end of your paper. In it you provide all of the bibliographic information for the sources you used when writing your essay. You have one entry for every source you refer to in the body of your paper, an entry that lists for your readers the information they would need to locate the source and read it themselves.

With in-text documentation you indicate where you found the specific information or language you used in your paper, usually including only the last name of the author and the page number on which the material is located. In your reference list you will give your reader much more information concerning this reading: the author's full name, the full title of the piece, and the place and year of publication. Also, while in-text documentation indicates a specific page where the material can be found, a reference list citation indicates all the page numbers of the reading.

A works cited or reference list is sometimes also called a *bibliography*, but actually the two are not the same. While the entry format for each is the same, in a bibliography you include an entry for every source you *consulted* when researching your paper; in a works cited list you include an entry only for the sources you actually *included* in your paper. Suppose you consulted ten books or articles when researching a topic for a paper but used only seven of them in your final draft. If your teacher asked you to put together a bibliography for your essay, you would have ten entries. If she asked you for a works cited or reference list, you would have only seven entries.

Putting together a works cited or reference list can be tedious and time-consuming because there are specific forms you have to follow, forms dictated by the type of source you are using and the style manual you are following. Your job is to follow these forms exactly. However, there is a reason for this uniformity. When you put together a works cited list in the proper form, you are providing a valuable service for your readers: when writers in a discipline agree to follow the same format for reference lists, readers can easily determine where to locate the sources that interest them because they know how to read the entries.

Complicating your efforts to put together a proper reference list is the fact that each field of study has its preferred ways of structuring entries. While the information in the entries generally stays the same across the disciplines, the order in which you present that information varies widely. As described in the previous chapter, teachers in the humanities tend to follow the guidelines established by the Modern Language Association (MLA), those in the social sciences typically employ the guidelines established by the American Psychological Association (APA), and those in the natural sciences often follow the guidelines established by the Council of Science Editors (CSE).

When putting together a works cited or reference list, your best approach is to follow the guidelines and sample entries as closely as you can, placing the information from your source exactly where it appears in the model. Pay very close attention to capitalization, spacing, and punctuation.

The samples provided below follow the guidelines of the major style manuals, but they are not comprehensive. As you write a paper, you may use types of readings not covered in this chapter. If this occurs, you can obtain a copy of each style manual at your library and follow the sample entry it contains for the type of text you are employing.

APA FORMAT

SAMPLE REFERENCE LIST ENTRIES

In an APA reference list, you include the name of the author, the title, and the publishing information for all of the readings you use in the body of your essay. You include the authors' last names and the initials of their first and middle names. If a source has more than one author, list their last names first followed by their initials and a comma; use an ampersand (&) to introduce the final name. Book and journal titles are italicized; article titles are not (neither are they placed in quotation marks). In the titles of books and articles, you capitalize only the first word of the title and subtitle (if any) and any proper nouns and proper adjectives. The format for listing the publishing information varies by the type of source, so pay close attention to the sample entries below and follow them precisely. The first line of every entry is flush with the left margin; all other lines are indented one-half inch or five spaces, and all entries end with a period.

Journal Article, One Author

Gollub, E. L. (2008). A neglected population: Drug-using women and women's methods of HIV/STI prevention. *AIDS Education & Prevention, 20* (2), 107–120.

Minkel, J. R. (2006, July). Dangling a carrot for vaccines. *Scientific American, 295,* 39–40.

- Note how the author's first and middle initials are used.
- Note where the year of publication is noted (because *Scientific American* is a monthly magazine, the month of publication is included as well).
- Note how the title of the article is not placed in quotation marks.
- Note which words are capitalized and which are not in the title of the article.
- Note how the journal title and volume numbers are italicized.

Journal Article, Two Authors

Broadhead, R. S., & Heckathorn, D. D. (1994). AIDS prevention outreach among injection drug users: Agency problems and new approaches. *Social Problems, 41,* 473–495.

- Note the order of the names: last name first followed by initials. The names are separated by a comma and the second name is introduced by an ampersand.
- The year of publication comes next, noted parenthetically.
- Note that the "A" in "Agency" is capitalized because it is the first word in the subtitle.
- Note that the volume number follows the title of the journal; it is also italicized.

Journal Article, Three to Six Authors

Kalichman, S., Eaton, L., Cain, D., Cherry, C., Pope, H., & Kalichman, M. (2006). HIV treatment beliefs and sexual transmission risk behaviors among HIV positive men and women. *Journal of Behavioral Medicine, 29,* 401–410.

- When there are three to six authors, list all of their names.

Journal Article, More Than Six Authors

Laga, M., Alary, M., Nzila, N., Manoka, A. T., Tuliza, M., Behets, F., et al. (1994). Condom promotion, sexually transmitted diseases treatment, and declining incidence of HIV-1 infection in female Zairian sex workers. *The Lancet, 344,* 246–248.

- When there are more than six authors, list the first six then include "et al." to indicate that the piece has additional authors.
- When you cite an article like this in the body of your essay, you will use the first author's surname followed by "et al." (Laga, et al., 1994).

Journal Article from Periodical with Continuous Pagination

Many academic journals employ **continuous pagination**: they number the pages of each volume consecutively even if that volume is published in several issues. For example, many academic journals are published quarterly—a single volume of the journal is published in four "numbers" or "issues" over the course of a year: volume 100, issue 1; volume 100, issue 2; and so forth. Suppose volume 100, issue 1, is published in April and contains 200 pages: the first page would be numbered "1" and the last page "200." Suppose volume 100, issue 2, is published in July of the same year: with continuous pagination, its first page number would be "201."

In a reference list citation for a journal using continuous pagination, you do not need to include the source's issue number or the month it was published. You need to include only the volume and page numbers:

Mitchell, R. E., Florin, P., & Stevenson, J. F. (2002). Supporting community-based prevention and health promotion initiatives: Developing effective technical assistance systems. *Health Education & Behavior, 29,* 620–639.

- Note that the volume number and specific page number of the article follow the title of the journal. You do not include the issue number.

Journal Article from Periodical without Continuous Pagination

When a journal does not employ continuous pagination, every issue of the journal begins with page "1." When this is the case, your citation needs to include both volume and issue numbers. The issue number follows the volume number, is noted parenthetically, and is not italicized:

Gollub, E. L. (2008). A neglected population: Drug-using women and women's methods of HIV/STI prevention. *AIDS Education & Prevention, 20* (2), 107–120.

- Note the order of information at the end of the citation and the punctuation: include the title of the journal and the volume number (both italicized), the issue number (noted parenthetically but not italicized), then the inclusive page numbers.

Article from a Monthly Periodical

Minkel, J. R. (2006, July). Dangling a carrot for vaccines. *Scientific American, 295,* 39–40.

- For a monthly periodical, indicate the month of publication after the year, separating the two with a comma.
- Be sure to include the volume number as well, after the journal title.

Article from a Weekly Periodical

Clinton, B. (2006, May 15). My quest to improve care. *Newsweek, 147,* 50–52.

- Indicate the month and day of publication after the year, separating the year and month with a comma.
- Include the volume number after the journal title.

Newspaper Article

Dugger, C. W. (2008, March 9). Rift over AIDS treatment lingers in South Africa. *New York Times,* p. 8.

Chase, M. (2005, April 20). Panel suggests a Peace Corps to fight AIDS. *Wall Street Journal,* pp. B1, B5.

- Note the placement of the date: year followed by month and day, with a comma separating the year and month.
- The title of the newspaper is capitalized and italicized.
- Precede the page number with "p." if the article is on one page and with "pp." if it runs longer than one page.

Newspaper Article, No Author

Children and AIDS. (2005, February 16). *New York Times,* p. 16.

- When there is no author, begin the citation with the title.
- Note how the section is noted with the page number when the newspaper is divided into sections.

Book with One Author

Hinds, M. J. (2008). *Fighting the AIDS and HIV epidemic: A global battle.* Berkeley Heights, NJ: Enslow.

- Note that the order of information for citing a book parallels the order of information for citing an article.
- Book titles are italicized. The first word in the title is capitalized and so are all proper nouns and proper adjectives and the first word in the subtitle.
- Following the title, indicate the city of publication and the publisher.

Books with Multiple Authors

Douglas, P. H., & Pinsky, L. (1991). *The essential AIDS fact book.* New York: Pocket Books.

Wanjama, L. N., Kimani, E. N., & Lodiaga, M. L. (2007). *HIV and AIDS: The pandemic*. Nairobi: Jomo Kenyatta Foundation.

- List multiple authors by their last names and initials, separating them with commas, and using an ampersand to introduce the final author.
- If a book has more than six authors, list all of their names in your reference citation, but in the body of your paper, when you cite them parenthetically for documentation, use only the first author's name followed by "et al." and the year of publication.

Two or More Works by the Same Person

Squire, Corinne. (1997). *AIDS panic*. New York: Routledge.

Squire, Corinne. (2007). *HIV in South Africa: Talking about the big thing*. London: Routledge.

- Arrange the citations in chronological order, the earliest first.

Book, Corporate Author

National Gay and Lesbian Task Force. (1987). *Anti-gay violence: Victimization and defamation in 1986*. New York: Author.

- If the publisher is the same as the corporate author, simply write "Author" after the city where the work was published.

Book, Later Edition

Fan, H. Y., Conner, R. F., & Villarreal, L. (2007). *AIDS: Science and society* (5th ed.). Sudbury, MA: Jones and Bartlett.

- If you are using a later edition of a book, list the edition number parenthetically after the title.

Edited Book

Cohen, A., & Gorman, J. M. (Eds.). (2008). *Comprehensive textbook of AIDS psychiatry*. New York: Oxford University Press.

- If one person edited the book, place "(Ed.)" after his name. If more than one person edited the work, place "(Eds.)" after their names.
- Pay particular attention to the periods in this citation. It is easy to leave some of them out.

Book, No Author or Editor

Corporate responses to HIV/AIDS: Case studies from India. (2007). Washington, DC: World Bank.

- When the title page of a book lists no author, begin your citation with the title.
- Note that in this entry, the edition number precedes the year of publication.

Multivolume Book

Daintith, J., Mitchell, S., & Tootill, E. (Eds.). (1981). *A biographical encyclopedia of scientists* (Vols. 1–2). New York: Facts on File.

- Indicate for your reader how many volumes comprise the work. This information follows the title.

One Volume of a Multivolume Book

Daintith, J., Mitchell, S., & Tootill, E. (Eds.). (1981). *A biographical encyclopedia of scientists* (Vol. 1). New York: Facts on File.

- When you use just one volume of a multivolume work, indicate the volume number parenthetically after the title.

English Translation of a Book

Jager, H. (Ed.). (1988). *AIDS phobia: Disease pattern and possibilities of treatment* (J. Welch, Trans.). New York: Halsted Press.

- Open the citation with the name of the author or editor.
- Following the title, give the translator's name followed by "Trans."
- Note that in giving the translator's name, you begin with her initials, followed by the last name.
- Again, pay attention to all the periods included in this citation.

Article or Chapter from an Anthology

Many times in writing a source-based paper you will use a work contained in an anthology of readings. When this is the case, follow this format in your reference list:

Bethell, T. (2006). The African AIDS epidemic is exaggerated. In Leone, D. A. (Ed.), *Responding to the AIDS epidemic* (pp. 18–22). Detroit: Greenhaven Press.

Patton, C. (1993). With champagne and roses: Women at risk from/in AIDS discourse. In C. Squire (Ed.), *Women and AIDS* (pp. 165–187). London: Sage.

- Open your citation with the name of the author whose ideas or language you included in your paper. Your in-text documentation for this source would be "(Patton, 1993)."
- Next, give the title of the specific reading you referred to in the body of your essay.

- Next, give the name of the author or editor of the anthology and the larger work's title (the title of the book is italicized). Precede this information with the word "In" (note capitalization).
- Follow the title with the specific page numbers on which the article can be found. In this case, Patton's article can be found on pages 165–187 of Squire's book; Bethell's article can be found on pages 18–22 of Leone's book.
- Close the entry with the publishing information.

Article in a Reference Work

Acquired immune deficiency syndrome. (1990). In *The new encyclopaedia Britannica* (Vol. 1, p. 67). Chicago: Encyclopaedia Britannica.

Haseltine, W. A. (1992). AIDS. In *Encyclopedia Americana* (Vol. 1, pp. 365–366). Danbury, CT: Grolier.

- When the entry in the reference work is signed, begin the citation with the author's name; when it is not signed, begin the citation with the title of the entry.
- Include the year the reference work was published, the title of the work (italicized), the volume number and inclusive page numbers of the entry (noted parenthetically), followed by the publishing information.

Personal Interview

Under APA guidelines, all personal communications are to be cited in the text only. Include the name of the person you interviewed (first and middle initials, full last name), the words "personal communication," and the date of the interview (month, day, year), all separated by commas:

(F. Smith, personal communication, June 24, 1995)

Electronic Sources of Information

The standards for citing electronic sources of information are still in flux. You can find the most current version of the APA's standards online at www.apa.style.org/elecref.html.

   In 2007, APA updated its guidelines for including electronic sources of information in reference lists. The major changes include these:

- When possible, include the Digital Object Indicator (DOI) number rather than the URL for online articles.
- Still include the URL for online reference sources, such as dictionaries and encyclopedias.
- Including the name of the database used to locate online articles is no longer required.
- Include the retrieval date only if the material is likely to be changed or updated.

Information on CD-ROM or Diskette

AIDS. (1995). *The 1995 Grolier multimedia encyclopedia.* [CD]. Danbury, CT: Grolier.

- List the name of the author or authors (if known), last name first followed by first and middle initials. Because this source text has no author, the entry begins with the title.
- List the date of publication in parentheses.
- Give the title of the chapter or entry you consulted for your paper.
- Give the title of the publication that contained the chapter or entry.
- Indicate the electronic medium (i.e., CD) in square brackets.
- List the publication information.

Online Information Databank

AIDS. (2008). In *Encyclopaedia Brittanica Online.* Retrieved July 1, 2008, from http://www.britannica.com

- Give the author's name. If the entry is unsigned, begin with the entry's title.
- Give the date of publication.
- Give the title of the database (preceded by "In").
- Give the retrieval date.
- Give the database's URL.
- DO NOT end the entry with a period (someone might think the period is part of the URL).

Article from an Online Publication

This is the format to use if your source text exists only electronically. If the article does not also appear in print somewhere, use this form for your reference list entry:

Ambinder, M. (2007, December 8). Huck and AIDS. Retrieved from http://theatlantic.com

- Give the name of the author followed by the date of publication.
- Give the title of the article.
- Give the URL where the article can be retrieved.
- You do not need to give the date of retrieval.

Previously Published Article Found Online

Underwood, A. (1999, February 8). How the plague began. *Newsweek, 133,* 59. Retrieved from http://www.newsweek.com

Kalichman, S. C., Eaton, L., Cain, D., Cherry, C., Pope, H., & Kalichman, M. (2006). HIV treatment beliefs and sexual transmission risk behaviors among HIV positive men and women. *Journal of Behavioral Medicine, 29*(5), 401–410. doi: 10.1007/s10865-006-9066-3

- Give the name of the author(s).
- Give the date of publication.
- Give the title of the article.
- Give the journal's title and volume number (along with the issue number when relevant).
- Give the inclusive page numbers of the article.
- If the article has a DOI indicator, give it.
- If the article does not have a DOI indicator, give the retrieval URL.

E-Mail

The fifth edition of APA's *Publication Manual* considers e-mail messages to be "personal communication," which should be cited in text only. In parentheses, include the name of the person who sent you the e-mail message (first and middle initials followed by the full last name), the words "personal communication," and the date of the communication (month, day, year):

(F. Smith, personal communication, December 1, 1998).

SAMPLE APA-STYLE REFERENCE LIST

List all of your references at the end of your paper, beginning the list on a new page. At the top of the page, center the word "References." After the heading, double-space and list your citations in alphabetical order according to the last name of the author or first key word in the title if there is no author. Indent the first line of every citation five spaces or one-half inch, and double-space all entries.

References

AIDS. (2008). In *Encyclopaedia Brittanica Online*. Retrieved July 1, 2008, from http://www.britannica.com

Ambinder, M. (2007, December 8). Huck and AIDS. Retrieved from http://www.theatlantic.com

Bethell, T. (2006). The African AIDS epidemic is exaggerated. In Leone, D. A. (Ed.), *Responding to the AIDS epidemic* (pp. 18–22). Detroit: Greenhaven Press.

Chase, M. (2005, April 20). Panel suggests a Peace Corps to fight AIDS. *Wall Street Journal*, pp. B1, B5.

Children and AIDS. (2005, February 16). *New York Times*, p. 16.

Clinton, B. (2006, May 15). My quest to improve care. *Newsweek, 147*, 50–52.

Cohen, A., & Gorman, J. M. (Eds.). (2008). *Comprehensive textbook of AIDS psychiatry*. New York: Oxford University Press.

Corporate responses to HIV/AIDS: Case studies from India. (2007). Washington, DC: World Bank.

Douglas, P. H., & Pinsky, L. (1991). *The essential AIDS fact book*. New York: Pocket Books.

Dugger, C. W. (2008, March 9). Rift over AIDS treatment lingers in South Africa. *New York Times*, p. 8.

Fan, H. Y., Conner, R. F., & Villarreal, L. (2007). *AIDS: Science and society* (5th ed.). Sudbury, MA: Jones and Bartlett.

Gollub, E. L. (2008). A neglected population: Drug-using women and women's methods of HIV/STI prevention. *AIDS Education & Prevention, 20* (2), 107–120.

Hinds, M. J. (2008). *Fighting the AIDS and HIV epidemic: A global battle*. Berkeley Heights, NJ: Enslow.

Kalichman, S. C., Eaton, L., Cain, D., Cherry, C., Pope, H., & Kalichman, M. (2006). HIV treatment beliefs and sexual transmission risk behaviors among HIV positive men and women. *Journal of Behavioral Medicine, 29* (5), 401–410. doi: 10.1007/s10865-006-9066-3

Laga, M., Alary, M., Nzila, N., Manoka, A. T., Tuliza, M., Behets, F., et al. (1994). Condom promotion, sexually transmitted diseases treatment, and declining incidence of HIV-1 infection in female Zairian sex workers. *The Lancet, 344*, 246–248.

Minkel, J. R. (2006, July). Dangling a carrot for vaccines. *Scientific American, 295*, 39–40.

Mitchell, R. E., Florin, P., & Stevenson, J. F. (2002). Supporting community-based prevention and health promotion initiatives: Developing effective technical assistance systems. *Health Education & Behavior, 29*, 620–639.

Squire, Corinne. (1997). *AIDS panic*. New York: Routledge.

Squire, Corinne. (2007). *HIV in South Africa: Talking about the big thing*. London: Routledge.

Underwood, A. (1999, February 8). How the plague began. *Newsweek, 133*, 59. Retrieved from http://www.newsweek.com

Wanjama, L. N., Kimani, E. N., & Lodiaga, M. L. (2007). *HIV and AIDS: The pandemic*. Nairobi: Jomo Kenyatta Foundation.

CSE FORMAT

SAMPLE REFERENCE LIST ENTRIES

The CSE style manual describes two different ways of citing material in papers—the citation-sequence system and the name-year system—and two corresponding types of reference list citations. The material contained in both types of citation is the same, but the order of the information and some of the punctuation are different. The CSE style manual also notes that individual scientific journals may require slightly different versions of these two basic types of citation. Therefore, as you examine the models offered below, keep in mind that you might see slight variations in the journals you consult while doing research. As always, if you have any question concerning proper form, consult your instructor or the style manual itself.

In general, CSE citations include the author's last name followed by first and middle initials, the title of the work, and publication information. The names of multiple authors are separated by commas. Article and book titles are not underlined, italicized, or placed in quotation marks, and only the first word and any proper nouns and proper adjectives are capitalized; do not automatically capitalize the first word of a subtitle. Journal names are not underlined or italicized, and those longer than one word are abbreviated following the *American National Standard for Bibliographic References* (you can get a copy of this work from your school's reference librarian). Do not use "p" or "pp" to indicate specific page numbers: simply list the page numbers at the appropriate place in the citation. For books, include the total number of pages in the work. All entries are single-spaced and end with a period.

If you are employing the citation-sequence system, the entries in the reference list at the end of your paper will be numbered and listed in the order they are cited in the text: source "1" will be the first work listed, source "2" the second one listed, and so on. If you are using the name-year system, the sources are listed in alphabetical order by the authors' last names on the reference page at the end of your paper. Under both systems, second and subsequent lines of an entry begin under the first letter of the first line. Some journals leave a blank line between entries; some do not. See the sample reference lists below for further explanations and examples.

Journal Article, One Author

Citation-Sequence System

[1]Gollub EL. A neglected population: drug-using women and women's methods of HIV/STI prevention. AIDS Ed & Pre 2008;20(2):107–20.

- Note the punctuation of the author's name: do not include a comma after the last name or periods between the initials.
- Note the capitalization in the article title: only the first word and any proper nouns and proper adjectives are capitalized.
- The article title is neither underlined nor placed in quotation marks.
- The journal title is abbreviated without periods and is followed by year and month of publication (because *Scientific American* is a monthly

magazine), the volume number, the issue number (in parentheses), and inclusive page numbers.
- The date of publication is followed by a semicolon; the issue number is followed by a colon.
- Note the lack of spaces between the month of publication, volume number, issue number, and page numbers.

Name-Year System

Gollub EL. 2008. A neglected population: drug-using women and women's methods of HIV/STI prevention. AIDS Ed & Pre 20(2):107–20.

- Note that the year of publication follows the author's name.
- Again, note the lack of punctuation in the title and the lack of spaces between the volume number, issue number, and page numbers.

Journal Article, Two Authors

Citation-Sequence System

[2]Broadhead RS, Heckathorn DD. AIDS prevention outreach among injection drug users: agency problems and new approaches. Soc Prob 1994;41:473–95.

- Note how the authors' names are listed: last name followed by first and middle initials. There is no comma between the author's last name and his initials and no periods between the initials. The names of the authors are separated by commas.
- Note the placement of the year of publication and volume number.
- Because this journal employs continuous pagination, you do not need to list an issue number.

Name-Year System

Broadhead RS, Heckathorn DD. 1994. AIDS prevention outreach among injection drug users: agency problems and new approaches. Soc Prob 41:473–95.

- Note how to punctuate and separate the authors' names properly.
- The year of publication follows the authors' names.
- The volume number follows the title of the periodical.

Journal Article, Three to Ten Authors

Citation-Sequence System

[3]Mitchell RE, Florin P, Stevenson JF. Supporting community-based prevention and health promotion initiatives: developing effective technical assistance systems. Health Ed & Behav 2002;29(5):620–39.

[4]Kalichman S, Eaton L, Cain D, Cherry C, Pope H, Kalichman M. HIV treatment beliefs and sexual transmission risk behaviors among HIV positive men and women. J Behav Med 2002;29:401–10.

- List all of the authors up to ten. If there are more than ten authors, list the names of the first ten authors, and then write "and others."

Name-Year System

Mitchell RE, Florin P, Stevenson JF. 2002. Supporting community-based prevention and health promotion initiatives: developing effective technical assistance systems. Health Ed & Behav 29(5):620–39.

Kalichman S, Eaton L, Cain D, Cherry C, Pope H, Kalichman M. 2002. HIV treatment beliefs and sexual transmission risk behaviors among HIV positive men and women. J Behav Med 29:401–10.

- List all of the authors up to ten. If there are more than ten authors, list the names of the first ten authors, and then write "and others."

Journal Article from Periodical with Continuous Pagination

For a definition of "continuous pagination" see the APA example on page 254.

Citation-Sequence System

[2]Broadhead RS, Heckathorn DD. AIDS prevention outreach among injection drug users: agency problems and new approaches. Soc Prob 1994; 41:473–95.

- Note how the authors' names are listed: last name followed by first and middle initials. There is no comma between the author's last name and her initials and no periods between the initials. The names of the authors are separated by commas.
- Note the placement of the year of publication and volume number.
- Because this journal employs continuous pagination, you do not need to list an issue number.

Name-Year System

Broadhead RS, Heckathorn DD. 1994. AIDS prevention outreach among injection drug users: agency problems and new approaches. Soc Prob 41:473–95.

- Note how to punctuate and separate the authors' names properly.
- When a journal employs continuous pagination, you do not need to include the issue number, only the volume number.
- Be sure to list all the page numbers for the article in your citation.

Journal Article from Periodical without Continuous Pagination

Citation-Sequence System

[1]Gollub EL. A neglected population: drug-using women and women's methods of HIV/STI prevention. AIDS Ed & Pre 2008;20(2):107–20.

- When a journal does not use continuous pagination, indicate the issue number in parentheses following the volume number.

- Note the lack of spaces between the volume number, the issue number, and the page numbers.

Name-Year System

Gollub EL. 2008. A neglected population: drug-using women and women's methods of HIV/STI prevention. AIDS Ed & Pre 20(2):107–20.

- Note the issue number parenthetically following the volume number.
- Note where the year of publication is placed.

Article from a Monthly Periodical

Citation-Sequence System

[5]Minkel JR. Dangling a carrot for vaccines. Sci Am 2006 Jul;295(1):39–40.

- Indicate the month of publication after the year of publication.
- Be sure to include the volume and issue numbers as well.

Name-Year System

Minkel JR. 2006 Jul. Dangling a carrot for vaccines. Sci Am 295(1):39–40.

or

Minkel JR. 2006. Dangling a carrot for vaccines. Sci Am 295(1):39–40.

- Note that the year of publication follows the author's name.
- Including the month of publication is optional.
- Again, note the lack of punctuation in the title and the lack of spaces between the volume number, issue number, and page numbers.

Article from a Weekly Periodical

Citation-Sequence System

[6]Clinton B. My quest to improve care. Newsweek 2006 May 15;147(20):50–2.

- Indicate the month and day of publication following the year.
- Note the lack of punctuation between the year, month, and day.

Name-Year System

Clinton B. 2006 May 15. My quest to improve care. Newsweek 147(20):50–2.

- Indicate the year, month, and day of publication after the author's name. Do not place commas between the year, month, and day.
- Note the issue number parenthetically after the volume number.

Newspaper Article

Citation-Sequence System

[7]Dugger CW. Rift over AIDS treatment lingers in South Africa. New York Times 2008 Mar 9; 8(col 1).

- After indicating the author and title of the piece, give the title of the newspaper (note that the title is not underlined).
- Next, give the year, month, and day of publication followed by the section (if applicable) and page and column numbers where the article begins.

Name-Year System

Dugger CW. 2008 Mar 9. Rift over AIDS treatment lingers in South Africa. New York Times;8(col 1).

- Note how the year, month, and day of publication follow the author's name.

Newspaper Article, No Author

Citation-Sequence System

[8]Chase M. Panel suggests a Peace Corps to fight AIDS. Wall Street Journal 2005 Apr 20;Sect B:1(col 2).

[9][Anonymous]. Children and AIDS. New York Times 2005 Feb 22;16(col 1).

- In place of the author's last name, write "Anonymous" in square brackets.

Name-Year System

Chase M. 2005 Apr 20. Panel suggests a Peace Corps to fight AIDS. Wall Street Journal;Sect B:1(col 2).

[Anonymous]. 2005 Feb 22. Children and AIDS. New York Times;16(col 1).

- "Anonymous" in square brackets takes the place of the author's name.

Book with One Author

Citation-Sequence System

[10]Hinds MJ. Fighting the AIDS and HIV epidemic: a global battle. Berkeley Heights, NJ: Enslow; 2008. 128 p.

- Note the way author's name is arranged, capitalized, and punctuated: last name first followed by initials. No comma between the last name and the initials, no periods between the initials.
- Note that book titles are not underlined or italicized.
- In book titles, only the first word and proper nouns and proper adjectives are capitalized.
- A semicolon precedes the date of publication and a period follows.
- At the end of the entry, give the total number of pages in the book.

Name-Year System

Hinds MJ. 2008. Fighting the AIDS and HIV epidemic: a global battle. Berkeley Heights, NJ: Enslow. 128 p.

- Here, the year of publication follows the author's name.
- Be sure to include the total number of pages in the book.

Book with Two or More Authors

Citation-Sequence System

[11]Douglas PH, Pinsky L. The essential AIDS fact book. New York: Pocket Books; 1991. 108 p.

[12]Wanjama LN, Kimani EN, Lodiaga ML. HIV and AIDS: the pandemic. Nairobi: Jomo Kenyatta Foundation; 2007. 128 p.

- If a book has multiple authors, list all of them, last name first followed by initials. Use commas to separate authors.

Name-Year System

Douglas PH, Pinsky L. 1991. The essential AIDS fact book. New York: Pocket Books. 108 p.

Wanjama LN, Kimani EN, Lodiaga ML. 2007. HIV and AIDS: the pandemic. Nairobi: Jomo Kenyatta Foundation. 128 p.

- Note where to place the year of publication and how to separate the authors' names.

Two or More Works by the Same Person

Citation-Sequence System

[13]Squire C. AIDS panic. New York: Routledge; 1997. 254 p.

[14]Squire C. HIV in South Africa: talking about the big thing. London: Routledge; 2007. 229 p.

Name-Year System

Squire C. 1997. AIDS panic. New York: Routledge. 254 p.

Squire C. 2007. HIV in South Africa: talking about the big thing. London: Routledge. 229 p.

- Arrange the citations in chronological order, the earliest first.

Book, Corporate Author

Citation-Sequence System

[15] National Gay and Lesbian Task Force. Anti-gay violence: victimization and defamation in 1986. New York: National Gay and Lesbian Task Force; 1987. 113 p.

- List the corporate author first.
- Note that the first word of a subtitle is not capitalized.

Name-Year System

[NGLTF] National Gay and Lesbian Task Force. 1987. Anti-gay violence: victimization and defamation in 1986. New York: NGLTF. 113 p.

- With the name-year system, open the entry with an abbreviation of the corporation's name; you can use this abbreviation for in-text documentation, as well.

Book, Later Edition

Citation-Sequence System

[16]Fan HY, Connor RF, Villarreal L. AIDS: science and society. 5th ed. Sudbury, MA: Jones and Bartlett; 2007. 252 p.

- If you use a later edition of a book, list the edition number after the title.

Name-Year System

Fan HY, Connor RF, Villarreal L. 2007. AIDS: science and society. 5th ed. Sudbury, MA: Jones and Bartlett. 252 p.

- Again, the edition number follows the title of the book.

Edited Book

Citation-Sequence System

[17]Cohen A, Gorman JM, editors. Comprehensive textbook of AIDS psychiatry. New York: Oxford UP; 2008. 619 p.

- Write "editor" after the editor's name, "editors" if more than one person edited the work.
- Note that there is no period after the editor's initials.
- Note the semicolon between the publisher's name and the year of publication.

Name-Year System

Cohen A, Gorman JM, editors. 2008. Comprehensive textbook of AIDS psychiatry. New York: Oxford UP. 619 p.

- The year of publication follows the editor's name.

Book, No Author or Editor

Citation-Sequence System

[18][Anonymous]. Corporate responses to HIV/AIDS: case studies from India. Washington, DC: World Bank; 2007. 88 p.

- If there is no author, open the entry with "Anonymous" placed in square brackets.

Name-Year System

[Anonymous]. 2007. Corporate responses to HIV/AIDS: case studies from India. Washington, DC: World Bank. 88 p.

Multivolume Book

Citation-Sequence System

[19]Daintith J, Mitchell S, Tootill E. A biographical encyclopedia of scientists. 2 volumes. New York: Facts on File; 1981. 935 p.

- For multivolume works, indicate the total number of volumes between the book title and city of publication.

Name-Year System

Daintith J, Mitchell S, Tootill E. 1981. A biographical encyclopedia of scientists. 2 volumes. New York: Facts on File. 935 p.

One Volume of a Multivolume Book

Citation-Sequence System

[20]Daintith J, Mitchell S, Tootill E. A biographical encyclopedia of scientists. Volume 1. New York: Facts on File; 1981. 458 p.

- If you use only one volume of a multivolume work, list that volume number after the title.
- If the volume has a separate title, give it after the volume number, preceded by a comma.

Name-Year System

Daintith J, Mitchell S, Tootill E. 1981. A biographical encyclopedia of scientists. Volume 1. New York: Facts on File. 458 p.

English Translation of a Book

Citation-Sequence System

[21]Jager H, editor. AIDS phobia: disease pattern and possibilities of treatment. Welch J, translator. New York: Halsted; 1988. 124 p. Translation of: AIDS-phobie.

- First, list the author or editor of the work, then the translated title.
- Next, give the name of the translator, last name first followed by "translator."
- Following the publication information, give the original title of the work.

Name-Year System

Jager H, editor. 1988. AIDS phobia: disease pattern and possibilities of treatment. Welch J, translator. New York: Halsted. 124 p. Translation of: AIDS-phobie.

Article or Chapter from an Anthology

Citation-Sequence System

[22]Bethell T. The African AIDS epidemic is exaggerated. In: Leone DA, editor. Responding to the AIDS Epidemic. Detroit: Greenhaven; 2006. p 18–22.

- Begin with the name of the author who wrote the article you are using.
- Next, give the title of the piece you use in your paper.
- Next, give the name of the person who edited the longer work, last name first, preceded by "In" and a colon.
- Next, give the title of the longer piece that contains the material you are using.
- Close with the publication information and the inclusive page numbers of the article, preceded with "p" for an article of any length.

Name-Year System

Bethell T. 2006. The African AIDS epidemic is exaggerated. In: Leone DA, editor. Responding to the AIDS Epidemic. Detroit: Greenhaven. p 18–22.

- Note where the year of publication is included.
- Note the period following the publisher.

Article in a Reference Work

The CSE style manual offers no specific instructions on how to cite entries from reference works. However, a survey of scientific journals shows that a common practice is to follow the form used for a work contained in a collection of essays (the preceding form).

Citation-Sequence System

[23][Anonymous]. Acquired immune deficiency syndrome. In: The new encyclopaedia Britannica. Volume 1. Chicago: Encyclopaedia Britannica; 1990. p 67.

[24]Haseltine WA. AIDS. In: Encyclopedia Americana. Volume 1. Danbury, CT: Grolier; 1992. p 365–6.

- When the piece in the reference work is signed, begin your entry with the writer's name; when it is not, begin with "Anonymous" in square brackets.
- Include the title of the entry and volume number of the reference work.
- Include the page number or numbers of the entry.

Name-Year System

[Anonymous]. 1990. Acquired immune deficiency syndrome. In: The new encyclopaedia Britannica. Volume 1. Chicago: Encyclopaedia Britannica. p 67.

Haseltine WA. 1992. AIDS. In: Encyclopedia Americana. Volume 1. Danbury, CT: Grolier. p 365–6.

- Note where you place the year of publication.

Personal Interview

Personal communications are noted only in text, not in reference lists. After the material, place in parentheses the words "personal communication."

Electronic Sources of Information

The sixth edition of the CSE style manual offers little guidance on constructing reference list entries for electronic sources of information. The sample entries offered below are based on current practice.

Information on CD-ROM or Diskette

Citation-Sequence System

[25][Anonymous]. AIDS. In: The 1995 Grolier multimedia encyclopedia. [CD-ROM]. Version 7.05. Danbury, CT: Grolier; 1995.

- Give the name of the author or authors. If none is listed, put "Anonymous" in square brackets followed by a period.
- Give the title of the chapter or entry you referred to in the body of your paper.
- Give the complete title of the work, preceded by "In" and a colon.
- Indicate the electronic medium (i.e., CD-ROM or diskette) in square brackets.
- Give the version or edition number.
- Supply the publication information: city of publication, publisher, and date of publication.
- Titles of entries or chapters are not placed in quotation marks, and titles of complete works are not underlined.
- Note which words are capitalized in the title of the complete work.

Name-Year System

[Anonymous]. 1995. AIDS. In: The 1995 Grolier multimedia encyclopedia. [CD-ROM]. Version 7.05. Danbury, CT: Grolier.

- Give the name of the author or authors. If none is listed, put "Anonymous" in square brackets followed by a period.
- Give the date of publication.
- Give the title of the chapter or entry you referred to in the body of your paper.
- Give the complete title of the work, preceded by "In" and a colon.
- Indicate the electronic medium (i.e., CD-ROM or diskette) in square brackets.

- Give the version or edition number.
- Supply the remaining publication information: city of publication and publisher.

Online Information Databank

Citation-Sequence System

[26][Anonymous]. AIDS. In: Encyclopaedia Britannica online. 1999. Available via the Internet; http://www.eb.com. Accessed 1999 July 22.

- Give the name of the author or authors. If none is listed, put "Anonymous" in square brackets followed by a period.
- Give the title of the chapter or entry that supplied the information you used in your paper.
- Give the title of the database you consulted.
- Give the date the database was published or last updated.
- Give the URL of the database.
- Give the date you accessed the information.

Name-Year System

[Anonymous]. 1999. AIDS. In: Encyclopaedia Britannica online. Available via the Internet; http://www.eb.com. Accessed 1999 July 22.

- Give the name of the author or authors. If none is listed, put "Anonymous" in square brackets followed by a period.
- Give the date of publication.
- Give the title of the chapter or entry that supplied the information you used in your paper.
- Give the title of the database you consulted.
- Give the electronic address of the database.
- Give the date you accessed the information.

Article from an Online Publication

Citation-Sequence System

[27]Ambinder M. Huck and AIDS. TheAtlantic.com [serial online]. 2007 Dec 8. Available from: http://www.theatlantic.com. Accessed 2008 Jul 2.

- Give the name of the author or authors (last name first followed by initials).
- Give the title of the article.
- Give the title of the online publication.
- Give the type of medium (e.g., online monograph or online serial) in square brackets.
- Give the date of publication.
- Give the availability information (the search engine used to locate the source text).
- Give the date you accessed the information.

Name-Year System

Ambinder M. Huck and AIDS. 2007 Dec 8. TheAtlantic.com [serial online]. Available from: http://www.theatlantic.com. Accessed 2008 July 2.

- Give the name of the author or authors (last name first followed by initials).
- Give the date of publication.
- Give the title of the article.
- Give the title of the online publication.
- Give the type of medium (e.g., online monograph or online serial) in square brackets.
- Give the availability information (the search engine used to locate the source text).
- Give the date you accessed the information.

Previously Published Article Found Online

Citation-Sequence System

[28]Shadlen KC. The political economy of AIDS treatment: intellectual property and the transformation of generic supply. Internat Stu Q [online] 2007;51(3):559–81. Available from: Academic Search Complete via the Internet. Accessed 2008 July 5.

- Give the name of the author or authors.
- Give the title of the article.
- Give the title of the magazine or journal.
- Indicate, in square brackets, the electronic medium.
- Give the publication information of the magazine or journal article. (Because *Newsweek* is a weekly publication, list the day, month, and year of publication along with the volume and issue numbers.)
- Indicate the search engine that was used to find the article.
- Give the date of access.

Name-Year System

Shadlen KC. 2007. The political economy of AIDS treatment: intellectual property and the transformation of generic supply. Internat Stu Q [online]; 51(3):559–81. Available from: Academic Search Complete via the Internet. Accessed 2008 July 5.

- Give the name of the author or authors.
- Give the date of publication.
- Give the title of the article.
- Give the title of the magazine or journal.
- Indicate, in square brackets, the electronic medium.
- Give the volume number, issue number, and pagination for the magazine or journal article.
- Indicate the search engine that was used to find the article.
- Give the date of access.

E-Mail

Personal communications are noted only in the text, not in reference lists. After the material, place in parentheses the words "e-mail communication" or "personal communication."

SAMPLE CSE-STYLE REFERENCE LISTS

Begin your reference list on a new page at the end of your paper under the heading "References" or "Cited References" centered at the top of the page. Double-space after the heading and begin your citations.

If you are using the citation-sequence system in your paper, the reference entries will be numbered and listed in the order they are cited in the text. Source "1" will be the first work listed, source "2" the second one listed, and so on. If you list your sources on the reference page using superscript numerals, align the second and subsequent lines of an entry under the first letter of the first line. If, instead, you list your sources with standard numerals, follow the number with a period, and then indent five spaces. Align the second and subsequent lines of an entry under the first letter of the first line. Here are two examples:

[1]Greene WC. AIDS and the immune system. Sci Am 1993 Sep;269(3):99–105.

[2]Broadhead RS, Heckathorn DD. AIDS prevention outreach among injection drug users: agency problems and new approaches. Soc Prob 1994;41:473–95.

1. Greene WC. AIDS and the immune system. Sci Am 1993 Sep;269(3):99–105.
2. Broadhead RS, Heckathorn DD. AIDS prevention outreach among injection drug users: agency problems and new approaches. Soc Prob 1994;41:473–95.

If you are using the name-year system, the entries are listed in alphabetical order by the authors' last names. Begin every line of these entries on the left margin. Some journals leave a blank line between entries; some do not. See the sample reference lists below for examples.

Citation-Sequence Format

References

[1]Gollub EL. A neglected population: drug-using women and women's methods of HIV/STI prevention. AIDS Ed & Pre 2008; 20(2):107–20.

[2]Broadhead RS, Heckathorn DD. AIDS prevention outreach among injection drug users: agency problems and new approaches. Soc Prob 1994;41:473–95.

[3]Mitchell RE, Florin P, Stevenson JF. Supporting community-based prevention and health promotion initiatives: developing effective technical assistance systems. Health Ed & Behav 2002;29(5):620–39.

[4]Kalichman S, Eaton L, Cain D, Cherry C, Pope H, Kalichman M. HIV treatment beliefs and sexual transmission risk behaviors among HIV positive men and women. J Behav Med 2002;29:401–10.

[5]Minkel JR. Dangling a carrot for vaccines. Sci Am 2006 Jul;295(1):39–40.

[6]Clinton B. My quest to improve care. Newsweek 2006 May 15;147(20):50–2.

[7]Dugger CW. Rift over AIDS treatment lingers in South Africa. New York Times 2008 Mar 9; 8(col 1).

[8]Chase M. Panel suggests a Peace Corps to fight AIDS. Wall Street Journal 2005 Apr 20;Sect B:1(col 2).

[9][Anonymous]. Children and AIDS. New York Times 2005 Feb 22;16(col 1).

[10]Hinds MJ. Fighting the AIDS and HIV epidemic: a global battle. Berkeley Heights, NJ: Enslow; 2008. 128 p.

[11]Douglas PH, Pinsky L. The essential AIDS fact book. New York: Pocket Books; 1991. 108 p.

[12]Wanjama LN, Kimani EN, Lodiaga ML. HIV and AIDS: the pandemic. Nairobi: Jomo Kenyatta Foundation; 2007. 128 p.

[13]Squire C. AIDS panic. New York: Routledge; 1997. 254 p.

[14]Squire C. HIV in South Africa: talking about the big thing. London: Routledge; 2007. 229 p.

[15]National Gay and Lesbian Task Force. Anti-gay violence: victimization and defamation in 1986. New York: NGLTF. 113p.

[16]Fan HY, Connor RF, Villarreal L. AIDS: science and society. 5th ed. Sudbury, MA: Jones and Bartlett; 2007. 252 p.

[17]Cohen A, Gorman JM, editors. Comprehensive textbook of AIDS psychiatry. New York: Oxford UP; 2008. 619 p.

[18][Anonymous]. Corporate responses to HIV/AIDS: case studies from India. Washington, DC: World Bank; 2007. 88 p.

Name-Year Format

References

Ambinder M. Huck and AIDS. 2007 Dec 8. TheAtlantic.com [serial online]. Available from: http://www.theatlantic.com. Accessed 2008 July 2.

[Anonymous]. 2005 Feb 22. Children and AIDS. New York Times;16(col 1).

[Anonymous]. 2007. Corporate responses to HIV/AIDS: case studies from India. Washington, DC: World Bank. 88 p.

Bethell T. 2006. The African AIDS epidemic is exaggerated. In: Leone DA, editor. Responding to the AIDS Epidemic. Detroit: Greenhaven. p 18–22.

Chase M. 2005 Apr 20. Panel suggests a Peace Corps to fight AIDS. Wall Street Journal;Sect B:1(col 2).

Clinton B. 2006 May 15. My quest to improve care. Newsweek 147(20):50–2.

Cohen A, Gorman JM, editors. 2008. Comprehensive textbook of AIDS psychiatry. New York: Oxford UP. 619 p.

Douglas PH, Pinsky L. 1991. The essential AIDS fact book. New York: Pocket Books. 108 p.

Dugger CW. 2008 Mar 9. Rift over AIDS treatment lingers in South Africa. New York Times;8(col 1).

Fan HY, Connor RF, Villarreal L. 2007. AIDS: science and society. 5th ed. Sudbury, MA: Jones and Bartlett. 252 p.

Gollub EL. 2008. A neglected population: drug-using women and women's methods of HIV/STI prevention. AIDS Ed & Pre 20(2):107–20.

Hinds MJ. 2008. Fighting the AIDS and HIV epidemic: a global battle. Berkeley Heights, NJ: Enslow. 128 p.

Kalichman S, Eaton L, Cain D, Cherry C, Pope H, Kalichman M. 2002. HIV treatment beliefs and sexual transmission risk behaviors among HIV positive men and women. J Behav Med 29:401–10.

Minkel JR. 2006 Jul. Dangling a carrot for vaccines. Sci Am 295(1):39–40

Mitchell RE, Florin P, Stevenson JF. 2002. Supporting community-based prevention and health promotion initiatives: developing effective technical assistance systems. Health Ed & Behav 29(5):620–39.

Shadlen KC. 2007. The political economy of AIDS treatment: intellectual property and the transformation of generic supply. Internat Stu Q [online]; 51(3):559–81. Available from: Academic Search Complete via the Internet. Accessed 2008 July 5.

Squire C. 1997. AIDS panic. New York: Routledge. 254 p.

Squire Corinne. 2007. HIV in South Africa: talking about the big thing. London: Routledge. 229 p.

Wanjama LN, Kimani EN, Lodiaga ML. 2007. HIV and AIDS: the pandemic. Nairobi: Jomo Kenyatta Foundation. 128 p.

MLA FORMAT

SAMPLE WORKS CITED ENTRIES

In a works cited list following MLA style, include the name of the author and full title of the works you cited in the body of your essay, along with relevant publication information. When listing the authors, include their full names, last name first. Titles of articles are placed in quotation marks; titles of books are italicized. In titles, the first and last words are capitalized along with any key words, proper nouns, and proper adjectives in between. Journal titles are italicized, and you should list all the pages you read in the source text. Do not precede page numbers with "p." or "pg."; simply list inclusive page numbers. Finally, MLA style employs reversed indentation: begin the first line of each entry at the left margin and indent all subsequent lines one-half inch or five spaces.

Note: 2008 saw the publication of the third edition of the *MLA Style Manual and Guide to Scholarly Publishing*. In this edition of its style manual, MLA substantially revised its guidelines for works cited entries. Over the next few years, as teachers and scholars become more familiar with these new guidelines, expect to see articles in print that use both old and new versions. The sample works cited entries below follow the new, third edition guidelines.

Major changes made in the third edition of the *MLA Style Manual and Guide to Scholarly Publishing* include the following:

- Add the medium of publication to each entry (e.g., "Print," "Web," or "CD").
- Place book, journal, or Web titles in italics; do not underline them.
- Include the volume and issue number for every journal citation.
- When working with online sources, do not include the URL.

Journal Article, One Author

Gollub, Erica L. "A Neglected Population: Drug-using Women and Women's Methods of HIV/STI Prevention." *AIDS Education & Prevention* 20.2 (2008): 107–120. Print.

- Give the full name of the author as it is printed with the article, last name first. Place a period after the name.
- The title of the article is placed in quotation marks. Note how the first and last word of the title are capitalized as are all key words in between. Also note that the period at the end of the article title goes inside the closing quotation mark.
- The title of the journal is italicized. Because *Scientific American* is a monthly publication, provide the month of the issue containing the information you used.
- Indicate the inclusive page numbers of the article.
- Indicate the medium of publication.

Journal Article, Two or Three Authors

Broadhead, Robert S., and Douglas D. Heckathorn. "AIDS Prevention Outreach among Injection Drug Users: Agency Problems and New Approaches." *Social Problems* 41.3 (1994): 473–95. Print.

Mitchell, Roger E., Paul Florin, and John F. Stevenson. "Supporting Community-based Prevention and Health Promotion Initiatives: Developing Effective Technical Assistance Systems." *Health Education & Behavior* 29.5 (2002): 620–639. Print.

- When there are two or three authors, list all of them in the order they appear in the article. Give the first author's last name, then his first name. Give the other authors' names first name first. Separate the names with commas and introduce the last name with "and."

Journal Article, More Than Three Authors

Kalichman, Seth, et al. "HIV Treatment Beliefs and Sexual Transmission Risk Behaviors among HIV Positive Men and Women." *Journal of Behavioral Medicine* 29.5 (2006): 401–410. Print.

- When there are more than three authors, list only the first author, last name first. Follow that name with the expression "et al." (which means "and others").

Article from a Monthly Periodical

Minkel, J. R. "Dangling a Carrot for Vaccines." *Scientific American* Jul 2006: 39–40. Print.

- Note the month of publication after the title. Months can be abbreviated.
- Note that there is *no* comma between the month and year.
- Note that you do *not* include the volume number of the work, only the month and year.

Article from a Weekly Periodical

Clinton, Bill. "My Quest to Improve Care." *Newsweek* 15 May 2006: 50–52. Print.

- After giving the title of the piece, list the day, month, and year of its publication in that order, without any punctuation between them.

Newspaper Article

Chase, Marilyn. "Panel Suggests a 'Peace Corps' to Fight AIDS." *Wall Street Journal* 20 Apr. 2005: B1+. Print.

Dugger, Celia W. "Rift Over AIDS Treatment Lingers in South Africa." *New York Times* 9 Mar. 2008: 8. Print.

- If the newspaper article is signed, give the writer's name, last name first.
- After the title of the piece, give the name of the newspaper, italicized.
- Next, give the date of publication: day, month, then year without any intervening punctuation.
- Give the page number, indicating the section number or letter when applicable.
- Use a plus sign (+) to indicate interrupted pagination.

Newspaper Article, No Author

"Children and AIDS." *New York Times* 22 Feb. 2005: 16. Print.

- If the article is unsigned, begin the entry with the title.

Book with One Author

Hinds, Maurene J. *Fighting the AIDS and HIV Epidemic: A Global Battle.* Berkeley Heights, NJ: Enslow, 2008. Print.

- If you think your reader will not recognize the city of publication, add the state abbreviation.
- Again, note how the entry begins with the author's last name.
- Note how the title is italicized and how the first, last, and key words are capitalized.

Book with Multiple Authors

Douglas, Paul Harding, and Laura Pinsky. *The Essential AIDS Fact Book.* New York: Pocket Books, 1991. Print.

Wanjama, Leah Niambi, et al. *HIV and AIDS: The Pandemic.* Nairobi: Jomo Kenyatta Foundation, 2007. Print.

- When a book has two or three authors, list all their names. Begin with the last name of the first author; the names of the other authors are listed first name first. Separate the names with commas and use "and" before the last name.
- If there are more than three authors, list only the first author and follow it with "et al." (Smith, John, et al.)

Two or More Books by the Same Person

Squire, Corinne. *AIDS Panic.* New York: Routledge, 1997. Print.

---. *HIV in South Africa: Talking about the Big Thing.* London: Routledge, 2007. Print.

- When you have two or more books by the same author or authors, list them on your works cited list in alphabetical order by the first key word in the title.
- For the first work by the author, give his or her full name, last name first. For subsequent entries by the author, instead of repeating the name, type three hyphens followed by a period. Then list the title of the work and the relevant publishing information.

Book, Corporate Author

National Gay and Lesbian Task Force. *Anti-gay Violence: Victimization and Defamation in 1986.* New York: National Gay and Lesbian Task Force, 1987. Print.

- Treat a corporate author just as you would an individual author.

Book, Later Edition

Fan, Hung Y., Ross F. Conner, and Luis Villarreal. *AIDS: Science and Society.* 5th ed. Sudbury, MA: Jones and Bartlett, 2007. Print.

- Indicate the edition number after the title.

Edited Book

Squire, Corinne, ed. *Women and AIDS: Psychological Perspectives.* London: Sage, 1993. Print.

Cohen, Ann, and Jack M. Gorman, eds. *Comprehensive Textbook of AIDS Psychiatry.* New York: Oxford UP, 2008. Print.

- If one person edited the work, place "ed." after his name. If there is more than one editor, use "eds."

Book, No Author or Editor

Corporate Responses to HIV/AIDS: Case Studies from India. Washington, DC: World Bank, 2007. Print.

- When there is no author, begin the entry with the title.

Multivolume Book

Daintith, John, Sarah Mitchell, and Elizabeth Tootill, eds. *A Biographical Encyclopedia of Scientists.* 2 vols. New York: Facts on File, 1981. Print.

- Indicate the number of volumes in a multivolume work after the title.

One Volume of a Multivolume Book

Daintith, John, Sarah Mitchell, and Elizabeth Tootill, eds. *A Biographical Encyclopedia of Scientists.* Vol. 1. New York: Facts on File, 1981. Print.

- If you use only one volume of a multivolume work, indicate the volume number after the title.

English Translation of a Book

Jager, Hans, ed. *AIDS Phobia: Disease Pattern and Possibilities of Treatment.* Trans. Jacquie Welch. New York: Halsted, 1988. Print.

- Begin the entry with the name of the author or editor whose work has been translated, followed by the title of the work.
- Next, write "Trans." followed by the name of the translator, first name first.

Article or Chapter from an Anthology

Bethell, Tom. "The African AIDS Epidemic Is Exaggerated." *Responding to the AIDS Epidemic*. Ed. Daniel A. Leone. Detroit: Greenhaven, 2006. 18–22. Print.

Patton, Cindy. "'With Champagne and Roses': Women at Risk from/in AIDS Discourse." *Women and AIDS*. Ed. Corinne Squire. London: Sage, 1993. 165–87. Print.

- First, list the name of the author whose article or chapter you are using.
- Next, give the title, in quotation marks. If the title of an entry already contains quotation marks, the original quotation marks are shifted to single quotation marks in the citation.
- Next, give the title of the work that contained the article and the name of the editor or editors, preceded by either "Ed." if one person edited the work or "Eds." if more than one editor was involved.
- Finally, list the publication information and the page numbers in the larger work where the article or chapter can be found.

Article in a Reference Work

"Acquired Immune Deficiency Syndrome." *Encyclopaedia Britannica: Micropaedia*. 1990 ed. Print.

- If the author of the entry in the reference work is listed, begin with that. If it is not, begin with the heading of the entry, in quotation marks.
- After indicating the heading of the entry, list the name of the reference work and the edition.

Personal Interview

Alexander, Jane. Telephone interview. 16 June 2008.

Smith, John. Personal interview. 16 June 2008.

- List the name of the person interviewed, the nature of the interview (whether done in person, over the telephone, etc.), and the date of the interview: day, month, and year.

ELECTRONIC SOURCES OF INFORMATION

The most up-to-date information on MLA formats for citing electronic sources of information is available at www.mla.org.

Information on CD-ROM or Diskette

"AIDS." *The 1995 Grolier Multimedia Encyclopedia*. Danbury, CT: Grolier, 1995. CD.

- Give the name of the author (if known), last name first.
- Give the title of the chapter or entry from which you drew the information (in quotation marks).
- Give the title of the CD.
- Indicate the place of publication, the publisher, and the date of publication.
- Indicate the medium of publication (in this case, CD).

Online Information Databank

"AIDS." *Encyclopaedia Brittanica Online*. Encyclopaedia Britannica, 2008. Web. 1 July 2008.

- Give the author's name (if known), last name first.
- Give the title of the article or entry. This particular source text is unsigned, so the entry begins with the title.
- Give the title of the online database, in italics.
- Give the name of the databank's sponsoring institution or organization and the date of publication.
- Indicate the medium of publication (in this case, "Web").
- List the date of access. Note how it is listed and punctuated.

Article from an Online Publication

This is the format to use if your source text exists only electronically. If the article does not also appear in print somewhere, use this form for your works cited entry:

Ambinder, Marc. "Huck and AIDS." *TheAtlantic.com*. Atlantic Monthly, 8 Dec. 2007. Web. 2 July 2008.

Underwood, Anne. "How the Plague Began." *Newsweek.com*. Newsweek, 8 Feb. 1999. Web. 3 July 2008.

- Give the author's name, last name first.
- Indicate the title of the work, in quotation marks.
- Give the title of the online database, in italics.
- Give the name of the databank's sponsoring institution or organization.
- Give the date of publication or posting.
- Indicate the medium of publication.
- Indicate the date of access.

Work from an Online Service

"AIDS: Education Cuts the Toll." *Business Week* 5 Dec. 2005: 112. *Academic Search Premier*. Web. 1 July 2008.

Parkhurst, Justin O. "'What Worked?': The Evidence Challenges in Determining the Causes of HIV Prevalence Decline." *AIDS Education & Prevention* June 2008: 275–283. *Academic Search Premier*. Web. 1 July 2008.

Shadlen, Kenneth C. "The Political Economy of AIDS Treatment: Intellectual Property and the Transformation of Generic Supply." *International Studies Quarterly* 51.3 (2007): 559–581. *Academic Search Complete*. Web. 5 July 2008.

- Give the name of the author, last name first.
- Give the title of the article in quotation marks.
- Give the title of the publication (in italics) and the relevant dates of publication and volume/issue numbers (the first sample is from a weekly publication, the second from a monthly publication, and the third from a quarterly publication).
- Give the inclusive page numbers of the article.
- Give the name of the database, in italics.
- Give the medium of publication.
- Give the date of access.

E-Mail

Give the name of the writer (last name first), the title of the message (taken from the "subject" line), an indication of who received the message, and the date of the message.

Edwards, John. "Re: AIDS Sources." Message to author. 31 July 2008. E-mail.

Francis, Heather. Message to Karen Wilhoit. 24 June 2007. E-mail.

- If the subject line of the message is blank, leave out that part of the entry.
- Note how the date of the message is listed: day, month, year.
- Note the medium of publication (in this case, "E-mail").

SAMPLE MLA-STYLE WORKS CITED LIST

Begin the works cited list on a separate sheet of paper at the end of your essay. Centered at the top, write "Works Cited" and then double-space before you begin listing your entries. Entries are alphabetized by the author's last name or by the first key word in the title if there is no author. The first line of each entry begins on the left margin, and all subsequent lines of each entry are indented one-half inch or five spaces. The entire list is double-spaced.

Works Cited

"AIDS." *Encyclopaedia Brittanica Online*. Encyclopaedia Britannica,

  2008. Web. 1 July 2008.

"AIDS: Education Cuts the Toll." *Business Week* 5 Dec. 2005: 112.

  Academic Search Premier. Web. 1 July 2008.

Alexander, Jane. Telephone interview. 16 June 2008.

Ambinder, Marc. "Huck and AIDS." *TheAtlantic.com*. Atlantic Monthly,

  8 Dec. 2007. Web. 2 July 2008.

Bethell, Tom. "The African AIDS Epidemic Is Exaggerated." *Responding

  to the AIDS Epidemic*. Ed. Daniel A. Leone. Detroit: Greenhaven

  P., 2006. 18–22. Print.

Broadhead, Robert S., and Douglas D. Heckathorn. "AIDS

  Prevention Outreach among Injection Drug Users: Agency

  Problems and New Approaches." *Social Problems* 41.3 (1994):

  473–495. Print.

Chase, Marilyn. "Panel Suggests a 'Peace Corps' to Fight AIDS." *Wall

  Street Journal* 20 Apr. 2005: B1+. Print.

"Children and AIDS." *New York Times* 22 Feb. 2005: 16. Print.

Clinton, Bill. "My Quest to Improve Care." *Newsweek* 15 May 2006:

  50–52. Print.

Cohen, Ann, and Jack M. Gorman, eds. *Comprehensive Textbook of

  AIDS Psychiatry*. New York: Oxford UP, 2008. Print.

Corporate Responses to HIV/AIDS: Case Studies from India.

  Washington, DC: World Bank, 2007. Print.

Douglas, Paul Harding, and Laura Pinsky. *The Essential AIDS Fact Book*. New York: Pocket Books, 1991. Print.

Dugger, Celia W. "Rift Over AIDS Treatment Lingers in South Africa." *New York Times* 9 Mar. 2008: 8. Print.

Edwards, John. "Re: AIDS Sources." Message to author. 31 July 2008. E-mail.

Fan, Hung Y., Ross F. Conner, and Luis Villarreal. *AIDS: Science and Society*. 5th ed. Sudbury, MA: Jones and Bartlett, 2007. Print.

Francis, Heather. Message to Karen Wilhoit. 24 June 2007. E-mail.

Gollub, Erica L. "A Neglected Population: Drug-using Women and Women's Methods of HIV/STI Prevention." *AIDS Education & Prevention* 20.2 (2008): 107–120. Print.

Hinds, Maurene J. *Fighting the AIDS and HIV Epidemic: A Global Battle*. Berkeley Heights, NJ: Enslow, 2008. Print.

Kalichman, Seth, et al. "HIV Treatment Beliefs and Sexual Transmission Risk Behaviors among HIV Positive Men and Women." *Journal of Behavioral Medicine* 29.5 (2006): 401–410. Print.

Minkel, J. R. "Dangling a Carrot for Vaccines." *Scientific American* July 2006: 39–40. Print.

Mitchell, Roger E., Paul Florin, and John F. Stevenson. "Supporting Community-based Prevention and Health Promotion Initiatives: Developing Effective Technical Assistance Systems." *Health Education & Behavior* 29.5 (2002): 620–639. Print.

National Gay and Lesbian Task Force. *Anti-gay Violence: Victimization and Defamation in 1986*. New York: National Gay and Lesbian Task Force, 1987. Print.

Parkhurst, Justin O. "'What Worked?': The Evidence Challenges in Determining the Causes of HIV Prevalence Decline." *AIDS Education & Prevention* June 2008: 275–283. *Academic Search Premier*. Web. 1 July 2008.

Patton, Cindy. "'With Champagne and Roses': Women at Risk from/in AIDS Discourse." *Women and AIDS*. Ed. Corinne Squire. London: Sage, 1993. 165–187. Print.

Shadlen, Kenneth C. "The Political Economy of AIDS Treatment: Intellectual Property and the Transformation of Generic Supply." *International Studies Quarterly* 51.3 (2007): 559–581. *Academic Search Complete*. Web. 5 July 2008.

Smith, John. Personal interview. 16 June 2008.

Squire, Corinne. *AIDS Panic*. New York: Routledge, 1997. Print.

---. *HIV in South Africa: Talking about the Big Thing*. London: Routledge, 2007. Print.

Underwood, Anne. "How the Plague Began." *Newsweek.com*. Newsweek, 8 Feb. 1999. Web. 3 July 2008.

Wanjama, Leah Niambi, et al. *HIV and AIDS: The Pandemic*. Nairobi: Jomo Kenyatta Foundation, 2007. Print.

Chapter 14

TIMED WRITING ASSIGNMENTS

DEFINITION

Regardless of your major, in college you will write a number of timed, in-class essays. Teachers who assign these papers usually expect you to compose a complete, fully developed essay or test answer in one class period. When the allotted time is up, you have to turn in your work for evaluation—whether you are finished or not.

Timed writing assignments are so common in college because they serve a number of purposes. Some teachers use them to determine how well you understand the material covered in class, asking you to summarize course material in your essay. Other teachers use timed essays to determine whether you can critique the course material. Their assignments require you to analyze, evaluate, or synthesize class readings, lectures, demonstrations, or presentations. Still other teachers ask you to apply in new ways material you covered in class. You might be asked, for example, to explain how certain theories you studied could explain a hypothetical case or solve a problem you are seeing for the first time. Finally, some teachers use timed, in-class writing assignments to determine how well you can write essays without assistance. You can get help writing papers outside of class, but under controlled, timed conditions, you are on your own. In fact, teachers often require students to complete both out-of-class and in-class assignments for this very reason, to assess their ability to write both with and without assistance.

Writing a timed essay is stressful for any writer. However, understanding the purpose of the assignment and approaching the task in a systematic way can help you write with confidence.

A RANGE OF TIMED WRITING ASSIGNMENTS, PURPOSES, AND CONDITIONS

Among the most common timed writing assignments are essay test questions, comprehensive finals, and take-home examinations. The writing conditions for these assignments can vary. Sometimes teachers give you the actual assignment or a list of possible writing tasks prior to the test so you can plan your answer; other times, they do not. Sometimes you can consult your notes and source texts as you compose your answer; other times, you may not. Each type of timed writing assignment and each set of test conditions call for a different type of preparation and a different set of test-taking skills.

COMMON TIMED WRITING TASKS

When teachers assign *essay test questions*, they usually expect fully developed, clear, organized responses that directly answer the question being asked and reveal your understanding of the course material. Assignments may ask you to summarize readings or lectures, critique the course material, draw connections among the authors studied in class, explore the relationship between the course material and your own experience, apply course material to new situations, or argue for or against positions or theories presented in the course. Most teachers expect essay test answers to have a solid beginning, middle, and end; to be clearly written; and to make appropriate references to material studied in the course. Being able to write strong responses to essay test questions is an especially important skill for college writers. A number of studies of writing requirements across the curriculum reveal that answering essay test questions is the most common writing task for students regardless of their major.

Given at the end of a course, *comprehensive finals* ask you to work with information presented over the entire term. You typically have more time in class to write these responses than you do when writing essay test answers, so you must plan your essays more carefully. Teachers typically expect you to make multiple references to course material in a comprehensive final; to present fairly sophisticated critiques of the readings, lectures, or laboratory exercises; to synthesize information in new and interesting ways; and to develop your own positions on issues covered in class.

Unlike the other types of timed writing tasks, you can complete *take-home examinations* outside of class. Take-home examinations can consist of a series of essay test questions or a single, comprehensive writing task. Teachers will typically tell you how much time they expect you to spend writing your response and trust you to keep to those guidelines. Sometimes they will require you to type your answer; other times, they will want you to turn in handwritten responses, perhaps in examination booklets they distribute in class. Teachers who ask you to write take-home examinations typically expect your answers to be more comprehensive, more organized, and more formally correct than responses written in class. They typically do not, however, expect the prose to be as polished as it would be in a formal essay. Remember to discuss the grading criteria with your teacher if you have any questions. Because most timed writing assignments in college are not completed outside of class, the rest of this chapter focuses on in-class essays.

RHETORICAL AIMS

In-class, timed writing assignments usually have one of three rhetorical goals: exposition, argument, or personal expression. Understanding the rhetorical goal of the assignment—whether you are being asked to convey information, argue a point, or share your own responses to course material—is the most important aspect of composing a successful timed essay. If you write an expository essay when the teacher expects an argument, you will be missing the entire point of the assignment.

Expository assignments ask you to inform your reader about a topic. Some expository assignments ask you to recapitulate information covered in class ("What were the major judicial reforms instituted by Henry V?"). Others require you to compare and contrast various source texts ("What are the theories of childhood language acquisition offered by Piaget and Vygotsky?"). These assignments do not ask you to assert and defend a position of your own; instead, your grade is largely based on how clearly you convey information.

Argumentative assignments, in contrast, ask you to explain and support a position of your own on a topic ("How successful were the judicial reforms instituted by Henry V?" or "In presenting his theory of language acquisition, who is more convincing, Piaget or Vygotsky?"). Your thesis asserts a position that you then explain and defend in the body of your essay. When evaluating argumentative timed writing assignments, teachers tend to focus on the clarity and accuracy of your position, the quality of textual support you supply, and the sophistication of your reasoning skills. Writing successful timed arguments is difficult, requiring you to employ a wide range of reading, writing, and reasoning skills. As discussed later in this chapter, dividing this task into manageable subtasks and preparing yourself thoroughly before you begin to write can help you complete the assignment successfully.

Responsive timed assignments ask you to convey your subjective reactions to course material ("What do you think about the judicial reforms instituted by Henry V?" or "Based on your own experience, whose theories of language acquisition make more sense, Piaget's or Vygotsky's?"). Here the teacher wants to know your reaction to the information covered in class, what you liked or did not like, understood or did not understand, found useful or did not find useful. More important, the teacher also wants to know the basis of your response—you need to explain why you responded in a particular way. When evaluating these assignments, teachers typically look for clarity and comprehensiveness—whether they fully understand your response to the material and the basis for your reaction.

ACCESS TO SOURCE MATERIAL

In most cases, when writing your timed essay, you will not be able to consult the material you studied in class. Nevertheless, your teachers will expect you to refer to this material in your essay, citing specific and relevant authors, studies, findings, dates, or criticism. While they may not expect direct quotations of this material, they will certainly expect you to summarize and paraphrase information and data accurately and appropriately.

Sometimes teachers will assign open-note tests, allowing you to consult readings, class notes, or other source material as you compose your response. Having access to this course material can be both a blessing and a curse. Being able to consult the material means you have less to memorize; as you write, you can look up information you need. You are also in a better position to quote material in your answer since you can copy it directly from your readings or notes. However, since you have access to the material when you write, your teachers are likely to expect your answers to be more thorough and precise, criteria they will employ when evaluating your response. Open-note tests also require you to manage your time more carefully than do closed-note tests. Many students fail to finish their essays in the allotted time because they spend too much time flipping through their textbooks to find information they need or copying long quotations into their answers. You ought to prepare yourself equally well for both open- and closed-note tasks so that you spend most of your time responding to the question or questions being asked.

ACCESS TO POSSIBLE ASSIGNMENTS

College teachers differ in letting students know prior to the test day what the assignment will be. Some teachers distribute the assignment days or weeks in advance, answer any questions you have about the task, and even encourage students to discuss the assignment with each other outside of class. Other teachers may distribute several possible questions or assignments ahead of time but not tell you before the day scheduled for the timed writing which assignment they want you to complete. Still other teachers never let their students know prior to the test day what the assignment will be. When the students come to class, they see the question for the first time.

QUALITIES OF A GOOD TIMED ESSAY

Timed essays can assume many forms. Successful responses, however, have several features in common. They are appropriate, concise, supported, organized, and clear and correct.

- *Appropriate*—the response addresses the question being asked.
- *Concise*—the response is direct and to the point.
- *Supported*—the response correctly and effectively refers to course material to explain or defend statements or assertions.
- *Organized*—the response is built around an introduction, body, and conclusion united by a thesis statement, topic sentences, and transitions.
- *Clear and correct*—the response avoids sentence-level errors and word choice errors that inhibit understanding.

APPROPRIATE

The most common—and most costly—error students make when completing timed writing assignments is failing to answer the question being asked. They may write an interesting essay, but—given the assigned task—their response is inappropriate. Students write inappropriate responses when they misunderstand or disregard the wording of the assignment, develop an idea that does not relate clearly to the rest of their essay, panic and write anything to fill the page, or compose an essay that tries to achieve the wrong rhetorical aim—for example, composing an expository essay when the assignment calls for an argumentative response. Preparing yourself to write prior to the test day, carefully analyzing the wording of the assignment, and asking the right questions as you compose and revise your work can help ensure that your responses are appropriate.

CONCISE

Because you are writing under timed conditions, your prose has to be direct, focused, and precise. Your response should focus on the question being asked, so avoid the temptation to follow tangents that take you too far afield. In addition, make your sentences as precise and economical as possible. With timed writing, if you can say something in two words rather than three, say it in two; if you can adequately develop an idea in one paragraph rather than two, develop it in one. Remember, the time you take to work on one section of your response leaves less time to work on other sections.

SUPPORTED

Almost all of the timed essays you write in school will ask you to work with the material you covered in class. When appropriate, your response to the assignment should refer to this material—the more specific you can be, the better. Generally, in academic writing—even in timed essays—supported assertions carry more weight and are more convincing than unsupported assertions. In open-note tests, try to quote source material in your response. In closed-note tests, you are more likely to summarize and paraphrase information. Integrating course material into your answer will help you produce effective, convincing timed essays.

ORGANIZED

Timed essays require careful planning and organization. Like any formal writing assignment, a timed essay ought to have an effective opening paragraph, a clear thesis that guides and controls the body of the essay, topic sentences that direct the paragraphs, and transitions throughout that help unite the piece and lead readers through the essay. Perhaps more than any other type of assignment, timed writing tasks test your ability to plan responses quickly, apply the organizational skills you have learned in school, and solve problems as they arise.

CLEAR AND CORRECT

When evaluating timed writing assignments, most instructors are less strict about sentence-level errors than they might be with more formal assignments. They know correct punctuation, spelling, and grammar are important, but they understand that writing under time constraints may prevent students from adequately revising and proofreading their work. Not every instructor, however, is so forgiving. It is a good idea, therefore, to talk to your instructor about her evaluation criteria. Of course, your essay will not succeed if errors make it too difficult to read the piece. If nearly every sentence contains a mistake, if sentence boundaries are confused, if the language is incomprehensible, you are much less likely to get a passing grade. As discussed in more detail later in this chapter, part of learning how to write timed essays successfully is understanding, locating, and correcting the errors that most seriously affect a reader's ability to understand your essay and the errors that you, as a writer, most commonly make.

WRITING TIMED ASSIGNMENTS

Adopting a process approach to composing timed writing assignments will help you complete them more easily and successfully. As with any other assignment, your best approach to composing a timed essay is to divide the task into a series of manageable steps: carefully analyze the assignment, engage in some planning, draft a response, and then reread and revise what you have written until you feel you have produced your best work. The trick with timed assignments is to complete the process before time runs out. Below are several steps you should consider following as you prepare for and draft timed writing assignments. Modify these suggestions to suit your individual composing style.

PREPARE FOR THE ASSIGNMENT OUTSIDE OF CLASS

Success at timed writing assignments depends on preparation well before you sit down to write the first word of the essay. Because timed writing assignments test not only your writing skills but also your study skills, engaging in a series of steps prior to test day can help you write a strong essay.

First, be sure you *review the course material* before you sit down to write your essay. Besides reviewing the assigned readings and your class notes, discuss the material with your classmates. Together, try to identify the most important information, findings, or theories covered in class. Even if you will be able to consult your notes or readings as you write your essay, studying the material and discussing it with others before the test will still be helpful: you will form a better understanding of the information, you will likely gain insights from others, and you will commit more information to memory, saving yourself time later as you write your response.

Second, if your instructor does not distribute the assignment prior to the test, *try to anticipate what he might ask*. Trying to imagine what the teacher is likely to ask will help you sort through the course material, identifying what is truly important. Instead of distributing test questions or timed writing assignments prior to the test day, some teachers, especially in the natural sciences, place copies of old examinations or assignments on a web page or on reserve at the library or department office. If your teacher does this, be sure to consult these old assignments as you study. Again, working with others to anticipate assignments or test questions can be very productive. Anticipating test answers can be dangerous, however, if you convince yourself that you have psyched out the teacher and know what the assignment will be or if you decide what you want to write even if it is not what the teacher ends up assigning. In either case, you will likely compose an inappropriate response. If you accurately predict the assignment, then you are that much more prepared on the day you write your essay. If you do not accurately predict it, you need to plan your essay in response to the task at hand.

Finally, as you study for the test, *work out possible responses or answers*. If the teacher distributes the assignment before the test, give yourself plenty of time to plan your answer. If you have to guess what the assignment might be, you should still determine how you would answer each possible question. When planning these responses, work closely with the course's source texts. Decide which readings or parts of readings would help you write particular responses, and select the quotes or examples you think would be good to incorporate into your essay. Even if you do not end up using this material in your response, simply working through it prior to the assignment will help you master the material.

Working with others to develop possible answers or responses can be quite helpful. As a group, you can brainstorm possible responses and critique ideas. However, such collaboration should only supplement your individual efforts to prepare for the timed writing assignment. Even when you work with others, you should still develop your own response to the assignment. Students composing nearly identical in-class essays will likely be suspected of plagiarism. The purpose of group work prior to writing a timed essay is to gain a better understanding of the course material, to work out a range of possible responses, and to establish the relative strengths and weaknesses of those responses, not to develop a single, shared "group" response.

READ AND ANALYZE THE ASSIGNMENT OR TEST QUESTION

Carefully analyzing the language of the assignment is crucial when you are writing timed essays. As you read the assignment, you need to make a series of decisions concerning the instructor's intention. First, you may need to identify the actual assignment itself. Sometimes teachers will ask a series of questions to get you thinking about the topic before they ask the test question or state the assignment. In such a case, it is easy to confuse the actual assignment and the accompanying questions. Consider, for example, the following assignment used in a course on Native American history. Assume you are a student seeing it for the first time and have only fifty minutes to write your response:

> Consider the relationship between the Hopewell and Fort Ancient cultures. Are they truly distinct? Do they represent separate cultures, or is it more accurate to claim they represent different stages of development of only one culture? How might researchers answer this question?

What, exactly, is the test question in this example? Should your answer address similarities and differences between the Hopewell and Fort Ancient cultures, or should it focus on research methodologies more generally, using ancient Native American cultures as examples? Should it do both? Making the wrong decision would lead to an inappropriate response. If you have trouble understanding the assignment, be sure to ask your teacher for clarification.

Second, pay particular attention to the verbs the teacher uses in the assignment. The verbs often will tell you what to write and indicate how you might organize your response. Below are some verbs you are likely to find in timed writing assignments, along with an explanation of their common meanings:

Verb	Writing Task
analyze	divide something into parts
compare	show similarities
contrast	show differences
define	explain the meaning of something
discuss	examine multiple sides of an issue, being as comprehensive as possible

explain   clarify what others think is confusing
illustrate   give examples of something
prove   defend a position with evidence that others will find
               convincing
summarize   briefly recount the main points of something

PLAN YOUR ESSAY OR ANSWER

Once you have a clear idea of what the teacher is asking you to do in your response, you need to plan your answer. A common mistake students make when writing timed essays is beginning their responses before adequately planning their answers. Without adequate planning, responses are usually unfocused and underdeveloped. Taking time to plan your answer may be nerve-racking—you may feel pressured to begin composing your response immediately. However, the three to five minutes you spend planning your response will actually make it easier for you to write your essay and will likely result in a better paper.

At a minimum, before you begin to draft your response, you need to develop your thesis and outline your essay. In most cases, your thesis should be a one-sentence answer to the question being asked. You will develop and support this thesis in the body of your essay. Write out and revise your thesis on scrap paper or even on the assignment sheet itself until you are satisfied with its wording. Next, outline your response on the same sheet of paper. This outline does not need to be formal or elaborate. It can be simply a list of the main points you want to make, preferably in the order you plan to present them. Make sure the order of ideas presented in your outline matches the order in which the ideas are presented in your thesis. Finally, you might want to indicate on your outline where you can insert source material into your response—which authors you can cite, which examples you can use, which quotations you can employ. The time you spend at this stage of the writing process will help you draft an effective answer, for you will continually refer to this outline as you write your essay.

DRAFT YOUR ESSAY OR ANSWER

Once you have taken a few minutes to draft your thesis and plan your response, you will be able to compose your response section by section. First, *write an effective opening*, one that introduces the topic of your essay, states your thesis, and captures your reader's interest through a provocative question, an interesting observation, a significant quotation, or some other device that will help your essay stand out from others completed in class. This opening section should remain brief—only a paragraph or two.

Once you have completed your introduction, *compose your response paragraph by paragraph using your outline as a guide.* Try to begin each new section of your essay with a clearly stated topic sentence that both introduces the idea you will develop and refers back to the language of your thesis. As you compose each paragraph, look for opportunities to make references to the material covered in class—quoting or paraphrasing readings or lectures, supplying documentation when necessary.

The actual process of writing your response may lead you to form some new ideas about the assignment, ideas you want to include in your essay. When this happens, do not trust your insight to memory—you already have too much on your mind in a timed writing situation. Instead, go back to your outline and quickly jot down the new idea where you think you might want to include it in your essay. If you need to insert this material in a section of the essay you have already written, you can do so: write out the passage, bracket it, and then indicate with marginal arrows, lines, or notes where you would like it to go. Most teachers will honor your intention and read the paragraphs in the order you indicate.

Finally, *be sure to write a concluding paragraph.* Many students forget to include a conclusion when they write timed essays, letting their responses end with the last point they make. Writing a conclusion gives you the opportunity to reemphasize important assertions, to bring your essay to a logical end, and to echo the strategy you employed to capture your reader's interest in the opening paragraph, giving your essay symmetry and your reader a sense of closure.

REVISE YOUR ESSAY OR ANSWER

Just as you should set aside time to plan your response before you begin to write, you need to reserve time at the end of the process to revise your work before you turn it in. Since you will have only a limited amount of time to revise, you need to work toward a limited set of revision goals.

First, as you reread your work, *make sure your response is appropriate.* Review the assignment, then your response, checking to see that you have met all of the assignment's requirements. Cut material that is not relevant, and add any examples, explanations, or elaborations you think you need. Delete material by drawing a single line through it. Add material by placing a caret below the place where you want it to go and write the material in the space above the line. As you revise your work at this point, you want to be sure you have met the demands of the assignment and have been true to your own intentions as well.

Second, *check each paragraph for adequate development.* Do you need to add another illustrative example? Can you make another reference to a source text? Does a particular assertion need further elaboration? Now is the time to add any needed support.

Next, *check for any problems with organization.* As you revise, add any transition words or phrases that might make your essay easier to read. If you need to insert a paragraph break, now is the time to indicate with a paragraph marker (¶) where you would like it to go. If you need to eliminate a paragraph break, in the margin of your paper write "no paragraph." If you failed to include an introductory or concluding paragraph, now is the time to add one.

Finally, *check for clear word choice.* Have you used any terms that might confuse your reader? Is your language as precise and economical as it can be? Make any needed changes.

PROOFREAD YOUR ESSAY OR ANSWER

Because you have very little time to proofread your work in a timed writing situation, first *proofread for the types of errors that seriously interfere with a reader's ability to understand your essay,* especially errors involving sentence boundaries. For example, try to correct any problems with sentence fragments, run-on sentences, comma splices, and missing end punctuation. Second, keeping in mind your known weaknesses as a writer, *proofread for the errors you are most likely to make.* If you know you typically forget to include apostrophes in possessive case constructions, proofread for that. If you know you misspell certain words, check them in your essay. If you have problems with capitalization, correct any such errors you find. Use standard proofreading symbols to indicate any corrections you make.

FINAL THOUGHTS

Writing in-class essays tests not only your ability to think, plan, and write under pressure, but also your ability to manage time. Here are a few tips to help you write successfully against the clock. First, *prepare, prepare, prepare.* The more time you spend preparing yourself for a timed writing assignment, the easier it will be for you to complete the task once the clock is running. Second, *adopt a process approach to completing the assignment.* When you get the assignment, do not dive right into writing. Instead, carefully analyze the assignment and reserve time to plan, revise, and proofread your work. As a general guideline, if you have fifty minutes to write your essay, take five minutes to plan your response, forty minutes to draft and revise your answer, and five minutes to proofread the final draft. Finally, *watch the clock as you write.* Many students become so focused on completing the assignment that they forget to monitor how quickly time is passing. If possible, bring a watch to class on the day you write your essay. If that is not possible, ask the teacher to keep track of time for you on the blackboard.

Summary Chart

HOW TO WRITE TIMED ESSAYS

1. **Prepare for the assignment outside of class.**
   - *Decide how to order your ideas, arguments, or findings.*
   - *Review the course material.*
   - *Analyze the assignment or test questions if the teacher distributes them prior to the test day.*
   - *Anticipate possible assignments or test questions if the teacher does not distribute them early.*
   - *Imagine possible responses to the assignments or test questions.*
   - *Discuss possible or actual assignments, test questions, and responses with classmates.*

2. **Read and analyze the assignment or test question.**
   - *Identify the assignment or test question.*
   - *Analyze the verbs to determine the nature of your response.*
   - *Clarify the rhetorical goal of the assignment or test question.*

3. **Plan your essay or answer.**
   - *Develop your thesis.*
   - *Outline your response, formally or informally.*
   - *Note on your outline where you might effectively incorporate source material.*

4. **Draft your essay or answer.**
   - *Write an opening paragraph that, at a minimum, introduces the topic of your response, indicates your thesis, and captures your reader's interest.*
   - *Construct your response paragraph by paragraph, following the outline you already designed.*
   - *When new ideas come to you as you compose your response, note them appropriately on your outline and include them in your essay.*
   - *Be sure to write a concluding paragraph.*

5. **Revise your essay or answer.**
   - *First, check to see that your response is appropriate, that it properly addresses the assignment or test question.*
   - *Check each paragraph for adequate development.*
   - *Check for problems with organization, especially the use of effective topic sentences and transitions.*
   - *Check for clear word choice.*

6. **Proofread your essay or answer.**
   - *Find and correct errors that might interfere with a reader's ability to understand your essay.*
   - *Find and correct the types of errors you most commonly make when writing.*
   - *Correct any spelling or grammatical errors you find.*

Appendix 1

REVISION CHECKLISTS

QUOTATION CHECKLIST

	Yes	No
1. Did you check your quoted passages against the original to make sure the wording is accurate?	_____	_____
2. Is the capitalization of words in the quotation proper and accurate?	_____	_____
3. Is the punctuation in the quotation proper and accurate?	_____	_____
4. Do you need to add italics, underline certain words, or use single quotation marks in the quotation?	_____	_____
5. Did you check the punctuation you employed to introduce the quotation?	_____	_____
6. Did you check the format of your block quotations?	_____	_____
7. If you added words to or deleted words from the source passage, did you confirm that you have not misrepresented the author?	_____	_____
8. Is the format of your documentation at the end of the quotation in the correct style?	_____	_____
9. Did you list the right page number or numbers in your documentation?	_____	_____

PARAPHRASE CHECKLIST

	Yes	No

1. Have you provided the full title of the source and identified its author?   _____ _____
2. Have you employed a variety of methods to paraphrase the material?   _____ _____
3. Have you checked to be sure your paraphrase accurately captures the author's ideas?   _____ _____
4. Have you remained as objective as possible in choosing language for your paraphrase?   _____ _____
5. Have you avoided offering your opinions on the topic of the reading or on the writer's style?   _____ _____
6. Have you checked your language to make sure each word you have chosen means what you think it means, has the connotation you want it to have, and fits the general tone of your paraphrase?   _____ _____
7. Have you reviewed your sentence structure for clarity and variety?   _____ _____
8. Have you provided appropriate transitions between the ideas you paraphrase?   _____ _____
9. Have you provided proper and accurate documentation?   _____ _____
10. Have you properly punctuated your documentation?   _____ _____

SUMMARY CHECKLIST

	Yes	No

1. In the opening section of your summary have you
   - introduced the topic of the essay?
   - given the full title of the source text?
   - given the full name of the author?
   - included *your* thesis?
2. In the body of your essay do you summarize only one point at a time?
3. Have you accurately and fairly put into your own words all of the author's important findings, arguments, or ideas?
4. Have you identified the primary means of support the author provides for each finding, argument, or idea?
5. By cutting material or words, have you tried to make your summary as brief as possible while still being comprehensive?
6. To be neutral, have you avoided comments on the
   - topic of the piece?
   - author's ideas?
   - author's style?
7. To help ensure that your summary will make sense to someone who has not read the original work, have you
   - defined any unusual or technical terms?
   - identified any people you refer to in your work?
   - provided a sufficient context for understanding the author's assertions or findings?
8. Do you have adequate paragraph breaks and transitions?
9. Have you supplied proper documentation?

RESPONSE ESSAY CHECKLIST

	Yes	No

1. In the introductory section of your essay, have you
   - introduced the topic of the reading? _____ _____
   - included the full and exact title of the reading? _____ _____
   - included the full name of the author? _____ _____
2. Have you included a thesis statement that captures your overall response to the reading, a response you develop in the body of your essay? _____ _____
3. Have you considered the accuracy and honesty of the responses you include in your essay? _____ _____
4. Have you clearly stated each of these responses? _____ _____
5. Have you explained the terms you used to characterize each of your responses? _____ _____
6. Have you tied each of your responses to some aspect of the source that gave rise to it? _____ _____
7. Have you explained how the material in the source text gave rise to your response? _____ _____
8. Have you developed only one response at a time in each section of your essay? _____ _____
9. Have you used language that helps your reader understand when you are moving from your discussion of one response to the next? _____ _____
10. Have you explained the connection between each response you explore and your overall thesis? _____ _____
11. Have you reviewed the language you use to make sure your word choice is clear and accurate? _____ _____

CRITIQUE CHECKLIST

	Yes	No
1. Have you included the title of the reading and the author's name in your introduction?		
2. Does your thesis make clear your overall assessment of the reading?		
3. Toward the beginning of your critique, have you provided a brief summary of the reading?		
4. In the body of your critique, do you examine only one element of the reading at a time?		
5. Do you clearly state a judgment concerning each element of the reading you explore?		
6. Do you provide examples from the reading to support and illustrate your judgment of each element you examine?		
7. Do you clearly and thoroughly explain your judgments concerning each example you provide from the reading?		
8. Have you employed proper evaluative criteria and standards?		
9. Have you provided clear transitions between the major sections of your paper?		
10. Is there a clear relationship between each section of your paper and your thesis?		
11. Have you provided proper documentation for all quoted, paraphrased, and summarized material?		
12. Have you revised your paper for accuracy? In other words, does the final draft reflect your honest appraisal of the reading?		
13. Have you reviewed the language in your paper to make sure your words adequately capture and communicate your judgments?		
14. As you review your work, do your judgments still stand? Do you need to change your thesis or any part of your paper?		

RHETORICAL ANALYSIS CHECKLIST

	Yes	No

1. Have you analyzed the assignment to determine who *your* audience is? _____ _____
2. Have you established the source text's rhetorical situation? _____ _____
3. Have you paraphrased the author's goal? _____ _____
4. Have you evaluated the author's rhetorical strategies in light of his or her goal? _____ _____
5. Have you determined which of the author's rhetorical strategies you will evaluate in your essay? _____ _____
6. Check the introductory section of your essay. Do you
   - introduce the topic of your source text? _____ _____
   - Introduce your source text? _____ _____
   - capture reader interest? _____ _____
7. Examine the wording of your thesis. Do you
   - state whether the author successfully achieves his or her goal? _____ _____
   - indicate which rhetorical strategies you will examine in your essay? _____ _____
8. Do you summarize the source text and describe its rhetorical situation? _____ _____
9. Check each section in the body of your essay. Do you
   - examine one rhetorical strategy at a time? _____ _____
   - support your judgments with specific examples from the source text? _____ _____
   - explain the link between your assertions and their supporting evidence? _____ _____
10. Have your revised your essay for
    - accuracy? _____ _____
    - development? _____ _____
    - organization? _____ _____
    - clarity? _____ _____
    - documentation? _____ _____

VISUAL TEXT EVALUATION CHECKLIST

	Yes	No

1. Have you carefully analyzed the assignment to determine whether you are supposed to describe, analyze, and/or evaluate the text? _____ _____
2. Have you carefully examined every aspect of the source text? _____ _____
3. Have you established the visual text's rhetorical situation? _____ _____
4. Have you established how the creators of the visual text attempt to achieve their rhetorical goal? _____ _____
5. Have you determined how well they achieve their goal? _____ _____
6. Have you expressed your findings in a clear thesis statement that can guide the development of your essay? _____ _____
7. In the introductory section of your essay, do you
   - introduce the topic? _____ _____
   - introduce the source text? _____ _____
   - state your thesis? _____ _____
   - attempt to capture reader interest? _____ _____
8. In the body of your essay, do you
   - provide an overview or description of the visual text? _____ _____
   - develop your essay one criterion at a time? _____ _____
   - cite specific examples from the text to support your claims? _____ _____
   - explain how those examples support your assertions? _____ _____
   - address possible objections to your interpretation? _____ _____
9. In the concluding section of your essay, do you
   - wrap up your essay in an interesting way? _____ _____
   - remind readers of your thesis? _____ _____
10. Have you revised your essay for
    - clarity? _____ _____
    - development? _____ _____
    - organization? _____ _____
11. Have you proofread your essay? _____ _____

INFORMATIVE SYNTHESIS CHECKLIST

	Yes	No

1. Have you checked your assignment to be sure you have written the proper kind of synthesis essay: informative or argumentative? _____ _____

2. In your introduction do you
   - introduce the topic of the paper? _____ _____
   - offer your thesis? _____ _____
   - capture your reader's interest? _____ _____

3. Examine the wording of your thesis. Does it clearly indicate what stance you will assume in your essay? _____ _____

4. Examine the structure of your essay. Does it follow the organizational plan indicated by your thesis? _____ _____

5. Check each section in the body of your essay. Do you
   - examine just one issue at a time? _____ _____
   - combine information from your source texts? _____ _____
   - explain the link between the examples you cite and the assertion you are making? _____ _____
   - make clear the relationship you see among your source texts? _____ _____

6. Examine your transitions. Have you provided adequate signals to help guide your reader through your work? _____ _____

7. The first time you introduce a source text do you give the full title of the piece and the author's full name? _____ _____

8. Have you properly documented all quoted, summarized, and paraphrased material? _____ _____

9. Have you reviewed your quotations for accuracy and variety? _____ _____

10. Is your works cited or reference list correct? _____ _____

11. Have you reviewed your essay to be sure the content accurately communicates your position and intention? _____ _____

12. Have you reviewed your word choice for clarity and accuracy? _____ _____

ARGUMENTATIVE SYNTHESIS CHECKLIST

	Yes	No
1. Have you checked your assignment to be sure you have written the proper kind of synthesis essay: informative or argumentative?	_____	_____
2. Have you carefully read, annotated, and critiqued all of the source texts you will use in your essay?	_____	_____
3. Examine the wording of your thesis statement. Does it clearly state the stance you will assume in your essay?	_____	_____
4. Check the opening section of your essay. Does it		
• introduce the topic of your paper?	_____	_____
• capture reader interest?	_____	_____
• include your thesis statement?	_____	_____
5. Examine each section in the body of your essay. Do you		
• focus on just one issue at a time?	_____	_____
• make clear assertions?	_____	_____
• support your assertions with evidence?	_____	_____
• explain the link between each assertion and its supporting evidence?	_____	_____
6. Check the organization of your essay. Do you		
• follow the organizational plan indicated by your thesis?	_____	_____
• provide transitions to help guide your reader through your essay?	_____	_____
7. Have you supported your assertions with some combination of quoted, summarized, and paraphrased source material?	_____	_____
8. Have you documented all the material that needs to be documented?	_____	_____
9. Have you checked the content of your essay to be sure it accurately communicates your position and intention?	_____	_____
10. Have you reviewed your sentences for accuracy and variety?	_____	_____
11. Have you reviewed your word choice for clarity and accuracy?	_____	_____
12. Is your works cited or reference list correct?	_____	_____

PLAGIARISM CHECKLIST

	Yes	No
1. Are all of your quotations properly documented?	_____	_____
2. Does your thesis make clear your overall assessment of the reading?	_____	_____
3. Is all paraphrased material properly documented?	_____	_____
4. Have you acknowledged or documented the help you have received in writing your paper?	_____	_____
5. If this is a group project, have you checked the original assignment to be sure your work conforms to the teacher's guidelines?	_____	_____
6. Does the paper truly represent your own work and effort?	_____	_____

Appendix 2

PEER REVIEW GUIDELINES

In most cases, your instructor will provide you with a set of guidelines to follow when you review a peer's writing. If your teacher does not give you a set of guidelines to follow, you may want to employ the peer review procedures outlined below. To apply any set of guidelines effectively, though, you need to understand the purpose of peer review and commit yourself to improving your peer's writing. When peers review your work, remember that they are merely suggesting ways you might improve your writing. As the author of the piece, you are responsible for all final editing decisions.

PURPOSE

When you review a peer's writing, you can play three related roles, each serving a unique purpose: average reader, adviser, and editor. As an **average reader**, you offer your genuine response to the manuscript. You should let your peers know which aspects of their writing you find interesting, which parts you find boring, what is clear, what is confusing, what you would like to know more about, what questions you have. As an **adviser**, along with offering your response to the manuscript, you also make specific suggestions to improve the piece. You can suggest changes in content, organization, format, or style. Finally, as an **editor**, you make specific suggestions for improving the piece and correct any problems you find in the writing.

Whatever role you play, your goal remains the same: to help your peer produce the most effective piece of writing possible. Peer review works best when it is truly reciprocal in nature: you do your best to improve your peer's writing because you know your peer is doing his or her best to improve your writing.

PROCEDURES TO FOLLOW

If you are asked to review a peer's writing, follow the guidelines your instructor distributes. If your teacher does not provide you specific guidelines to follow, employ the following procedures.

Step 1:   **Read through the entire paper** carefully without marking anything.

Step 2:   Consider whether the paper (or any part of it you are reviewing) **meets the needs of the assignment**. If it does not, tell your peer why you think it does not answer the assignment.

Step 3:   Examine the paper's **content**. Point out which sections of the essay are clear, which need further development, which specifically address the assignment, and which seem to stray from it. Offer any suggestions you have for improving the paper's content.

Step 4:   Examine the paper's **structure**. Note any problems with the paper's thesis statement or topic sentences. Comment on whether the writer provides clear and effective transitions between paragraphs or among sentences within the paragraphs. Note any passage where you lose track of the writer's train of thought. Finally, comment on the effectiveness of the opening and closing sections of the essay.

Step 5:   Examine the paper's **style**. Note any awkward or confusing sentences (if you have a suggestion about how to improve the sentence, offer it). Look for consistency in voice, diction, and point of view, commenting on any problems you find. If you think that any passage is stylistically inappropriate given the assigned audience, let the writer know.

Step 6:   **Proofread** for errors in spelling, punctuation, or typing. You can either circle errors you find and leave them for the author to correct or offer corrections of your own.

Step 7:   Examine the paper's **documentation**. First, check to see that the author has documented every passage that needs to be documented, noting any questions you have. Second, note any errors you find in the documentation the author provides, such as problems with the documentation's placement, formatting, or punctuation. Finally, proofread the paper's works cited or reference list if there is one.

ACTING ON PEER REVIEWS

As an author, you have the final say concerning the changes you make to your essay. You can accept or reject your peer's suggestions, but whatever decision you make, base it on a careful consideration of your peer's comments. Accepting every suggestion a peer reviewer offers is usually a bad idea, as is summarily rejecting every suggestion a reviewer makes. Consider each comment individually. Decide whether the peer reviewer's suggestion will improve your manuscript. If it will, make the change. If you think it will not, do not act on the suggestion. If you are unsure about making any change, talk it over with your instructor before you decide.

Appendix 3

WRITING FROM READINGS: REVISION GUIDELINES

Below is a series of steps you can follow to revise source-based essays. Regardless of the specific type of assignment you are writing, revising your work in stages is the best way to ensure that you produce strong essays. Though revising your writing this way takes some time, it will be worth the effort. You should start by examining your essay's content and structure, then move through your sentences, word choice, and punctuation. Finally, check your essay's format and use of source material.

With each pass through your essay, you will be focusing on just one aspect of your writing. This type of focused revision will help prevent you from overlooking errors and missing opportunities to improve your work. You can make your revision process even more effective if you take a break between each step and approach your paper fresh each time. Use these guidelines to supplement, not replace, directions or instruction offered by your teacher.

Step 1: Check the content of your essay
- Examine your essay in terms of the assignment and your intentions:
- Does the essay adequately and clearly answer the assignment?
- Have you covered everything you intended to cover in your essay?
- Does your essay state only what you intend it to state?
- Have you adequately addressed opposing views, exceptions, or alternatives to your assertions?
- Consider your essay from the perspective of your reader:
- Are there any assertions that need further explanation to be clear?
- Do you need to support any claims with additional examples?
- Do any assertions need additional support from readings?
- Are there any terms that need to be defined?

Step 2: Check the organization of your essay

- Is your thesis clearly and properly stated?
- Does your thesis guide the development of your essay?
- Do your topic sentences guide the development of their paragraphs?
- Are your topic sentences linked to your thesis statement through the repetition of key ideas?
- Does every topic sentence contain transition words or other devices that indicate its connection to the previous section of your essay?
- Do you employ transition words or other devices to link the sentences within your paragraphs?
- Examine the opening section of your essay:
    - Does it introduce the topic of your essay?
    - Does it introduce source texts when necessary?
    - Does it capture reader interest?
- Examine the closing section of your essay:
    - Does it offer a satisfying conclusion to your essay?
    - Does it remind readers of your primary assertion or thesis?
    - Does it maintain reader interest?

Step 3: Check the quality of your sentences one paragraph at a time

- Check to be sure your sentences are all grammatically correct.
- Check to be sure any material you quote is integrated smoothly into your essay.
- Check to be sure you have not created sentence problems by improperly quoting or paraphrasing material from readings:
    - Be sure you have defined all terms or abbreviations that need to be defined.
    - Be sure you have not created sentence fragments or run-on sentences by quoting or paraphrasing material.
- Check for sentence variety.
- Check for sentence clarity.
- Check for sentence economy:
    - Cut all unnecessary words.
    - Cut all padded expressions.

Step 4: Check the quality of your word choice

- Check the accuracy and precision of your word choice:
- Does each word capture exactly what you intend to communicate?
- Have you avoided vague, imprecise language?
- Have you avoided unnecessary jargon?
- Have you avoided slang or other language that is too informal?
- Are your words as accurate and precise as they can be?
- Check the clarity of your word choice:
    - Will your readers understand the language that you use in your essay?

- Are there terms in quoted or paraphrased passages that need to be defined?
- Check the connotation of your word choice:
  - Have you employed language that has appropriate connotative meanings?
  - Is the tone of your language appropriate given the assignment and audience?

Step 5: Check your use of punctuation
- Are your sentences punctuated correctly?
- Sentences can often be punctuated correctly in a variety of ways. Have you chosen the most effective punctuation, given your assignment and audience?

Step 6: Check the format of your essay
- Check to be sure you have adhered to assigned or expected format requirements, such as those concerning:
  - Cover page
  - Page margins
  - Page numbering
  - Use of headings and subheadings
  - Font size and type
  - Use, placement, and size of graphics
  - Placement of appendixes, works cited or reference lists, footnotes or end notes

Step 7: Check your use of source material
- Check the accuracy of all quoted or paraphrased material.
- Be sure all quoted and paraphrased material is properly documented.
- Check the content of your works cited or reference list:
  - Are all needed entries present?
  - Do any entries need to be cut because you do not refer to them in the body of your essay?
- Check the format of your works cited or reference list:
  - Is all the needed information present?
  - Is each entry punctuated correctly?
  - Are the entries listed in the correct order?

CREDITS

Allen, Josh. "Should Cell Phones" Be Banned from the Classroom? Yes." "Learning & Leading with Technology, vol. 35, no. 4 © 2008, ISTE ® (International Society for Technology in Education), www.iste.org. All right reserved.

Altschuler, Glenn C. "College Prep: Adapting to College Life In an Era of Heightened Stress," from *The New York Times*, August 6, 2000 Issue. Copyright © 2005 by The New York Times Co. Reprinted with permission.

Burr, Ty. "Bombs Trump Big Ideas in Potent 'Vendetta'" as originally appeared in Boston Globe March 16, 2006. © 2006 Globe Newspaper Company.

Corliss, Richard. "Can a Popcorn Movie also be Political? This One Can." As published in Time Magazine, Mar. 5, 2006. Copyright TIME INC. Reprinted by permission. TIME is a registered trademark of Time Inc. All rights reserved.

DeLiso, Ellen R. "Crafting a Workable Cell Phone Policy." Copyright © EducationWorld. com, Reprinted with permission.

Furr, Susan R., John S. Westefeld, Gaye N. McConnell, and J. Marshall Jenkins. "Suicide and Depression Among College Students" (In Professional Psychology: Research and Practice, 2001, 32, 97–100.) Copyright © 2001 by The American Psychological Association. Reprinted with Permission.

Goode, Erica. "More in College Seek Help for Psychological Problems," from *The New York Times*, February 3, 2003 Issue. Copyright © 2003 by The New York Times Co. Reprinted with permission.

Hunter, Stephen. "Quite the Bomb: 'V for Verdetta' Can Blow Away Parliament, But Not Its Audience" from the Washington Post, Style Section, 3/17/2006 Issue, Page(s) C1.

"Missing Link," *The New Republic*, Oct. 5, 1992. Reprinted by permission of *The New Republic*. Copyright © 1992 by The New Republic, Inc.

Moore, Patrick. "Hard Choices," edited version reprinted by the permission of the author.

Piel, Gerard. "AIDS and Population 'Control'." February 1994. Reprinted with permission. Copyright © 1994 by Scientific American, Inc. All rights reserved.

Portner, Jessica. "Complex Set of Ills Spurs Rising Teen Suicide Rate." 12 April 2000. As first appeared in *Education Week*, April 12, 2000.

Wechsler, Henry. "Getting Serious about Eradicating Binge Drinking," The Chronicle of Higher Education, November 20, 1998. Reprinted by permission of the author.

INDEX